Development, Ecology and Climate Change: Issues and Challenges

Editor

Mohinder Kumar Slariya, Ph.D.

Dedicated to My grandparents …who distributed sweets when I passed my matriculation examination..

ISBN-10: 1517103606
ISBN-13: 978-1517103606

Content

Preface and Acknowledgments

Increasing population put pressure on resources which is the need of the hour to make any type of development and development is to be planned in physical environment which is vital part of ecology and trespass in ecology to make life of human being more comfortable has innate relationship with climate change. This triangular relationship between development, ecology and climate change is one of the most emerging issues of 21st century and urgently required to understand issues and challenges associated with these.

To understand issues and challenges related to it, an international conference on Development, Biodiversity and Climate change: Issues and Challenges, popularly known as Chamba Climate Meet-2014 has been organised as a collaborative effort of many organisations round the globe from 3rd to 5th of October, 2014. Number of papers on 18 sub-themes in two categories have been received and scientific steering committee has finally selected more than hundred papers for final presentation in the conference. On the basis of recommendations of scientific steering committee more than hundred papers have been selected for publication in form of edited volumes in form of series entitled, "Advances in Environmental Sociology and Conservation Sciences". This volume, *"Development, Ecology and Climate Change: Issues and Challenges"* is an attempt to highlight issues and changes associate with development and climate change as an outcome of the conference. This volume is comprises of 21 chapters contributed by different scholars coming from different parts of the world and from different institutions. The editor is hopeful that this volume will prove beneficial to address issues and challenges associate with developmental processes and will justify the organisation of such conferences.

i

I gratefully acknowledged the collaborative efforts of all supporters' who made Chamba Climate Meet-2014 happened, speaking specifically Asia Climate Education centre, Jeju, South Korea, IUCN, International Sociological Association (WG-05), Sewa Himalayas and support of all participants coming from different countries of the globe. I extend my heartfelt thanks to all contributors of this volume. Hard work of scientific steering committee who supported at every step and put this book in final shape and also thankful to convenor of scientific steering committee for all sorts of support.

I sincerely own this academic contribution to my respected teacher Dr. RK Kaistha, Prof. Satish Sharma and Prof. OP Monga, because of whom what I am today. The emotional support of my friends, Dr. Vidya Sagar, Sachin, Ashwani, Yash Pal are few to count.

I am thankful to Principal and staff of Govt. PG College, Chamba to extend their cooperation in organising the conference.

Lastly, thanks to all my family members, my mother, my wife, my son (Abhishiant) and daughter (Abhidiksha) for their emotional support and my students for giving shape to this book.

I will be very happy to respond to your comments/quarries at mkslariya@gmail.com.

Dr. Mohinder Slariya

Chamba, India: 28.08.2015

Chapter- I

The Role of Rivers in Development

Apeksha Agarwal & Darpan Agarwal*

Abstract

Rivers in general embody many values. For example, rivers symbolize connections, human health, habitat, protecting freshwater ecosystems for fish and wildlife. Rivers greatly contribute in the developmental processes like generation of hydropower, irrigation facilities, recreational activities, preservation and enhancement of indigenous communities, supporting variety of flora and fauna etc. across the globe. It is difficult to isolate the different stresses on a system and to pinpoint one singular cause of the decline in the biodiversity but what we fail to see sometimes is that throughout a river course, human activities have significant impacts on rivers and these activities on a major perspective not only affecting riverine ecosystem but also causing deterioration of mountain ecosystem and biodiversity which is collectively resulting into exacerbating and speedy climate change, biodiversity loss and ecological imbalance. Rivers affected by extensive development will require significant management interventions to protect ecosystems and people. The paper aims to address issues like, protection, proactive restoration, rehabilitation, and management actions which are needed to enhance the resilience of riverine ecosystems to minimize impacts and to address the interests of primitive communities living in the vicinity of river.

Keywords- Deterioration, Development, Enhancement, Imbalance, Preservation

---

*Department of Environmental Sciences, The Global Open University, Nagaland, India

Introduction

Rivers are of immense importance geologically, biologically, historically and culturally. Although they contain only about 0.0001% of the total amount of water in the world at any given time, they are the vital carriers of water and nutrients to areas all around the earth. They are critical components of the hydrological cycle, acting as drainage channels for surface water - the world's rivers drain nearly 75% of the earth's land surface. They provide habitat, nourishment and means of transport to countless organisms; their powerful forces create majestic scenery; they provide travel routes for exploration, commerce and recreation; they leave valuable deposits of sediments, such as sand and gravel; they form vast floodplains where many of our cities are built; and their power provides much of the electrical energy we use in our everyday lives. It has always been an essential element for survival. The importance of a water secure future is fully recognized in all countries. With nearly half of the globe, facing acute water crisis due to increased pressure from both consumption pattern and population, the future water security in many countries stands threatened and turning into scarcity. According to United Nations estimates, more than half the global population will live in water-stressed or water-scarce countries by 2025.

Due to various developmental processes over Rivers, all of the plants, animals, and human that depends upon it are also negatively affected. Human intervention for the purpose of economic growth and modernization activities such as introducing exotic species, pollution the natural land systems through rising industrial production, expanding consumption in a growing middle class, raising animals for a more meat-centric diet and damming a river that provided essential nutrients and minerals, all have made the River a place of concern.

The attention to these subjects is distributed unevenly, with the impacts on river seen as an urgent concern in some places and less pressing in others. This uneven attention, or specificity, is linked to issues of *selectivity* (the inclusion of some cases and exclusion of others), example Within the Arctic and sub-Arctic, sea ice and adjacent coastal areas are the most important focus of concern, with some attention going to the tundra and permafrost, and relatively less devoted to boreal forests, though all these zones are highly sensitive to climate change. [1] Low-lying islands form only a small portion of coastal regions that are threatened by sea level rise, but the public pays more attention to island nations such as Tuvalu and the Maldives than to densely populated deltas of rivers such as the Nile, the Brahmaputra-Ganges, the Mekong, and the Mississippi. [2] Similarly, one portion of mountain regions, namely, the glaciers at high elevations, is discussed more extensively than the grasslands and forests in middle-elevation regions, which also face serious impacts, *historicity* (the long temporal depth of the pathways to inclusion or exclusion), example - The Brahmaputra basin which is a densely populated region being a lifeline to many communities crossing over the three different nations comprising of India China and Bangladesh has also been disputed ever since the independence of India as China claims some parts of the Indian territory to be of his which is the region where all the agrarian work is dependent upon the river system of Brahmaputra. The regions were the targets of colonial attention for material reasons (whether directly for the extraction of economically important resources or indirectly for geopolitical and strategic motives), but the regions, and their indigenous inhabitants, also appealed deeply to the cultural imagination of colonial travellers and scientists and of the colonial public at large; both these material and cultural forces contribute to the positioning of the regions in relation to climate change, and *consequentiality* (the effects of this specificity on claims of responsibility for climate change). Some change like the melting of ice in Polar Regions, the rising sea levels that threaten low-lying islands are recognized as harmful consequences of climate change, while other changes like shifts in mountain ecosystems, the spread of deserts are not seen as serious or as closely linked to it. [3]

In asking how and why impacts on rivers are more apparent in some regions than in others, we raise questions of recognisability. As for other matters of public concern, there is a gap between recognition and responsibility, between noting a problem and feeling an obligation to address it.

Some of the environmental problems which are generally associated with river basin development projects include the spawning of waterborne diseases, the filling of reservoirs with sedimentation, the drying-up of down-stream fisheries, the spread of salinization and water logging in associated irrigation projects, the inundation of valuable agricultural and forestry land, the displacement of population and the loss of mineral resources, wildlife areas or valuable historical sites.

Thus the paper will try to analyse the impacts on the riverine ecosystem with rising developmental activities over it, with special emphasis given to the sustainability of dams mainly in the vast populated region of the world i.e. the Ganga Brahmaputra basin. Some proactive restoration, rehabilitation and management actions has been illustrated to overcome the problems arising out of the developmental processes, through which the final conclusion has been drawn out with some suggestive measures and also calls for few limitations.

Development – Impacts on Riverine Ecosystem

River Ecosystem Composition River ecosystem is the complex biological communities in the river and river environment interaction, the system is the series of subsystems from land riparian ecosystem, aquatic ecosystems, and wetlands to marsh ecological system which is open and continuous. [4] The river ecological system is changed with the passage of time, precipitation change, human disturbance, temperature fluctuation. The river is a living, in morphology, channel change may need very long time, but human disturbance effects on the river do not need too long time, such as water pollution, excessive water etc. As the demands of agricultural, industrial and urban water users increase the water resources of river basins become stretched to the point that supplies remaining for environmental needs become marginal.

Human developments along the river have, as noted before, been going on for millennia. All cultures that have moved through the area have left their mark upon the river. The water remaining for environmental uses has been reduced beyond public acceptance levels.

Whether they wish to use it for transportation, take the fish that dwell in its depths, or even try to harness its mighty power, humans have indelibly made their impact on the river for better or for worse. Another problem that the river ecosystem faces is that of pollution, and the majority of this comes from human activity. There are many sources of this pollution. In rural areas, sewage is dumped into the river as a result of poor sanitation conditions.

River is affected, and all of the plants, animals, and humans that depend on the river are also negatively affected. The most significant threats are encroachment and forest and wetland clearing in areas of biodiversity value, increasing infrastructure development, and the wildlife trade.

Human activities such as introducing exotic species, pollution the natural land systems, and damming a river that provided essential nutrients and minerals, all have made the River a place of concern. Damming a river has the potential to impact on upper and downstream reaches of the river, the flow and function of the tributaries, the main stream aquatic habitats and biodiversity, forest habitats in the floodplain or basin, delta mangroves and coastal habitats, as well as the marine ecosystems such as sea grass, coral and the sediment and nutrient plume closely linked to fisheries productivity.

Who gains and who suffers from the big dams has become a global concern. The question of ecological sustainability and social justification cannot be answered without consideration of all the related issues. The debate on large dams is organised around the following positions. There are some who totally oppose big dams on the grounds of their not delivering the results that they are claimed to, and more; the social costs paid by certain sections are huge while the benefits accrue to others. There are others who agree to the concept of big dams but want proper treatment meted to the environment efficient planning and proper rehabilitation while another category is happy with the status quo and favour big dams as they exist without question.

A vast area of land gets submerged under the reservoirs of the dams. For a proper land and water management adequate forest cover is a must. Instead of proper afforestation, further deforestation is taking place. It is in the hilly areas that forests are submerged for the construction of dams. As most of the dams take nearly a decade or more to complete, the labourers working on the dam site put pressure on the forest resources to meet their requirements for food, fuel and shelter, putting enormous

pressure on the catchment forests.

Along with the flora there is the inevitable loss of precious fauna. It is difficult to imagine the extent of this loss as there is

no comprehensive study on them. These biological resources

have evolved over millions of years and contain within them genetic resources that are directly linked to the survival of human beings. Many other crucial ecological functions like soil preservation, water replenishment and microclimatic stabilization have been ignored.

A French seismologist remarks that, *"by building dams, man is playing the sorcerer's apprentice. In trying to control the energy*

of rivers, he brings about stresses whose energy can be suddenly and disastrously released." [6]

Dams are also a cause of adverse health impacts. Large-scale water projects have increased the incidence of water-borne diseases like malaria, fluorosis and schistosomiasis. The modern, perennial irrigation projects have acted as catalysts in both the increase and lethality of malaria, - much to the discomfort of the health authorities. Water seepage from the dam's reservoir and canals increases the level of the sub-soil water. As a result, the alkalinity level of the soil increases. This in turn has changed the fluoride, calcium and trace metals composition of the soil, thus aggravating fluorosis in its pristine form and in a new dimension in the syndrome of knock-knee

The construction of a dam leads to a reduction in the flow of water and silt downstream and eventually to the sea, causing a negative impact on the ecosystem downstream. The construction impedes the migration of aquatic mammals and reduces the silt flow which affects the fertility of the agricultural land downstream. A reduction of water flow at the mouth of the river leads to ingress of salt water up the river having negative consequences. Fisheries are important livelihood sources of large coastal population which has also been affected with climatic threats from sea level rise induced salinity and flooding and increasing frequency and damage intensity of cyclones.

There is depletion in the fish catch throughout the river basin causing an enormous reduction in the protein availability and marginalising the fisher folk. The increase in the salinity of many rivers also destroys the habitat of aquatic mammals. The reduction of silt, which contains nutrients, hampers the survival of fisheries downstream. Moreover, reservoirs and canals inevitably face an invasion of aquatic weeds which are not conducive to the survival of fishes and other aquatic mammals.

Continuous neglect of the problems of involuntary displacement, inadequate resettlement and rehabilitation, lack of transparency and questionable economic performance have eroded the credibility of large civil engineering constructions, evoking wide spread campaigns and the cohort of social activism against large dams. The social dislocation already caused by large-scale suffering from dam-related displacements of people and inadequate rehabilitation has extended the disasters from natural to human dimensions. The poor live in the uplands and also depend on common property resources (CPRs)

Scudder [1986] who has studied forced relocation concludes that, *"next to killing a man, the worst you can do is to displace him"*. He attributes this statement to the fact that there are various stresses that the individual faces social, cultural and psychological, which are a result of the breakdown of their social and economic lifestyle [8] One is not advocating that the tribals, their economy and culture be left untouched. But there is no disagreeing that they are a deprived lot. There is absolutely no talk about 'development-oriented resettlement' on the part of the authorities. Use of force is often resorted to. Where land is provided for relocation, it is of an inferior variety or not productive at all. At times forests are cut to provide resettlement sites. No effort is made to recreate the village as it was in the old site. Neither is any effort made to minimise the loss of essentials of social, cultural and spiritual values. They are the worst hit as dam sites essentially are in hilly areas where the dependency on common property resources is high.

We must point out explicitly that there are three categories of IDPs, i.e., environment, conflict and development induced. Most internally displaced persons are victims of environmental degradation, skewed development processes and ethnic conflicts. Though technically they are citizens of the country, empirically they are refugees. Rehabilitation of the oustees is one of the least satisfactory aspects of reservoir projects. Most dams are constructed in remote hilly areas, mostly inhabited by tribals and other weaker sections of the society. Big dams inevitably have huge reservoirs and therefore displace a large number of people. The landless labourers, marginal farmers, sharecroppers, tenant cultivators, artisans, cattle grazers, fisher folk and the like who depend on the regions natural resources are not compensated for

9

their loss. The relocation plan is aimed at satisfying only the elite, and that too marginally, who own land.

Floods are not a result of nature's action, rather are caused by the poor land and water management policies. Cutting down forests dramatically increases the risks of flooding. The magnitude and intensity of flooding is dependent on deforestation, rainfall and soil erosion factors as well as physical and anthropogenic causes. The problem is aggravated by the faulty and improper land use practices, shifting cultivation, lack of awareness and urbanisation in lower Brahmaputra river basin. Trees act as natural sponge, soaking up rain-fall and thereby recharging the ground water and eventually releasing it slowly to the river below. According to a UNESCO study, the watershed of one river released between 1 and 3 per cent of the total rainfall when forested, and once the trees were cut down, between 97 and 99 per cent[9] The volume of water carried by rivers in deforested areas can be huge, putting tremendous pressure and often breaching the flood control embankments. During the monsoons, the reservoir level should be kept low in order to receive flood-waters. However, these norms are not respected in order to maximise power generation. Excess water flow in the reservoir raises the reservoir level to the full posing a real danger of dam collapse. To prevent a disaster, water is suddenly released thereby causing floods downstream

It has been observed that, bigger the project, the more centralized it is. This centralization has a bias towards the economically powerful, while the localised and small projects of irrigation and power generation provide a greater chance of equitable distribution, as we shall discuss when examining alternatives. The introduction of social and environmental aspects would definitely put a brake on these projects. It has also seen that alternatives need to be taken seriously and extensive studies are required in the area. We agree that the technology and the environmental and social relations of large dams are inappropriate. If the technology of large dams is applied at all then it should be directed to benefit the weaker majority and not the privileged few. It is unfortunate that irrigation and power generation, which could play an important role in the alleviation of poverty and greater social justice, is doing just the opposite. A section rightly believes that irrigation by dams helps in strengthening the capitalist structure, largely because of the extreme in-equality in the distribution of land in the command area which gets further polarised with the introduction of irrigation by big dams. The ruling class due to the power that it enjoys is successful in diverting nearly all the benefits of large projects to itself.

'The cheapest form of alternate energy is energy saved'. Efforts should be directed towards curbing wasteful energy use on luxurious items by the pampered few. Equally important is exploring alternate forms of energy. We have the know-how for energy from petroleum, gas, earth's crust, biomass, solar, tidal waves, animal excreta and wind. There should be more research into their practicability and expanded application.

Sustainability of Dams-Special Reference to Ganga-Brahmaputra Basin

Studies have recognized dam building as the most substantial human impact on riverine ecosystems. The intensification and diversification of uses have made international water resource a valued, sometimes strategic resource, where nations attach great importance in securing access and control over it. Inevitably it leads to conflict among basin states. Though there are few instances in history where nations went to military confrontation over water, but dispute over such critical resource definitely affects adversely the cooperative development of water

11

resources, mutual trust and other areas of international relations.

We assessed impacts and trends of land-use changes from proposed dam building on terrestrial biodiversity with a special emphasis been given to the dam which the different nations like India and China propose to build in the Ganges and Brahmaputra Basin and on the Great band of Brahmaputra. Proposed locations of dams correlate with zones of species richness for angiosperms, birds, fishes, and butterflies.

The Brahmaputra river system flows through China, India, Bhutan, and Bangladesh. The drainage area of the Brahmaputra River is 234,000 square miles, of which 72,000 square miles is in India, 28,000 square miles is in Bangladesh, and almost the entire area of Bhutan lies within its drainage system. The Ganges and Brahmaputra plains are identified as one of the most densely populated regions of the world and one suffering from rapid population growth and increasing poverty. It is estimated that some 450 million people, or 9.6 percent of all mankind, occupy the 100 million acres of croplands in these basins. These people are among the poorest in the world, many of them earning not more than US$150 in a year. The vast majority relies on agriculture for their livelihood.

Yet, considering the general poverty level of the area, coupled with a high rate of population increase, more efforts in improving agricultural practices are urgently needed, most important of which include additional water resources, better water management methods, and improved agricultural services. The lower Brahmaputra river basin, Assam is especially vulnerable to earthquakes, major landslides and floods and unfettered dam development may have disastrous consequences.

Now focusing the debate on the seismic risks may extend the debate to a new dimension of upstream-downstream conflict in the region. When the upstream and the downstream areas fall in two different countries, as will be the case for dams all along the southern border of Nepal and Bhutan, and proposed dam building by China on Brahmaputra, under this situation, the question of dam safety will then be addressed singularly by the downstream country and governed by international law. This will create an additional factor for the downstream country to influence decisions in the upstream country. Since all the future water management projects will have to depend on the question of storage. The fear of domination and territorial sensitivities of smaller states lead to mistrust, reservation and delay about bilateral negotiations. Meanwhile, the smaller countries have also experienced a rising resource consciousness and pressures of economic development. However, When both the upstream and downstream areas of the dam fall within one nation-state, as in the case of Tehri, the decision-making process is often influenced more by the economic growth factors at the cost of social and environmental damage factors.

As Resource consciousness among nations has increased tremendously, the hydrology of major Asian rivers will be severely affected in the near future. Though the enormous water and hydroelectric resources in the Himalayas, and deep ground-water sources provide an important potential for successful development but the rush to harness hydroelectric power by building hundreds of dams on both sides of the earthquake prone Himalayas will further accelerate changes in hydrology and the effects of climate change.

The economic feasibility of future large dams in the Himalaya will finally depend on whether the politically powerful downstream economies will be ready to pay adequately higher price for water or power. Himalayan water need not tor ever be considered by the downstream plains as a free gift through in from the upstream areas by colonial laws used by the state.

India already plans to increase hydropower projects in the Himalayas from 74 to 355 over the next 15 years, increasing the capacity from 15,208 to 126,588 MW. [12] Whereas China is planning 750 projects in Tibet alone. Further, China may also divert water from the Tsangpo-Brahmaputra, one of the largest rivers in Asia, before it enters India. The diversion of the river if that is indeed on the agenda—would have the largest implications of all. [13] If true, dispute over political boundaries could extend to water resources. Exploitation of Himalayan resources is likely to be accelerated as energy consumption rises more rapidly in Asia than anywhere else.

China and India, respectively, are already the world's top and the fifth-largest emitters of greenhouse gases. Snow melt from Himalayan glaciers constitutes a principal water resource during the summer months for at least half of the world's population. The region is ecologically fragile and vulnerable to high intensity earth-quakes. Hence, there arises questioning on the very wisdom of such mega dam projects.

The synergistic effects of decreasing water resources, loss of biodiversity, increased pollution, and climate change may have negative social and economic consequences and, even worse, escalate conflicts within and between the two countries. [14]

An international river basin links all the riparian states in a complex network of environmental, economic, political and security interdependencies. In this process, it creates the potential for interstate conflict as well as the opportunities of cooperation. There are supreme legislative and judicial institutions to lay out modalities of cooperation and resolve disputes among sub-national political units. But in international water resource sharing projects the situation is different. States try to claim absolute right over, control -and use of the natural resources located within or flowing through their territory (the rule of "Territorial Sovereignty" or "Harmon Doctrine"). The notion compels states to appropriate more and more water before it crosses the boundary and share less and less with other basin states, automatically involving conflicts.

Three categories of factors have started exercising considerable influence on international water disputes/conflicts and resolution processes in a given basin (1) The UN Convention of non-navigational use of international watercourse which function as referred principles of international waters sharing (2) the international funding agencies of the project and supra-national organisations (3) civil society initiatives from respective nations which can be from research institutions/ forums/human rights or environmental campaigners. [15]

The present uncertainties related to the seismic risk from large dams in the Himalaya need to be addressed at the earliest. Otherwise there is a strong possibility that dam issues may become subject of international litigation.

Proactive Restoration, Rehabilitation and Management Actions

Ecosystem Based Adaptation (EBA) refers to use of natural resources through conservation and enhancing resilience of ecosystem to buffer the worst impacts of climate changes on species and well-being of community. [16] This can be done through cooperation between the countries which would help us to mitigate climate change, environmental damage, and biodiversity loss; both regionally and globally.

Moreover, sharing expertise policy frameworks for sustainable use of resources with the rest of the countries could contribute to reduction in deforestation and in the mitigation of climate change through both the preservation, and enhancement of forest carbon stocks.

Dams and particularly large dams have become a necessity for the country to meet the increasing demand for water, food grains, flood-control, power supply- particularly peaking power, and supply of carbon-free energy. The opposition to dams that was originally rooted in the human issue of involuntary displacement has now also evolved around the complex environmental risks and uncertainty, and far-reaching environmental impacts. We need to balance current needs with long-term sustainable development.

Considering the huge availability of hydel power in the riparian states, the generation of carbon free energy has become a major cause of concern as it will lead to the greenhouse effect due to higher rate of CO_2 emission mainly from the burning of fossil fuels and biomass, agricultural practices, deforestation.

Large dams impound large amount of water over a certain area of land, which creates ecological and seismic imbalance. The main apprehension comes on account of ecological and environmental concerns and also displacement of people by these projects- *Seismicity*: The impounding of water in big dams may accentuate big mass and pressure, which are enough to cause/initiate seismic activity; *Water logging*: Another negative impact attributed to dams and hydel projects, relates to water logging in areas around them. Water logging causes rise in water table in nearby areas leading to salinity and oxygen depletion; *Siltation*: The problem of soil erosion has become more acute because of massive degradation of forest due to cutting of trees for firewood and other purposes; *Displacement of people*: Displacement of people living on the proposed project site and the area to be submerged has become a very emotional issue. Most of the hydel projects are located in remote and inaccessible areas, where local population is either illiterate or have marginal means of employment; the per capita income of families is low. However, the moment any village is earmarked for take-over by dam or any other developmental activity, social transformation takes place immediately; *Submergence of large area*: The large dams are being constructed and they submerge large tracts of land; *Gestation period*: The gestation period of a hydel project is longer than others, owing to the following reasons: - longer period of assessment of the scheme , involvement of large number of agencies , longer period in determining and ascertaining ecological and environmental impact , formulation of rehabilitation and resettlement plan and its implementation, acquisition of land, general apathy of lenders towards project financing because of misplaced notions, remoteness of area of operations, relatively large percentage of work related to civil engineering, which is time consuming, geological surprises in the civil works and, development of infrastructural facilities; *Destruction of forests*: Loss of forest because of any activity is undoubtedly harmful. Major causes of deforestation in our country are cutting of trees for developmental projects, requirement of wood in construction and buildings, etc. Some other reasons are excessive grazing of cattle, shifting or jhuming cultivation etc.

Thus all these apprehensions can be solved to some extent through following alternatives- *Small dams*: They can be set up without much displacement and are therefore favored at some locations; *Non-conventional sources*: It is suggested by some, that we must make use of alternative sources of energy generation, which are more environmental friendly. It is said that renewable sources of energy like solar and wind power could be an ideal substitute for hydel and thermal power. The estimates by the Ministry of Non-conventional Energy resources (MNES) of the potential of renewable energy indicate that solar, hydel and ocean thermal power may have limited potential in comparison to our demand; *Conservation*: the prevailing shortage of energy and peak demand could be met through proper energy conservation and demand-side management (DSM). [17]

Moreover, there is a need to execute *environment impact assessment* in India according to the EIA notification of 1994. The evaluation criteria should include impact on soil in terms of degradation and productivity status, loss of genetic resources (flora and fauna) and loss of or damage to habitat. In the long term and popular interest, there is a need for breaking such a dead-lock and evolve more comprehensive criteria and guidelines for decision-making on dams. This process needs an interdisciplinary scientific approach and should have wide acceptability among the diverse stakeholders.

Displacement of the people would undoubtedly disconnect them from their past, culture, customs and traditions. The choice of the exact type and scale of any intervention should be guided by a better knowledge of the social and economic impact. Thus the national policy in India stipulates that the 'living standards of those displaced should be maintained at least at the same level, if not improved, to what they were, prior to their involuntary displacement'. Satisfactory rehabilitation is a term which is difficult to evaluate, especially when it is enforced through laws of imperial origin, like the Land Acquisition Act introduced by the British rulers of India. [18] Proper drafting and implementation of rehabilitation and resettlement plan can compensate for displacement of people and assuage their miseries. The effects of these dams on ecology require serious discussion. Indigenously developed and locally managed structural techniques are an important component of adaptation to floods which are frequently taking place during the developmental processes. Thus, Flood management is more effective than flood control. Integrated River Basin Management is comprehended as coordinated regional planning, sustainable development, agriculture, livelihood, use and management of land, water and related natural resources within hydrologic boundaries, in order to maximize the resultant economic and social welfare, in an equitable manner without compromising the sustainability of vital ecosystems.

Conclusion

We conclude that Asia's water towers are threatened by climate change, but that the effects of climate change on water availability and food security in Asia differ substantially among basins. At this stage of development, there is a need to interject some amount of lateral thinking, which will allow the hidden elements of the holistic picture to emerge and achieve salience. Ecology and environment are very fragile and all efforts should be made to cause least disturbance to it. Maintenance of it is an urgent concern and effort should be made to improve the environment of the country as a whole.

Rivers are the source of conflict between countries and people in the region. The alternatives need to be taken seriously and extensive studies are required in the areas of great concern like the Ganga Brahmaputra Basin which is said to be the most populous and resourceful basin in the world. There is a greater need to focus on to the slogan 'think globally, act locally'.

If we learn how to look at our problems from an ecological perspective, we can stand taller and see these problems more comprehensively, and achieve longer-term social development. Dams constitute an integral part of available technological interventions for integrated water resources development. The choice of the exact type and scale of any intervention would be guided by a process better informed of their social, economic

19

and ecological impacts.

Generalizations can't be drawn based on few examples thus the scope of the paper is very limited. The selection has been random and there has been no conscious attempt to distort figures. While agreeing that the study is not comprehensive and complete, we believe that there is enough proof to worry about the performance of large dams.

References

[1]   Hovelsrud, Grete, K., Birger Poppel, Bob van Oort, and James D. Reist. 2011. Arctic societies, cultures, and peoples in a changing cryosphere, Ambio 40(1):100–110.

[2]   Ericson, Jason, Charles Vorosmarty, S. Lawrence Dingman, Larry Ward, and Michel Meybeck. 2006. Effective sea-level rise and deltas: causes of change and human dimension implications, Global and Planetary Change 50(1–2): 63–82.

[3] Ben Olive, Heather Lazarus, Grete K. Hovelsrud, and Alessandra Giannini, Recognitions and Responsibilities: On the Origins and Consequences of the Uneven Attention to Climate Change around the World, Current Anthropology, Vol. 55, No. 3 (June 2014), pp. 249-275

[4] Stegner, W. (1992), where the bluebird sings to the lemonade spring, Living and Writing in the West, 256, 116-120

[5] J. Keller, A. Keller and G. Davids, River basin development phases and implications of closure, Journal of Applied Irrigation Science. Vol. 33, No. 2/1998, pp. 145-16

[6] Rothe, J P, 1978, 'Fill a Lake, Start an Earth-quake', New Scientist, Vol 39, No 605, July 11, p 78.

[7] J. Bandyopadhyay, B. Mallik, M. Mandal and S. Perveen, Dams and Development:
Report on a Policy Dialogue, Economic and Political Weekly, Vol. 37, No. 40 (Oct. 5-11, 2002), pp. 4108-4112

[8] Scudder, Thayer, 1986, The Relocation Com-ponent of Sardar Sarovar, Report to the World Bank.

[9] Goldsmith, E and Hildyard, N, 1984, Cornwall, The Social and Environmental Effects of Large Dams, W'adebridge Ecological Centre Vol 1: Overview

[10] Conservation International, www.biodiversityhotspots.org/xp/Hotspots/

[11] Singh, R.B. and Bortamuly, M. 2005. Impact of Flood on Biodiversity in the Brahmaputra Valley, MPMD-2005, eds. K. Takara, Y. Tachikawa and B. Nawarathna, Kyoto, Japan. pp. 599-606.

[12] J. W. van Gelder, C. Scheire, H. Kroes, New Trends in the Financing of Dams—a Research Paper Prepared for International Rivers, Bank Track and WWF Germany (Profundo, Castricum, Netherlands, 2008).

[13] K. Pomeranz, The Great Himalayan Watershed, New Left Rev. 58, 5 (2009).

[14] Kamaljit S. Bawa, Lian Pin Koh, Tien Ming Lee, China, India, and the Environment, Science vol 327, 19 March 2010.

[15] Rakesh Tiwary, Conflicts over International Waters, Economic and Political Weekly, Vol. 41, No. 17 (Apr. 29 - May 5, 2006), pp. 1684-1692.

[16] Vignola R, Locatelli B, Martinez C, Imbach P (2009) Ecosystem-based adaptation to climate change: what role for policy-makers, society and scientists? Mitig Adapt Strateg Glob Chang 14:691–696

[17] Pradip Baijal and P. K. Singh, Large Dams: Can We Do without Them?, Economic and Political Weekly, Vol. 35, No. 19 (May 6-12, 2000), pp. 1659-1666

[18] Jayanta Bandyopadhyay, Sustainability of Big Dams in Himalayas, Economic and Political Weekly, Vol. 30, No. 38 (Sep. 23, 1995), pp. 2367-2370

Chapter-II

Measuring Social Connectivity in Context of Rapid Environmental Change and Water Scarcity

Darwin Horning*

Abstract

Water resources are becoming increasingly threatened through human action, or inaction as a result of ineffective and often inappropriate water governance regimes. To address the broad call for water governance transition to more adaptive and sustainable models, re-conceptualization of water as a network of linkages or relationships between people and nature is required. Understanding these underlying socio-ecological networks and their influences on watershed management decisions, in light of climate change, loss of biodiversity, financial stress, and the water- food-energy nexus, has and will increasingly challenge water practitioners globally.

The ultimate goal is to develop a deeper and more comprehensive understanding of the social elements influencing the decision making and development associated with transitioning our current water governance regimes to more adaptive and sustainable models, particularly within a rural Canadian context.

Keywords: Water governance, institutions, sense-making, resilient, socio-ecological, adaptive

*University of British Columbia Okanagan, Canada

Introduction

Water governance has emerged as one of the key concerns for experts focused on water sustainability. Increased public awareness and an enhanced sense of stakeholder ownership in decision-making processes have escalated the pressure on water resource managers to accommodate non-state actors in the decision making phases of water governance. This has led to an increasingly diverse group of actors and sectors engaged in water management. The growing awareness of the multifaceted and multi-scalar nature of water governance, due in-part to the growing diversity of interconnected participants with a complex hydrological cycle, has however not been reflected in responses to water challenges (Molle et al., 2008). The rising socio-ecological awareness, but continued shortfall of current water governance responses, has led to a call for new, more innovative socio-ecological governance approaches. This broadening consensus is, however, tempered by the limited agreement on which particular governance model provides a 'best-fit' model for addressing current challenges (Collins & Ison, 2009; Godden et al., 2011). While there is limited agreement on the optimum model(s) of governance required for transitioning to resource sustainability, there is agreement that water institutions play a key role in transition.

In recent times water institutions have gained significant prominence as being fundamental in addressing the growing environmental and social challenges (Acheson, 2006; Ostrom, 2010; Poirier & de Loë, 2010). This is particularly salient as the transition of governance systems is driven not by technological resource imperatives alone, rather by an expanding perspective that recognizes the existence and importance of social-ecological inter-relationships. This paper begins with a look at the changing nature of water resource institutions as being central components in the transition from intra-perspective, stationary based mechanisms to more open, knowledge seeking phenomena which incorporate a grounded recognition of the rapidly changing environment associated with water resources.

The paper highlights some of the existing challenges associated with the progress in water institution development, beginning with the fundamental lack of agreement on what constitutes an institution. In a very broad sense, institutions can be generally understood as the 'rules and actions of the game, intended to reduce uncertainty by providing structure to everyday life' (Genus, 2014). The contestation over a more refined and precise institutional definition may be attributed to the increasingly complex nature of socio-ecological systems and the multiple scales in which water institutes operate (Poirier & de Loë, 2010; Scott, 2008).

Section 2 of the paper discusses *institutional inertial* as one of the key ongoing barriers to water governance transition. Sections 3-4 outline the changing nature of institutions and the ways institutional analysis is conducted. Specifically, institutions have begun to be viewed more holistically, incorporating both contextual and social aspects within a relational framework. In Sections 5-6 a new water governance 'sense-making' research methodology is proposed, one which incorporates both social network analysis (SNA), a research method rapidly becoming the preferred tool for relational network investigation, and Discourse Network Analysis (DNA), a new tool involving content discourse analysis within a relational reframing. The paper contends that a new mixed methods sense-making research agenda, involving both a network structure (SNA) and network content (DNA) analysis is required in order to address existing deficiencies and limitations in contemporary water governance research.

Coupling SNA and DNA (S-DNA) in a more whole- systems examination of the complex nature of water governance addresses the identified deficiency associated with SNA and provides a tool to incorporate the richer network content data in a whole systems examination. The paper concludes (Sections 6-7) with a discussion on the application of the mixed methods approach and how S-DNA will enable the investigation into alignment between structure and content and in so doing facilitate a clearer understanding of network content and the importance of aligning network content and network structure.

Institutional Inertia

As water environments continue to change and become less predictable, the need for adaptive rather than technical solutions increases. Adaptation by its fundamental nature, however, requires the identification, categorization, and development and learning. This in turn requires new and different ways of managing and operating from those currently being utilized (O'Brien, 2011). Current water decision-making processes have focused on supply side management, often referred to as the hydraulic mission due to a focus on engineered solutions such as pumps, pumps and storage (Moore, 2013). AS a result, water decisions such as allocation, have become highly institutionalized and normalized, making water regimes ridged and resistant to change and innovation (Moore, 2013). The embedded nature of the dominant supply side approach ultimately dictates what knowledge and lens is used to frame water decision-making responses such as government policy, funding initiatives and action re-enforcing the status quo (Steyaert & Olivier, 2007). In the case of allocation the status quo has often led to an increasing threat to water systems due to over allocation (Neef, 2007). Academics refer to this resistance to change as 'institutional inertia', and have identified it as one of the leading barriers to transformation of our current governance systems (Pahl-Wostl et al., 2007; Engle et al., 2011; Brown & Farrelly, 2009). Exacerbating institutional barrier is what Dorado (2005) refers to as the 'opaque' nature of a deep-seated scientific and technical approach.

Self-perpetuation of the scientific or supply-side approach is also due to the normalization of the use of generalized industry wide 'best practice' recommendations, research and depoliticised policy frameworks which continue to ignore the social, political and institutional dimensions associated with water decision making (Moore, 2013; Cleaver & Franks, 2007; Molle et al., 2008). Moore (2013) uses Integrated Water Resource Management, currently being used in many high profile organizations such as the Global Water Partnership, as an example of a 'best practises' approach which purports to achieve efficiency, equity and environmental sustainability through expert knowledge and sound science. Moore (2014, pg. 492-3) argues, "…good information (alone) is (not) the only ingredient required for multiple stakeholders to come together, cooperate and reconcile differences in the interest of a common good". Lautze et al. (2011) further argues that there may even be a fundamental conflict or incompatibility associated with the goals of efficiency, equity and sustainability. Lautze et al. (2011) conclude that popular usage of the term water governance has assumed a subordinated interpretation and approach of efficiency, equity and sustainability, as a panacea approach, utilizing predetermined and generic goals, rather than adopting an approach which includes, as a primary role of water governance, a process to define water management goals according to local preferences.

Institutional Change

Different resource users perceive ecosystems through different frames, and usually only operate within a limited knowledge reference. As mentioned earlier, historically, water has been managed as an exploitable resource, with emphasis being placed on the supply side bolstered by technological solution. This hydraulic approach has biased funding models, research and policy towards building hard infrastructure for water service projects which benefit industry like irrigators, industrial water users and domestic use in an often reactive manner (Moore, 2013; Swatuk, 2003). There has been over the past decade, however, a migration in the academic literature towards 'softer' approaches, ones that consider relational implications and impacts on water from a demand side perspective. AS this shift in water governance perspective occurs, attention is drawn to the significant challenges and risks associated with governing and managing with incomplete and insufficient knowledge within a complex and dynamic environment. Recognizing that governance of water must consider more than the utilitarian nature of water mandates that a more robust approach be taken to identify and address both the mono-focused and homophilia (individuals tend to associate with like individuals) tendencies of existing water governance systems.

Institutional Progress

The growing interest in institutional analysis over the past decade signifies the importance and central role institutions play in affecting sustainability solutions in the water field (Acheson, 2006; Ostrom, 1999). As we endeavour to transition from a time of government to governance our understanding of the importance of water institutions and impact of their inter-relationships water governance continues to grow (Hall & Taylor, 1996; Ostrom, 1999; Hotimsky et al., 2003; Hodgson,

2006; Poirier & de Loë, 2010). In the early-1970s, neo-institutionalism began to recognize that organizational structure resulted from more than just technology imperatives and resource dependencies (Thompson, 2003; Pfeffer & Salancik, 1978; Scott, 2008). Institutional theory , within organizational sociology, began to acknowledge that organizational structures reflected, "Institutional forces (then vaguely defined as rule-like frameworks), rational myths and knowledge legitimized through the education systems, by social prestige, laws …and the courts" (Meyer et al., 1977, p. 341-343)

In the late 1980s – early 1990s, the term 'new institutionalism' emerged describing the re-framing of governance from a linear process, conducted by rational actors (classic economics), to systems or organizations that were influenced by social, economic, and political factors, and informed by context and actor relationships (Powell & DiMaggio, 1991; Hall & Taylor, 1996).More recent institutional theory is focused on deeper and more resilient aspects of social structure through examination of the processes by which structures, including schemas, rules, norms, and routines, become established as authoritative guidelines for social behaviour. Despite the fact that, "regulatory elements have continued to received greater attention from scholars, in particular, institutional economists and rational choice political scientists" (Scott 2008, p. 429), recognition continues to grow, with regard to the significance of social relationships in resource governance, including the "softer" cultural cognitive elements, which provide deeper and more legitimate meaning to water resource systems. According to Scott (2008, p.147)

Although institutional elements are themselves symbolic, they are of interest insofar as they provide cognitive schema, normative guidance, and rules that constrain and empower social behaviours. Rules, norms and meaning arise in interaction and they are preserved and modified by the behaviour of social actors.

To demonstrate progress in the field of institutional analysis, Scott (2008) developed a brief history, starting from the mid-20th century. Although several major trends emerged from Scott's (2008) review. A detailed description of each is beyond the scope of this paper, however, a general sense of the progress and future direction of institutional analysis can be inferred from the following key trends (Scott, 2008)

[1] From looser to tighter conceptualization
[2] From determinant to interactive arguments
[3] From superficial to consequential change
[4] From assertion to evidence
[5] From organization-centric to field level approaches
[6] From non-rational formulations to rationality within institutional frameworks
[7] From institutional stability to institutional change

The final trend, *from institutional stability to institutional change*, highlights the growing awareness regarding both external (exogenous) and internal (endogenous) changes that continue to influence and modify institutions. The exogenous factors may include political (delegation and subsidiarity), environmental (changing hydrological cycles) or social (social capacity and capital). Endogenous sources of change may consist of gaps or mismatches between scales of systems or formal regulatory structures and informal activities and processes at the local level (Sewell, 1992; Scott, 2008; Dacin et al., 2012; Norman & Bakker, 2009).

Continued Challenges

Although the concept of the institution dates back as early as 1725 (Giambattista Vico's, *Scienza Nuova,* cited by (Hodgson, 2006), a universally accepted definition has yet to be developed. Moreover, no agreement has been reached with respect to the form of institution which is best suited for any given task or situation (Vatn, 2005; Acheson, 2006). This lack of agreement may be attributed to the growing awareness associated with the increasingly complex nature of coupling social systems needs with ecological system needs (Poirier & de Loe, 2010). This has led to a multitude of institutional solutions being advocated for (Poirier & de Loe, 2010; Ostrom et al., 2007; Pahl-Wostl et al., 2010; Acheson, 2006; Pahl-wostl et al., 2000; Berkes et al., 2003). Additional complexity arises from the multiple scales in which institutional elements operate, ranging from the micro (inter-actor) level, to the meso (inter-cluster or organization) level, to the macro (transnational system) level (Scott, 2008).

Historically, inter-institutional research has focused predominantly on the 'why' and 'when' relationships form (Scott, 2005) however; more recently, research have begun to consider institutions in a more holistic manner, by considering the contextual and social aspects relating to institutions within a network of relationships.

The re-framing of institutional development as a bi-directional (affecting and being affected by) network of relationships has provided useful insights into the mechanisms (e.g. role of social capital and environmental and structural interaction) within a given context. It is important to recognize that within this relational re-framing, water institutions consist of multiple political actors, or groups of actors, with varying levels of influence, pursuing agendas aligned with individual self-interest,

31

and this pursuit occurs within a context of unique social and cultural embeddedness which shapes both the institutional responses and ability and willingness to respond to particular issues. This is important when considering water institutions within a climate change context, and the central role that they play in identifying the issues, framing the subsequent discussions, driving the agendas and ultimately determine the final policies enacted. Although these institutions (i.e. technical committees, planning committees etc.) may be regarded as goal-directed inter-organisational networks, little is known about these organizational networks which give rise to questions regarding coordination, representation, accountability, knowledge creation, innovation, institutional performance and overall governance structure.

Relational Framework

To provide some clarity to water institutions and their constituent components, Menard & Saleth (2011), building on Saleth & Dinar (2004-5) and Ostrom (1990), developed a framework or environment identifying the components and subcomponents of a water governance with their associated institutional influences and linkages. The primary purpose for the framework was to identify existing barriers to effective governance processes such as coordination, knowledge transfer, and innovation for example. Saleth and Dinar's (2004-5) framework made explicit the interconnected nature of the intra- and inter-relationships of institutional sub-components within a water governance system. Menard and Saleth (2011) advanced Saleth and Dinar's framework by identifying and mapping inter and intra relationships of the water institute subgroups (water law, water policy, and water organizations) within a context influenced by change agents (environment, technology and economic) to produce water sector performance within an iterative or adaptive structure (Figure 1)

Table 1, further details Saleth and Dinar's (2004-5) water institutions and their sub-components. According to Menard and Saleth (2011), each of the institutions subcomponents are influenced by three primary forces or change agents: technology, economic and environment, further highlighting the complexity associated with water governance and the importance of understanding the structural and relational aspects of the water networks within a governance design. By making the institutional linkages explicit, Menard and Saleh's (2011) framework facilitates a deeper understanding of the social network associated with water governance and the network requirements for productive communication in policy development. Having a clearer understanding of network requirements enables the identification of potential inconsistencies between rule-making, network structure and resource management goals. Understanding the policy-network connectivity clarifies the development of policy and increases the likelihood of implementation success overall (Ostrom, 2009; 2010a, 2010b).

Figure 1: Water Governance Framework. (adapted from Menard & Saleth, 2011)

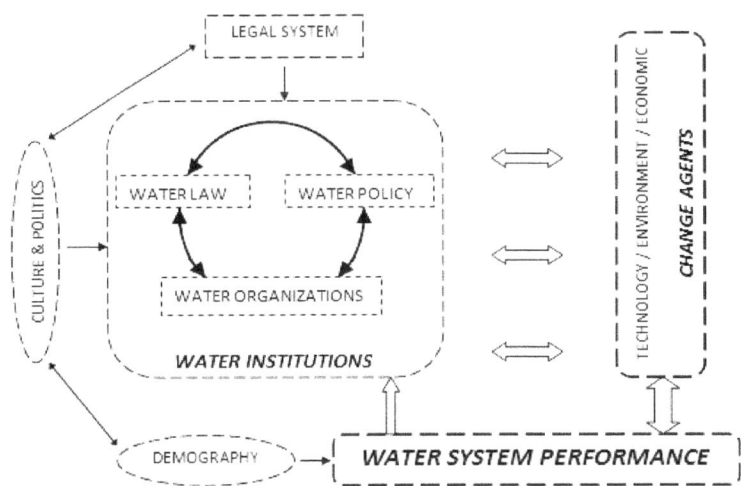

Table 1: Water Governance Framework-Water Institutions.
(Adapted from Saleth and Dinar, 2004)

Water law	Water Organization	Water Policy
Inter Source/Resource Links	Government Layers	Use Priority
Water Rights	Structure of Water Admin	Project Selection
Conflict Resolution	Financial/Staff Patterns	Cost Recovery
Accountability	Pricing/Fee Collection	Water Transfers/Rights
Private / Public Participation	Regulation/Accountability	Turn-over/Devolution
	Information Capability	Privatization
	Technical Capacity	Technology Policy

Water governance systems exist within a broader governance regime which either create or inhibit the contextual pressures for change. Regardless of purpose, water governance must retain a design unique to its context (i.e., rural, urban, regional) yet remain connected, at multi-scale levels, to the broader governance structures and issues to be effective (Moore, 2013). For example Integrated Water Resource Management (IWRM) has been promoted by organizations globally (e.g. Global Water Partnership) as an integrated approach to managing water by coordinating the management of water, land and other related resources in order to maximize the benefits (social, environmental and economic). The intersection or cross connections of the systems will depend on the context in which they evolve. Thus, the "one- size-fits-all" approach to water governance design should instead be viewed through a contextual frame, as proposed by Manard and Saleth (2011) and Saleth and Dinar (2004-5), whereby any alternative governance option must be informed by the context for which it is designed to ensure effective governance (Oestrum, 1990) at a multitude of scales. The advancements in a relational approach to institutional design that will ultimately provide key knowledge for understanding water governance systems at the institutional and sub-institutional levels are described in the following section.

Re-Conceptualization and Waterscapes

The growth of interest in water governance within the resource literature reflects both a changing conceptualization - from government to governance (Perramond, 2012; De Loë et al., 2009) and the changing role played by states in economic, political, and social life (Budds & Hinojosa, 2012). Re-conceptualization of water governance as a collaborative, adaptive and distributed (CAD) model has led to a debate concerning the optimal scale of governance, highlighting the importance of the political nature of existing and new governance models (Bridge & Perreault, 2009; Budds & Hinojosa, 2012; Horning & Bauer, pending). Associated with this re-conceptualization are fundamental questions relating to: the impacts of governance architectures; the overall effectiveness of more 'earth-system' oriented governance; the ways in which multiple agents at all levels can influence the processes; and, how environments (both human and natural) affect these agents and their involvement in governance (Budds & Hinojosa, 2012).

Bridges and Perrault (2009) propose a critical and dialectical approach for investigating how social (human) relationships of a governance system can influence and shape the water governance model and how different water governance structures can influence the evolving socio-natural arrangements. By locating water governance within a political framework, inquiry is focused on production, mobilisation, and contestation of control and distribution of the resource. Socio-political processes can play an important role for example, in determining the choice of scale and inclusion of locally developed knowledge. Socio-political processes however, run the risk of limiting, robust communication, innovation, and knowledge transfer processes, which are ultimately influenced by the power and control of a cluster of actors and the likely potential for homophile associations(Rat well & Peterson, 2012). These approaches may be viewed in what (Sproule-Jones et al., 2008) and Manard and Saleth (2011) refer to as the intra (structure) and inter (system) 'institutional interplay' of governance. Sproul-Jones et al. (2008, p. 8) define institutional interplay as:

The connections, interactions and effects that result from the presence of multiple institutions involved in a water governance system Institutional interplay is recognized by the common pool of resource researchers as the increasing institution and political complexity within the policy process inherent within water policy issues.

As resource systems shift from government to governance, there is an inherent recognition that water is, in its self, not a single purpose material resource to be harvested and allocated, rather it's the union of water's physical appliance and its social relational network which inhabits and express each other (Karen Bakker & Cook, 2011a) (K. J. Bakker, 2003; Linton, 2010; Loftus, 2009; Perrault, 2006; (Swynegedouw, 1999; Budds & Hinojosa, 2012). Budds and Hinojosa (2012, p. 120) argue that the starting point for characterising water (flows, forms, practices, and discourse) must reflect both, "the material and social processes through which instances of water become formed". Understanding the material and social processes of water requires attention to a broad spectrum of issues such as flow rates, access and allocation, equity, technology, emerging science, institution adaptation, current legislation, and governance frameworks, all which are defined and guided by the interrelationships among the participating actors and social constructs (Budds & Hinojosa, 2012). This dual conceptualization is known collectively as the 'waterscape' of a given context (Baviskar, 2007; Budds, 2008; Loftus, 2009; Loftus & Lumsden, 2008; Pares, 2011; Swyngedouw, 1999).

The waterscape approach de-emphasizes the limitations of a scalar focus debate that has dominated much of the water governance literature, by changing the conceptualization towards a multi-directional, multi-scale, relational perspective of water. In other words, social processes shape water and water shapes social processes (Bakker, 2003b; Linton, 2010; Perreault, 2006). This re-conceptualization enables effective water governance analysis to proceed without preconceptions or bounding limits (i.e., hierarchical limits). Budds and Hinojosa (2012, p. 120) argue that:

The concept of a 'waterscape' represents a useful lens with which to view the multiple processes and dynamics that mediate water over time and space, in a way that avoids the limitations of thinking about water in purely material terms, analysing water issues according to traditional spatial scales, and accepting hierarchical forms of institutional administration as given.

Responses to water dilemmas seldom consider the complexities of waterscapes associated with the interconnectedness water cycles and human-nature (Stein et al., 2011). Vogel (2012, p. 161) asserts that improved water governance outcomes will only come about through, "more interactive and longer-term models attentive to dynamic political-social geographies". In recent academic literature focusing on water governance, the emerging view was a "need for closer attention to the processes and interrelationships between power and social networks in water governance, with particular reference on both institutional dynamics and scalar construction." (Norman et al., 2012). Consequently, by taking a more relational approach to water and focusing on governance as a set of risk-trust relationships involving people and places, as opposed to merely a physical apparatus (Loftus, 2009) a clear conceptualization of the governance environment (system) and content) and structure (institutions) is possible (Saleth & Dinar, 2004). However, Saleth and Dinar fail to account for a key aspect of any water governance system, which is the content of the network which determines the development, and eventual structural makeup of the network itself. If the goal, as suggested in the water governance literature, is to improve the adaptive performance of our water systems, then developing comprehensible understanding of water governance environment, structure, and network content is an effective means to achieve this goal. The following section describes a new a sense-making research agenda which enables the consideration of all three essential water governance components in a whole systems approach.

Sense-Making Research

There is growing gap between scholarship, policy practise and practical knowledge relating to sustainable water management, due in large part to the fundamental lack in understanding of the roles, types of influence and power, authority, and legitimacy, actors have within water decision making arena (Moore, 2013). Academics over the past decade have, however, begun to focus more attention towards addressing this void. Much of the scholarly work emanating from leading water researcher institutes has attempted to address the deficiency in our social ecological knowledge as it pertains to governing water. Sense-making research methods have emerged as the preferred research method employed to make explicit, what has up until recently been implicit, information regarding water governance particularly at the local level. For example, (Moore, 2013, p. 493) in her empirical study of local watershed governance processes points out that, "while scholarship may have been presented as depoliticised in the past, the findings from her study of the MDBA (Murray-Darling Basin Authority, Australia) and the PRBC (Prachinburi River Basin Committee, Thailand) highlighted that those responsible for water governance 'on the ground' within watersheds may be far more aware of the social and political dimensions of their work than is recognised within the literature."

Sense-making research consists of a set of research methodologies used to organize and make sense of unknowns in order to be able to act and respond accordingly. Sense making involves determining a plausible understanding or map, testing this understanding through data collection and then refining, or abandoning the map depending on how credible it is (Ancona, 2012; Weber & Glynn, 2006; Weick, 1995). Sense-making research is particularly suited to the field of water governance due to its ability and purpose of making complex and unintelligible environments and information understandable (Heifetz et al., 2009). Sense-making research methods (Sardone & Wong, 2010) offer significant opportunities for developing a more cognitive and comprehensive understanding of central drivers and barriers to developing adaptive and sustainable water governance models. Sense-making research draws upon the premise that water governance occurs within a non-linear, dynamic environment while incorporating complex adaptive system thinking and complexity theory. The use of a sensemaker research analysis facilitates the capture of contextual data typically omitted during survey and questionnaire research methodologies (Kurtz & Snowden, 2003; Kurtz, 2009). Sense-making research is also well suited for multi-perspective analysis of fragmented narratives (text, dialogue etc.) associated with areas such as institutional network communication (knowledge exchange), decision-making, strategy development, and policy-making. One of the key goals is to enable both qualitative and quantitative analyses of the micro-narratives to reveal issues and trends (new knowledge) associated with the water governance networks that either exists or is emergent. The underlying premise of sense-making research is that the successful formulation and implementation of policy in water governance will only be achieved through the development of a deeper and more meaningful understanding of the increasing complexities associated with the governance context (environment), the structure (network), and the content (dialogue or narrative) of water decision-making processes.

Complexity Conundrum

The growing awareness of the deep-seated connections between biophysical environments and human health, security, economy, culture and social justice (Badin et al., 2011; Lubchenco, 1998; Liu et al., 2007) has provided insight into our inability to fully understand, the uncertainties associated with complex socio-ecological and our resultant inability to sustainably manage earth's water resources (Bodin et al., 2011; Levin, 1998). Throughout the water governance literature, there is a consensus that those responsible for governing water face increasing levels of complexity however, there is little discussion as to what the complexity is comprised of or how to address complexity within water governance system. In an attempt to address this deficiency, Moore (2013) developed a summary table from the literature of complexity within the water governance field, at both the global and local scales (Table 2):

Table 2: Complexity factors in water governance (adapted from Moore, 2013, p. 501)

	Global Scale	Local Scale
1.	- historical neglect of 'political' aspects within water research and governance practices - opaque governing context increasing system complexity	- political aspects obvious, and not all challenges considered complex - complexity resulting from severe ecological challenges which serve as disturbances within watershed that are difficult to understand, resolve, or prevent -highlights critical link between 'human' and 'ecology' - Sense-making required to draw on experience to understand factors contributing to challenges
2.	-diverse set of actors and institutions involved but lacking clarity of authority or leadership for water governance yet maintain influence over governance policy agendas contributing to complexity	- 'fuzziness' of roles and responsibilities may not be impediment for decision making and management on day-to-day basis - severe ecological challenges occurring without clear cause-effect relationships which challenged existing governance authority - lack of clarity in-turn potentially creates conflict among those responsible for governing at local scale
3.	-development and advocacy for competing definitions	-similar fragmentation at local scale from diversity of frameworks, ideas, interests and

and uncoordinated governance frameworks leading to fragmentation	values -true challenge is moral and ethical dilemmas posed by confronting this diversity and making decision - human degradation harms the environment and human health and livelihoods which makes determining concrete solutions in light of the potential risks very difficult increasing perceived sense of complexity	

Moore's findings reflect three key aspects associated with multi scale water governance; 1) there are local implications for global approaches to water governance; 2) understanding the linkages between human and ecology is critical in identifying water governance solutions (Bodine et al., 2011); and, 3) employing a sense-making (social relational approach coupled with a formal analytical framework (see Table 3, *Adaptive Management Network Structure Typology Assessment Framework*) can begin to address the lack of clarity surrounding roles, responsibilities and authorities at the local level (Bodin, O. & Prell, 2011).

Social Relational Network Perspective

One of the most effective means for studying social network relationships is social network analysis (SNA), which focuses on the patterns of relationships among actors and their implications (Bodine et al., 2011; Scott, 2000). SNA is guided by formal social theory within a mathematical framework and a systematic analysis of empirical data (Bodine et al., 2011). Identifying specific information such as network structure, actor characteristics and communication patterns is increasingly becoming common place in water governance and resource research. New technologies and the proliferation of easily accessible analysis software which enables capture, analysis and display of relational information has allowed water researchers the ability to pursue new research directions leading and expand the knowledge base of relational influences among actors and institutions and their impacts on water governance transition. SNA provides water governance specialists a new lens through which to identify and analyse drivers and barriers in water decision-making, facilitating better understanding of the relational underpinnings associated with water governance.

SNA has been used in a variety of organizational and social settings, within a range of fields including, but not limited to: military and terrorism studies; medical and health fields; and, geography and management studies (Stein et al., 2011) Although SNA has been in use since the 1960's, it has only recently emerged as the relational research method of choice within the resource (water) governance field. This recent expansion of SNA within the resource sector likely corresponds to an increasing awareness of the importance of the linkages between society and ecology in conjunction with the growing awareness that business-as-usual in water governance is failing to address the escalating number of failing water systems globally. Utilizing social network analysis requires that the social network be viewed as a set of actors, individually, or as an aggregated group or cluster, linked through one or more relationships (Marin & Wellman, 2010; Stein et al., 2011) The communication between the actors defines both the network and the social network data. In SNA, the unit of analysis is the relationship between the actors who provide information for the individual components of the system. "Analysing the relational data allows for the study of how localized interaction between individuals, organizations, or other social entities gives rise to larger-scale patterns – or structures – that both facilitate and constrain individual actors while revealing properties of the social system as a whole"

(Borgatti, et al., 2009; Diani & McAdam, 2003; Stein et al., 2011; Wasserman & Faust, 1994)

Through SNA, mapping of the social relations can be conducted at multiple scales, including actor level, aggregated cluster level and at the whole network scale. Mapping the social relationships reveals hidden characteristics, for example "communities of practice" associated with pockets of localized and/or specialized knowledge, which may have developed over time and place, but may not necessarily be widely known beyond the immediate users or community (i.e., localized conservation efforts). Being able to visualize the social network is the first step in the SNA process.

The social network perspective emphasizes multiple levels of analysis; the differences between the actors are traced to constraints and opportunities that arise from their embeddedness within the network; thus, the structure and behaviour of networks is grounded in and enacted by local interactions among the actors (Knoke & Yang, 2008).

SNA is unlike typical evaluation methodologies in that the program effects and outcomes are not averaged and compared across individuals or programs, rather, SNA assesses the unique structure of the interrelationships among individuals (Lurie et al., 2009; Wasserman, 1994; de Nooy, 2010). SNA enables characterization of communication at the individual actor level (degree of centrality, connectedness, and 'in-betweenness'), and provides a more aggregated metric for network cohesion, information flow, and degree of hierarchical organization (Lurie, 2009).

Adjacency Matrix

	A	B	C	D	E	F	G	H	I	J	K	L	M
1		LP4	LP3	LP2	LP7	LP6	C6F3	FP1	FN1	LP9	C3	LP10	L(
2	LP4	0	0	0	0	0	0	0	0	0	0	0	0
3	LP3	0	0	1	1	1	1	0	0	0	0	0	0
4	LP2	1	1	0	1	1	0	1	0	0	0	1	0
5	LP7	0	0	0	0	0	0	0	0	0	0	0	0
6	LP6	0	0	0	0	0	0	0	0	0	1	0	0
7	C6F3	0	1	0	0	0	0	1	0	0	0	0	0
8	FP1	0	0	0	0	0	0	0	0	0	0	0	0
9	FN1	1	0	0	0	0	0	0	0	0	0	0	0
10	LP9	0	0	0	0	0	0	0	0	0	0	0	0
11	C3	0	0	0	0	0	0	0	1	0	0	0	0
12	LP10	0	0	0	0	0	0	0	0	0	0	0	0
13	LG5	1	1	0	1	1	0	0	0	0	0	0	0
14	LG4	0	1	0	0	0	0	0	0	1	0	0	0
15	FP2	0	0	0	0	0	0	0	0	0	0	0	0

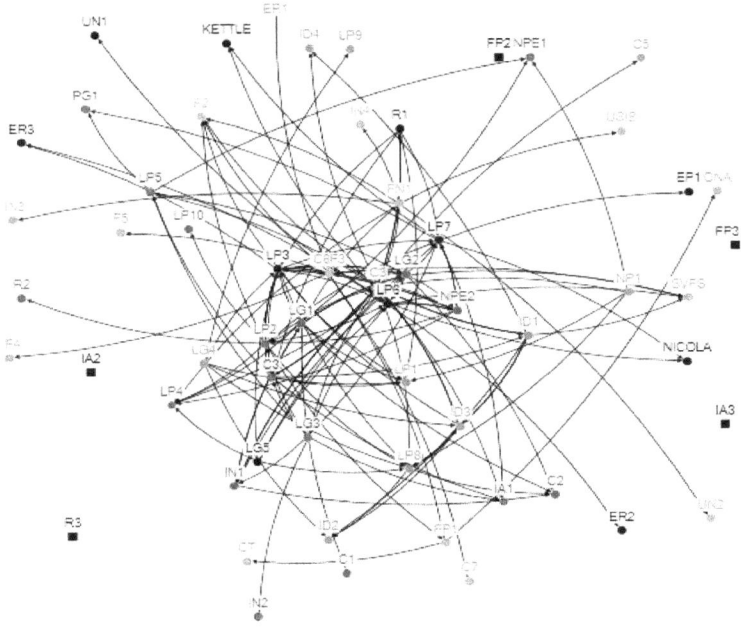

Two of the most common methods of illustrating a social network include an adjacency matrix, and a socio-gram, each having specific strengths and weaknesses. Figures 2a) and 2b) show a adjacency matrix (partial) and a directed socio-gram, with legend, respectively, for the rural watershed planning network, a small rural watershed challenged with increasing development pressures and climate change impacts within a water scarce region of British Columbia.

LP-Local Political LG-Local Gov. Staf.
PG-Prov.Gov St af
FG-Fed. Gov Staf
C–Consultant
F-First Nations (FN) FP-FN Political
USIB-Upper Sim. Ind.Band
CT-Colville Tribe
ONA – Ok. Nat.All.
NP-Non-profit
NPE-NP Environ. IA-Ind. Agriculture
IN-Ind. N. Resource
R-Rec-Tourism
ID- Irrigation Dist. EP-Energy Provider ER-Educ &Research
EO-Educ. Other
SVPS-SimV.Pl.Soc.
Kettle-Ket.Riv Rep
Nicola-Nic. WS Rep

While identifying actor (egocentric) scale characteristics such as centrality (position in network) and between (bridging), SNA can also show both aggregated and whole network information. For example in the given example (Figure 2a and b) the network shows a strong core (strongly linked)-periphery (weakly linked) network structure which may not be ideally suited for the given task of formulating a long range sustainable watershed plan requiring innovation and a broad knowledge base to draw upon (Ahuja, 2000; Saleth & Dinar, 2004). Investigating further, the core appears to consist predominantly of local political representatives and local government staff, which would appear to indicate a centralized *business-as-usual* approach to watershed planning. Alternative network content data would be required to determine actual knowledge bias and goal setting. Further empirically measureable, observations can be made regarding additional network characteristics such as *isolates* (actors within the network but not connected to other actors within the network) or *cliques* (actors connected to each other forming a small cluster but not connected to the larger network) for example. These measures reveal individual or groups of actors who are unlikely to become nodes of innovation and may be restricting information exchange (gate keepers) creating barriers to network advancement. Through analysis of the communication patterns, network strengths and deficiencies are readily identifiable and further in depth investigations can be conducted and recommendations made to address any barriers which may prevent network advancement or mismatched network structure.

The socio-gram (graph) method provides a much more intuitive means to convey network information, in a visual manner that is easily and quickly understood. Based upon Graph Theory, sociograms display the relationships between the actors, represented by lines (arcs, edges, and links) and points (actor, node, and vertices) within the network signifying the communication, communication direction and strength, and relative network positioning between actors and overall network structure. Sociograms however, do not support any mathematical or statistical manipulation (Knoke & Yang, 2008). Examples of additional possible network typologies include (Knoke and Yang, 2008):

- Transaction relations
- Communication relations
- Boundary penetration relations
- Instrumental relations
- Sentiment relations
- Authority/power relations
- Kinship and descent relations

The application of SNA in resource governance, although expanding due largely to the increasing interest in adaptive and co-management arrangements, which require a relational approach, has not been consistently applied. Bodin et al. (2011) have identified three broad categorical approaches (Table 3) identified within the literature:

While Bodine et al. (2011) refer to these as three different categorical approaches, it can be argued that these approaches are in fact a single approach to SNA at three varying stages of research evolution, representing progressive stages from a simplistic understanding towards a more refined and precise level of investigation. Alexander and Armitage (2014, p. 3) argue for a continued effort to evolve SNA, "It is an imperative to move beyond a binary view of social networks and thus offer concepts and tools to advance the understanding of establishment and governance…".

Structural Approach to Adaptive Watershed Governance

One of the key characteristics of the *structurally explicit approach* (Table 3) involves the analysis of systematically collected data using formally defined models and methods to allow the identification of inferred relationships between quantified structural aspects of social networks and outcomes. Bodin et al. (2006) provides an example of this in the *Adaptive*

SNA Approach	Category Descriptions
Binary metaphorical approach	-social networks are treated as a metaphor for saying that there is an exchange of knowledge, information or other resources between actors -social networks treated as unspecified binary variables, either there is a network or there is not -network structure is not explicitly addressed -actors are either socially tied or not -characterized by studies where social networks in natural resource governance are identified as instrumental, but where little is said about the actual structure or pattern of the social networks
Descriptive approach	-this category starts to address some of the key characteristics of the studied social networks -descriptors (e.g. vertical, bonding, bridging) are used and often tied to social concepts such social capital or capacity -further separation enables a more precise analysis - builds on the notion that not all social networks are created equally -studies generally lack methodological studies on how to empirically investigate and analytically distinguish between different descriptions of social network structure, lowering studies ability to explain or increase understanding of how social network structure matters
Structurally explicit approach	-studies where social network has been measured using systematic data collection methods -relational data have been analysed using formally defined models and methods -objective is to infer relationships between formally defined and quantified structural characteristics of social network and various outcomes in natural resource governance

	-structural characteristics may include, whole network characteristics such as clustering, cliqueism, multi-model, central, fragmented or isolates (e.g. (Smythe et al., 2014); various types of ties including strength, directionality (e.g. Stein et al., 2011); and even specific actor characteristics such as bridging actors (organizations) (e.g. (Vignola et al., 2013).

(adapted from Boding et al., 2011, p. 17-18, in Alexander & Armitage, 2014)

Range of SNA approaches in Watershed Governance adaptive management typology from Table 3:- 1) social memory, 2) heterogeneity, 3) redundancy (resilience), 4) learning, 5) adaptive capacity, and 6) trust.

Management (AM) – Network Structure Typology Framework (Table 4). Governance research has shown that the existence of social networks is an important aspect of effective multi-stakeholder natural resource decision making processes (Bodin & Crona, 2009). More specifically, "...the structural patterns or typology of the network can have significant impact on how actors behave", (Bodine and Corona, 2009, p. 366), and how actors ultimately make decisions with respect to resource

Tompkins and Adger, (2004) content that the existence of social linkages between stakeholders has the potential to both increase community resilience and adaptive capacity to change. Increased adaptive capacity within our governance systems can be achieved through a balance of network structural attributes is required (Newman and Dale 2005). Specifically, the following six network attributes were identified as being central to an

Table 4: Adaptive Management Network Structure Typology Assessment Framework (Source: Adapted from Bodin et al. 2006) - Note: x- values indicate a negative influence on adaptive network feature with the presence of higher SNA metric values

management. Contrary to current advocacy for the broad

adoption of collaborative governance as a panacea for all natural resource challenges (Horning and Bauer, 2014) while Newman and Dale (2003) recognized that, 'not all social (governance) networks were created equal.

While not an exhaustive listing of adaptive management (AM) network features, the six listed features are well supported within the literature as primary characteristics associated with adaptation (Bodine et al., 2006; Newman & Dale, 2005; Tompkins & Adger, 2004). Bodine et al. (2006, p. 1) describe the six features as, "... important for the adaptive management of natural resources and the ways in which they are linked to social network structure". The following Framework (Table 4) has been adapted from Bodine et al.'s (2006) matrix linking key features for adaptive management and natural resources and their linkages to social network structures. An expanded description for each of the individual adaptive management network structure features is contained in Appendix 1.

Adaptive Management - Network Structure Typology		SNA Quantitative Metric			
		Reachibility	Density	Betweeness / Modularity	Centrality
Network Structure Features	Social Memory	X	X		
	Heterogeneity		X-	X	
	Redundancy		X		
	Learning	X		X	X-
	Adaptive Capacity	X	X-		X
	Trust		X	X-	

Building on Tomkins and Adger's (2004) and Newman and Dale's (2005) earlier adaptive management and social network research, Bodine et al.'s AM Framework allows for a systematic collection and analysis of data, supported by AM theory, facilitating the comparison of water governance networks.

Through the use of the AM Framework, the implicit relationship between structure and functionality of the social networks can be examined. *Learning,* for example, has been identified within the adaptation literature (Pahl-Wostl et al., 2010) as one of the key aspects associated with a network's ability to adapt to the 'non-stationarity' prevalent in contemporary natural resource systems. Linked to the *Learning* network structure typology are the quantitative social network metrics of `betweenness, *modularity* and *reachability* (indicated by an `x` with either a`+` or `-`, indicating either a positive or negative relationship to the adaptive metric). It should also be noted that other network characteristics such as high degree of *centrality*, may be counterproductive to the networks ability to adapt due to a more centralized network structure (see discussion for Figure 2b) resulting in less experiential learning (Leavitt, 1951; Shaw, 1981)

Utilizing sense-making research techniques, and specifically SNA methods guided by Bodin et . al.'s AM – Network Framework, is particularly important when considering the ongoing challenges facing water governance regimes, particularly in rural environments where challenges may include the following (Norman & Bakker, 2005)

- mismatch in governance structures and integration between levels and jurisdictions particularly when watersheds span national borders;
- distinct and sometimes incompatible governance cultures and mandates (political);
- limited institutional capacity, financial resources, participation capacity and data availability, which is particularly common the more rural the watershed;
- distance (both spatial and social); and

- Psychological-sociological factors, such as mistrust and lack of leadership.

Many of these challenges are often associated with the existing formal governance structures and actors such as local political representatives (Norman & Bakker, 2005). Social network analysis provides a means, through quantitative network data, relational mapping and empirical network analysis techniques, to examine social network drivers and potential barriers to sustainable water governance development. Information from social network analysis makes possible the delineation of key network aspects, such as structure (i.e., density, size, intensity, and spatial proximity), network dynamics (i.e., access, gaps, norms, and rules), and context (formal/informal arrangements, historical or contemporary remnants, pathological barriers, and others).

When coupled with an analysis framework like Bodin et al.'s (2006) AM - *Network Structure Framework*, sense-making (SNA) can provide an effective tool for identifying and analysing existing social network structures, their influence on water governance networks ability to adapt to escalating water governance challenges (e.g. institutional inertia, fragmentation, etc.). However, there remains a gap in SNA research. While network structural and context can be examined through SNA, little information is revealed with respect to the network content that ultimately determines these network characteristics. The following section will elaborate on these limitations.

Social Network Analysis Challenges and Limitations

It is also argued that sense-making research and specifically social network analysis is a research methodology well suited to understand the complex and multi-level socio-ecological processes associated with governing water. However, for the field of social network analysis to continue to grow and advance, several challenges and limitations must be overcome. These identified challenges include: the dynamic development nature of social networks; the multi-level complex characteristics of water governance networks; and, the broad variety of factors beyond communication, between actors, which influence water governance (Albrecht et al., 2014). Challenges commonly associated with the assessment of networks include; network analysis, which is mostly carried out through statistical analysis that tends to ignore network processes; network focus which is often one dimensional; and, data collection and analysis that is limited to communication processes at the exclusion of examination of external impacts and possibly even more importantly the influences of informal network development (Albrecht et al., 2014; Norman & Bakker, 2010). Although challenges and limitation associated with SNA research methodology may in some cases be more applicable in non-water governance related fields, such as military and medical research, it is important for water governance researchers to be aware of their possible implications. For example (Hannan, 2005) identified the challenge of 'garbage-in-garbage-out' as one of the key challenges within the military field, when collecting and mapping social information relating to, for example, possible terrorists networks. Assuming far greater access to water network actors with far more benign social information, should increase the quality of data being collected and analysed in water governance. There remains however, the opportunity for poor or misleading information (i.e. peer bias, confirmation bias or agenda promotion, etc.) stemming from the perceived, or real risk, associated with revealing potentially personal information and the possible repercussions (i.e. loss employment, loss of stature, impact on existing relationships, agenda promotion, etc.) and the general reluctance to reveal intimate information to researchers, leading to reduced overall data quality and reliability, potentially leading to false or misleading observations.

On a more fundamental level, one of the key methodological limitations associated with SNA is the lack of contextual information. While there is significant and important information pertaining to nodes and network structure connecting them, there is limited or no consideration of the network content that ultimately determines relational ties (Moser et al., 2013). The following sections of this paper will discuss the contextual nature of networks and propose an 'enhanced sense-making' research approach in the form of SNA - Discourse Network Analysis (S-DNA), as a complementary mixed-methods, sense-making research design to overcome the contextual limitation of SNA and incorporate a more whole systems approach to water governance.

Discourse Network Analysis

There has been significant growth in the use of SNA research over the past decade due in part to: scientific innovation, and advancements in technology and statistical modelling. The proliferation of the World Wide Web and social media applications, coupled with an increasing interest in relational aspects of resource governance (e.g. co-management). Advancements in technology have included the development and proliferation of easily accessible relational analysis software (e.g. Gephi, Node XL, Packet, Ucinet, etc.) providing scientists, social and otherwise, the tools necessary to investigate relational aspects of social networks through SNA. The increased use of SNA has, however, come at a cost. As the research focus shifts towards relational investigations, researchers tend to disregard the contextual information that facilitates deeper understanding of the very determinants of these networks (Moser et al., 2013)

To address this gap in knowledge and process, its argued that Discourse Network Analysis, as a new tool, would provide category-based content analysis, (i.e. interview data) coupled with social network analysis (Wasserman & Faust, 1994), resulting in a mixed-methods research methodology designed to capture and analyse both the rich qualitative contextual information as well as the quantitative structural network information. By combining research methods, perceived or real deficiencies of either approach will be overcome in a synergistic manner (Leifeld & Haunss, 2012) while meeting the increasing call within academia to incorporate more mixed methods and integrated research. For example the implementation of a purely statistical research analysis is perceived as insufficient and lacking the ability to scrutinize rich qualitative data in a more inductive manner. While at the same time, qualitative research has been criticized for being too diverse and not structured in a way to allow for generalization at a more macro level (Moser et al., 2013). By combining the interpretive approach of discourse analysis (DA) with the more quantitative network analysis (NA) methods, the results will provide a more holistic network data set based upon relational information within a richer adaptive management framework. For example when investigating the network structure of a watershed planning process illustrated in Figure 2, using S-DNA would reveal network characteristics at the actor level (e.g. centrality of specific actors or clusters or who the bridging actors-groups may be) and at the whole network level revealing information such as network fragmentation and appropriate network structure (e.g. core-periphery versus distributed). Once the structural characteristics are determined through SNA, DNA could be utilized to provide a deeper analysis into network content to determine discussion framing, goal setting and ultimately the end policy; and, whether there is existing alignment between network discourse and network structure.

While social network analysis focuses on the relations (links or edges) and patterns of relationships, DNA focuses on the specific motives and actions of the actors within the network, enabling both the network structure and the individual actor motivational data to be investigated. Discourse analysis focuses on the use of language used by actors to assign meaning and ultimately sense-making (Phillips & Jørgensen, 2002). The assumption in DA is that discourse is a social practise involving communication and coordination providing a means to define and align goals (Leifeld, 2013; Habermas, 1981). In the field of water governance, specifically watershed planning, the goals of long term water sustainability, and ultimately the meaning of sustainability itself, are defined through the language employed by the network actors.

(Foucault, 1991) argues that discourse is an exercise in power established through linguistic pattern usage and frame setting within the dominant network clusters or actors. The rural watershed planning network for example, represented in the sociograph (Figure 1b), illustrates this phenomenon through its core-periphery network structure with the core being dominated by local government and local political actors.

Discourse Analysis can take on many forms depending upon the questions that are being investigated and, the subject of analysis. There are various methodological approaches associated with discourse analysis including: critical discourse analysis, category-based content analysis, argumentative discourse analysis and semantic networks, to more hybrid approaches including decomposition analysis and policy network analysis (see Leifeld, 2013). It has been argued that discourse analysis approaches that employ actor-centered approaches (e.g.

advocacy coalition framework, collective symbolic coping) overlook the richer contextual data contained in the discourse while the content oriented approaches (e.g. critical discourse analysis, category based content analysis, etc.) fail to adequately consider the actor level information (Leifeld, 2013). While the various discourse analysis methods allow for the collection and analysis of data sets that are richer in content, Leifeld (2013) argues that there remains a gap between relational network information and the rich content which ultimately determines the networks under investigation, or what Moses (2013, p. 548) refers to as the 'content of ties'. This paper contends that to address this gap S- DNA be used to investigate both the social network characteristics and the network content which determine the social network characteristics to ultimately identify the level of alignment or misalignment between the two.

Aligning Network Discourse and Structure within an Adaptive Framework

The main purpose of Discourse Network Analysis (DNA) is the analysis of actor-based discourse (Leifeld, 2013). DNA involves a two stage process; the first stage involves content analysis where dialogue is coded into categories from which network data is then extracted. The process of grouping coherent linguistic units, or 'frames', into categories is repeated until there are a sufficient number of categories to answer the original research question(s). Although content analysis can be both inductive and deductive, the preferred method is inductive particularly in investigations where the categories are unknown. For example in a case where the goal may be to determine the central themes of discourse involving the process of establishing a watershed plan and the alignment of this discourse with stated goals or identified issues or concerns needing to be addressed such as climate change adaptation and water sustainability, inductive categorization would reveal the true framing and content of the governance process.

Determining alignment between discourse and identified issues and goal setting is a critical and crucial step in establishing if our governance systems are currently 'transitioning to sustainability' or whether institutional inertial continues to hinder this transition (Genus, 2014). For example, in a recent study looking at legally binding emissions treaty to advert catastrophic climate change, the traditional discourse from developing nations argued that, "any international agreement must be based on historical and per capita carbon emissions and developed countries must be responsible for reducing their emissions first and funding mitigation and adaptation in other countries", (Thaker & Leiserowitz, 2014).

Recently, however, discourse analysis in India, as an example, has revealed that traditional climate change discourse (government) is shifting in recognition of the "co-benefits" and alignment between India's; development aspirations; concern for energy access; and recognition of climate change vulnerability coupled with an alignment of climate change and development goals (Thaker & Leiserowitz, 2014). Additionally, new actors and institutions have also contributed to increased governance 'flexibility', with potential implications for climate change policies in India.

This study highlights two key interrelated elements associated with transitioning our water governance systems; network content, and network structure, each playing a key role in shaping the other in the evolution of our current water systems to more sustainable governance regimes. Developing a deeper and more comprehensive understanding of the influences content and structure have on each other and the overall network transition through S-DNA provides a first and important step in ensuring alignment between intention and application in water governance. Utilizing S-DNA as a new and more holistic mixed methods approach to governance research will provide researchers with the means to answer critical questions pertaining to network structure (e.g. fragmentation) and key actor characterization (e.g. bridging actors) along with developing a deeper understanding of the underlying drivers and barriers to reducing complexity and facilitating water governance adaptation.

Conclusion

As most water regimes around the world struggle with transitioning water governance to more adaptive and sustainable models, addressing challenges including but not limited to the following become essential for any governance transition success (Norman & Bakker, 2005):

- standardization of laws and regulations (harmonization) versus delegation of decision-making and policy implementation to more local levels of government (subsidiarity);
- aligning mismatched governance structures;
- integrating often incompatible intra-jurisdictional governance cultures and mandates;
- overcoming deficiencies in institutional and citizen capacity;
- inadequate and insufficient resources, including financial;
- active non-participation of key stakeholders;
- data availability; and,
- social/psychological factors including mistrust and lack of leadership

Common to all of these challenges is the growing gap between scholarship, policy and practical knowledge relating to the understanding of the roles, types of influence and power, and authority and legitimacy actors and institutions have within water decision making arena. As a result, water related decisions often fail to consider the interconnected nature of human-nature with the natural water cycle (Stein et al., 2011).

Increasingly attention within water governance literature has shifted towards institutions as viewed through a socio-ecologically lens. A growing number of water experts have begun to argue for a re-conceptualization of water institutions as more than technical, rational, and actor-driven phenomena.

This re-conceptualization frames water institutions as consisting of multiple political actors, or groups of actors, with varying levels of influence, pursuing agendas aligned with individual self-interests. This pursuit occurs within a context of unique social and cultural embeddedness shaping both the institutional responses and their ability and willingness to respond. This is particular important when considering climate change and water institutions which occupy central roles in identifying the issues, framing the subsequent discussions, driving the agendas and ultimately determine the final policies enacted. Although these institutions (i.e. technical committees, planning committees etc.) may be regarded as goal-directed inter-organisational networks, little is known about these organizational networks giving rise to questions such as: coordination, representation, accountability, knowledge creation, innovation, institutional performance and overall governance structure.

A broad recognition of institutions as being embedded in a complex socio-ecological environment, where inter- and intra-actor relationships both influence and are influenced by the context and structural elements of the system, has led to a rising number of academics promoting a more relational approach to water as opposed to merely approaching water as a consumptive resource. Saleth & Dinar (2004) argue that a clear re-conceptualization of the water governance includes both the environment (system) and structure (institutions). This paper extends this conceptualization by arguing that content (dialogue), as a driver for the network structure, is also a critical consideration in reconceptualising water governance. In a reconceptualised water governance paradigm, the social and political dimensions of water governance must be made explicit in a generalized manner. If the goal, as suggested in the water governance literature, is to improve the performance of our water systems, then a deeper and clear understanding of water governance from a relational perspective is an effective means by which we can achieve this goal. To achieve this, water governance researchers have begun to employ emerging sense-making research methods, specifically social network analysis, in an attempted to facilitate a deeper understanding of the social underpinnings of human behavior in water decision making. Social Network Analysis, as a preferred sense-making research methodology, provides key quantitative network investigation tool, through sociogram mapping of network communication and empirical network analysis techniques. Employing social network analysis enables the delineation of network aspects, such as structure (i.e., density, size, intensity, and spatial proximity), and network dynamics (i.e., access, gaps, norms, and rules), and context (formal/informal arrangements, historical or contemporary remnants, pathological barriers, and others). There are however limitations in the use of SNA as a standalone research approach.

This paper argues that successful water governance transition to sustainability requires a deeper understanding of network content in addition to network structure and context. To achieve this, a proposed new mixed method, sense-making research agenda, combining social network analysis with discourse network analysis. Using a more synergistic S-DNA research approach will provide researchers with an effective tool able to quantify relational and content aspects of water governance networks. Employing S-DNA as a mixed-methods research program provides researchers with the means to examine critical water concerns which continue to confound water experts, concerns such as; the ongoing fragmentation – connectivity conundrum; or, determining the role bridging actors - institutions play in transitioning water governance systems for example.

These questions are particularly relevant in a Canadian context where the wide variety of regions and unique hydrology contexts has resulted in one of the most decentralized and fragmented water governance systems in the developed world (Bakker & Cook, 2011).This high degree of decentralization has continued to challenge water system integration and coordination, creating a significant barrier to sustainability transition for many of the water governance systems across Canada approaching, or already in a state of crisis.

Bibliography

Acheson, J. M. (2006).   Institutional Failure in Resource
         Management. Annual Review of Anthropology,
         35(1), 117–134.
         doi:10.1146/annurev.anthro.35.081705.123238

Ahuja, H. (2000). Collaboration Networks , Structural Holes
         , and Innovation : Longitudinal Study Gautam
         Ahuja. Administrative Science Quarterly, 45(3),
         425–455.

Albrecht, M., Elbe, J., Elbe, S., & Meyer, W. (2014).
         Analyzing and evaluating regional governance
         networks: Three challenges for applications.
         Evaluation, 20(1), 58–74.
         doi:10.1177/1356389013518457

Alexander, S. M., & Armitage, D. (2014). A social relational
         network perspective for MPA science.
         Conservation Letters, 00(0), n/a–n/a.
         doi:10.1111/conl.12090

Ancona, D. (2012). Sensemaking: Framing and acting in the
         unknown. The Handbook for Teaching
         Leadership: Knowing, Doing, and Being.

Bakker, K. (2003).   An uncooperative commodity :
         privatizing water in England and Wales (p. 224).
         New York: Oxford University Press.

Bakker, K., & Cook, C. (2011a).   Water Governance in
         Canada: Innovation and Fragmentation.
         International Journal of Water Resources
         Development, 27(2), 275–289.
         doi:10.1080/07900627.2011.564969

Bakker, K., & Cook, C. (2011b). Water Governance in

Canada: Innovation and Fragmentation. International Journal of Water Resources Development, 27(2), 275–289. doi:10.1080/07900627.2011.564969

Bakker, K. J. (2003).   From public to private to … mutual? Restructuring water supply governance in England and Wales. Geoforum, 34(3), 359–374. doi:10.1016/S0016-7185(02)00092-1

Baviskar, A. (2007). The dream machine: the model development project and the remaking of the state. In M. C. H. H. R. Kanchan Chopra (Ed.), Growth, Equity, Environment and Population: Economic and Sociological Perspectives (p. 287). New Delhi: Sage Publications.

Berkes, F., Colding, J., and Folke, C. (Ed.). (2003). Navigating social-ecological systems : building resilience for complexity and change (p. 393). New York: Cambridge University Press.

Bodin, Ö., & Crona, B. I. (2009). The role of social networks in natural resource governance: What relational patterns make a difference? Global Environmental Change, 19(3), 366–374. doi:10.1016/j.gloenvcha.2009.05.002

Bodin, Ö, Ramirez-Sanchez, S., and Prell, C. (2011).   A Social Relational Approach to Natural Resource Governance. In Social Networks and Natural Resource Management: Uncovering the Social Fabric of Environmental Governance (pp. 3–28). New York: Cambridge University Press.

Bodin, Ö., and Prell, C. (2011). Social Networks and Natural Resource Management: Uncovering the Social Fabric of Environmental Governance. (C. Bodin, Ö., and Prell, Ed.)Social Networks and Natural Resource Management: Uncovering the Social Fabric of Environmental Governance (p. 376). New York: Cambridge University Press.

Borgatti, S. P., Mehra, A., Brass, D. J., & Labianca, G. (2009). Network analysis in the social sciences. Science (New York, N.Y.), 323(5916), 892–5. doi:10.1126/science.1165821

Bridge, G., & Perreault, T. (2009). Environmental governance. In A companion to environmental geography (Noel Castr., pp. 475–497). Wiley-Blackwell.

Brien, K. O. (2011). Global environmental change II : From adaptation to deliberate transformation, 36(5), 667–676.

Brown, R. R., & Farrelly, M. a. (2009). Delivering sustainable urban water management: a review of the hurdles we face. Water Science and Technology : A Journal of the International Association on Water Pollution Research, 59(5), 839–46. doi:10.2166/wst.2009.028

Budds, J. and Hinojosa, L. (2012). Restructuring and Rescaling Water Governance in Mining Contexts: The Co-Production of Waterscapes in Peru. Water Alternatives, 5(1), 119–137.

Cleaver, F., & Franks, T. (2007). Distilling or Diluting ? Negotiating the Water Research-Policy

Interface, 1(1), 157–176.

Collins, K. B., & Ison, R. L. (2009). Trusting Emergence: Some Experiences of Learning about Integrated Catchment Science with the Environment Agency of England and Wales. Water Resources Management, 24(4), 669–688. doi:10.1007/s11269-009-9464-8

Dacin, M. T., Goodstein, J., & Scott, W. R. (2012). Forum Special Instructional Change, 45(1), 43–56.

De Loë, R. C., Armitage, D., Plummer, R., Davidson, S., & Moraru, L. (2009). From Government to Governance: A State-of-the-Art Review of Environmental Governance. (p. 67).

Diani, M., and McAdam, D. (2003). Social movements and networks : relational approaches to collective action. (D. Diani, M., and McAdam, Ed.) (p. 348). New York: oxford University Press.

Dorado, S. (2005). Institutional Entrepreneurship, Partaking, and Convening. Organizational Studies, 26(3), 385–414.

Engle, N. L., Johns, O. R., Lemos, M. C., & Nelson, D. R. (n.d.). Integrated and Adaptive Management of Water Resources : Tensions , Legacies , and the Next Best Thing, 16(1).

Foucault, M. (1991). Governmentality. In. In & P. M. B. Graha, C. Gordon (Ed.), The Foucault effect: Studies in governmentality (pp. 87–104). Harvester Wheatsheaf.

Genus, A. (2014). Governing Sustainability: A Discourse-Institutional Approach. Sustainability, 6(1), 283–305. doi:10.3390/su6010283

Godden, L., Ison, R. L., & Wallis, P. J. (2011). Water Governance in a Climate Change World: Appraising Systemic and Adaptive Effectiveness. Water Resources Management, 25(15), 3971–3976. doi:10.1007/s11269-011-9902-2

Habermas J. (1981). The Theory of Communicative Action. Polity. Cambridge University Press.

Hall, A., & Taylor, C. R. (1990). Political Science and the Three New Institutionalisms , (1996), 936–957.

Hannan, M. J. (2005). Operational Net Assessment: A Framework for Social Network Analysis and Requirements for Critical Debate (Vol. 298, p. 25).

Heifetz, R., Grashow, A., & Linsky, M. (2009). Leadership in a (Permanent) Crisis. Harvard Business Review, 87(7/8), 62–69.

Hodgson, S. (2006). Modern Water Rights: Theory and Practice (p. 120). Rome, Italy: FAO Legislative Study (FAO).

Hotimsky, S., Cobb, R., & Bond, A. (2003). Contracts or Scripts ? A Critical Review of the Application of Institutional Theories to the Study of Environmental Change, 11(1).

Knoke, D., & Yang, S. (2008). Social network analysis: Quantitative applications in the social sciences

(2nd ed.). Los Angeles: Sage Publiscations.

Kurtz, C. F. (2009). The Wisdom of Clouds, 1–20.

Kurtz, C. F., & Snowden, D. J. (2003). The New Dynamics of Strategy sense-making in a complex-complicated world, 1–23.

Lautze, J., de Silva, S., Giordano, M., & Sanford, L. (2011). Putting the cart before the horse: Water governance and IWRM. Natural Resources Forum, 35(1), 1–8. doi:10.1111/j.1477-8947.2010.01339.x

Leavitt, H. (1951). Some effects of certain communication patterns on group performance. Journal of Abnormal and Social Psychology, 46, 38–50.

Leifeld, P. (2013). Reconceptualizing Major Policy Change in the Advocacy Coalition Framework : A Discourse Network Analysis of German Pension Politics, 169–198.

Leifeld, P., & Haunss, S. (2012). Political discourse networks and the conflict over software patents in Europe. European Journal of Political Research, 51(3), 382–409. doi:10.1111/j.1475-6765.2011.02003.x

Levin, S. A. (1998). Ecosystems and the Biosphere as Complex Adaptive Systems. Ecosystems, 1(5).

Linton, J. (2010). What is water?: the history of a modern abstraction. UBC Press.

Loftus, A. (2009). Rethinking Political Ecologies of Water.

Third World Quarterly, 30(5), 953–968.
doi:10.1080/01436590902959198

Loftus, A., & Lumsden, F. (n.d.). Reworking Hegemony in
the Urban Waterscape. Centre for Civil Society
Research Report No. 43 (pp. 101–124).

Lurie, S. J., Fogg, T. T., & Dozier, A. M. (2009). Social
network analysis as a method of assessing
institutional culture: three case studies.
Academic Medicine : Journal of the Association
of American Medical Colleges, 84(8), 1029–35.
doi:10.1097/ACM.0b013e3181ad16d3

Menard, C., & Saleth, R. M. (2011). The effectiveness of
alternative Water Governance Arrangement.
Towards a Green Economy, 1–29.

Meyer, J. W., & Rowan, B. (n.d.). Institutionalized
Organizations : Formal Structure as Myth and
Ceremonyl, 2.

Molle, F., Mollinga, P. P., & Wester, P. (2008). Hydraulic
Bureaucracies and the Hydraulic Mission :
Flows of Water , Flows of Power, 2(3), 328–
349.

Moore, M. (2013). Perspectives of Complexity in Water
Governance : Local Experiences of Global
Trends, 6(3), 487–505.

Moser, C., Groenewegen, P., & Huysman, M. (2013).
Extending Social Network Analysis with
Discourse Analysis: Combining Relational with
Interpretive Data (pp. 547–561). Vienna:
Springer.

Neef, A. (2007). Transforming Rural Water Governance :
Towards Deliberative and Polycentric Models ?,
2(1), 53–60.

Newman, L., & Dale, A. (2003). Network Structure ,
Diversity , and Proactive Resilience Building : a
Response to Tompkins and Adger, 10(1).

Nooy, W. De. (2010). Communication in Natural Resource
Management : Agreement between and
Disagreement within Stakeholder Groups, 18(2).

Norman, E. S., & Bakker, K. (2009). Transgressing Scales:
Water Governance Across the Canada–U.S.
Borderland. Annals of the Association of
American Geographers, 99(1), 99–117.
oi:10.1080/00045600802317218

Norman, E. S., Bakker, K., & Cook, C. (2012). Introduction
to the Themed Section : Water Governance and
the Politics of Scale, 5(1), 52–61.

Norman, E., & Bakker, K. (2005). Drivers and Barriers of
Cooperation in Transboundary Water
Governance: A Case Study of Western Canada
and the United States.

Ostrom, E. (1968). COPING WITH TRAGEDIES OF, 493–
535.

Ostrom, E. (1990). Governing the commons: The evolution
of institutions for collective action.

Ostrom, E. (2009). Understanding institutional diversity.
Princeton university press.

Ostrom, E. (2010). Beyond Markets and States : Polycentric Governance of Complex Economic Systems †. American Economics Review, 100(3), 641–672. doi:10.1257/aer.100.3.641

Ostrom, E. (2010). Polycentric systems for coping with collective action and global environmental change. Global Environmental Change, 20(4), 550–557. doi:10.1016/j.gloenvcha.2010.07.004

Ostrom, E., Janssen, M. A., & Anderies, J. M. (2007). No Title, 15176–15178.

Pahl-Wostl, C., Jeffrey, P., Isendahl, N., & Brugnach, M. (2010). Maturing the New Water Management Paradigm: Progressing from Aspiration to Practice. Water Resources Management, 25(3), 837–856. doi:10.1007/s11269-010-9729-2

Pahl-wostl, C., Sendzimir, J., Jeffrey, P., Aerts, J., Berkamp, G., & Cross, K. (2000). Managing Change toward Adaptive Water Management through Social Learning, 12(2).

Perramond, E. P. (2012). The Politics of Scaling Water Governance and Adjudication in New Mexico, 5(1), 62–82.

Perreault, T. (2006). From the Guerra Del Agua to the Guerra Del Gas : Resource Governance , Neoliberalism and Popular Protest in Bolivia, (October 2003).

Pfeffer, J.S., Salancik, G. (1978). The external control of organizations: a resource dependence perspective. New York.

Phillips, L. & Jørgensen, M. W. (2002). Discourse analysis: as theory and method. London: Sage Publications.

Poirier, B. a., & de Loë, R. C. (2010). Analyzing Water Institutions in the 21st Century: Guidelines for Water Researchers and Professionals. Journal of Natural Resources Policy Research, 2(3), 229–244. doi:10.1080/19390459.2010.486162

Political Science and the Three New Institutionalisms Peter A . Hall and Rosemary C . R . Taylor. (n.d.), (June 1996).

Powell, W. W., & DiMaggio, P. J. (1991). The New Institutionalism in Organizational Analysis. (W. W. Powell & P. J. DiMaggio, Eds.)The New Institutionalism and Organizational Analysis (Vol. 17, p. 478). University of Chicago Press. doi:10.2307/258726

Rathwell, K. J., & Peterson, G. D. (2012). Connecting Social Networks with Ecosystem Services for Watershed Governance: a Social-Ecological Network Perspective Highlights the Critical Role of Bridging Organizations. Ecology and Society, 17(2), art24. doi:10.5751/ES-04810-170224

Saleth, R. M., & Dinar, A. (2005). Water institutional reforms : theory and practice, 7, 1–19.

Saleth, R. M., & Dinar, A. (2004). The institutional economics of water: a cross-country analysis of institutions and performance.

Scott, W. R. (2005). Institutional theory: Contributing to a theoretical research program. Great Minds in Management: The Process of Theory Development,, 460–484.

Scott, W. R. (2008). Approaching adulthood: the maturing of institutional theory. Theory and Society, 37(5), 427–442. doi:10.1007/s11186-008-9067-z

Sewell, J. W. H. (1992). A Theory of Structure: Duality, agency, and transformation. American Journal of Sociology, 1–29.

Shaw, M. E. (1981). Group dynamics : the psychology of small group behavior. (3rd ed.). New York: McGraw-Hill.

Smythe, T. C., Thompson, R., & Garcia-Quijano, C. (2014). The inner workings of collaboration in marine ecosystem-based management: A social network analysis approach. Marine Policy, 50, 117–125. doi:10.1016/j.marpol.2014.05.002

Sproule-Jones, M., Johns, C. and Heinmiller, T. (2008). Canadian water politics: conflicts and institutions (p. 390). Montreal: McGill University.

Stein, C., Ernstson, H., & Barron, J. (2011). A social network approach to analyzing water governance: The case of the Mkindo catchment, Tanzania. Physics and Chemistry of the Earth, Parts A/B/C, 36(14-15), 1085–1092. doi:10.1016/j.pce.2011.07.083

Steyaert, P., & Ollivier, G. (2005). The European Water

Framework Directive : How Ecological Assumptions Frame Technical and Social Change, 12(1).

Swatuk, L. A. (2003). A Political Economy of Water in Southern Africa, 1(1), 24–47.

Swynegedouw, E. (1999). Modernity and Hybridity : Nature , Regeneracionismo , and the Production of the Spanish Waterscape , 1890-1930. Annals of the Association of American Geographers, 89(3).

Thaker, J., & Leiserowitz, A. (2014). Shifting discourses of climate change in India. Climatic Change, 123(2), 107–119. doi:10.1007/s10584-014-1059-6

Thompson, L. (n.d.). Improving the creativity of organizational work groups.

Tompkins, E. L., & Adger, W. N. (2004). Does Adaptive Management of Natural Resources Enhance Resilience to Climate Change ? Ecology & Society, 9(2).

Vatn, A. (2005). Rationality, institutions and environmental policy. Ecological Economics, 55(2), 203–217. doi:10.1016/j.ecolecon.2004.12.001

Vignola, R., McDaniels, T. L., & Scholz, R. W. (2013). Governance structures for ecosystem-based adaptation: Using policy-network analysis to identify key organizations for bridging information across scales and policy areas. Environmental Science & Policy, 31, 71–84. doi:10.1016/j.envsci.2013.03.004

Vogel, E. (2012). Parcelling out the Watershed : The Recurring Consequences of Organising Columbia River Management within a Basin-Based Territory, 5(1), 161–190.

Wasserman, S. & Faust, K. (1994). Social Network Analysis: Methods and Applications. Cambridge: Cambridge University Press.

Weber, K., & Glynn, M. a. (2006). Making Sense with Institutions: Context, Thought and Action in Karl Weick's Theory. Organization Studies, 27(11), 1639–1660. doi:10.1177/0170840606068343

Weick, K. E. (1995). Sensemaking in Organizations (Vol. 3., p. 231). CA: Sage.

Chapter-III

Sustainability Analysis and Stakeholders' Perception for Small Hydropower Development in Western Himalayan Region of India

Deepak Kumar & S.S. Katoch*

Abstract

Small hydropower projects (SHPs), though generally considered more environmentally benign and socially acceptable as compared to large projects, yet their overall sustainability is under suspicion especially in the Indian Himalayan Region (IHR). Almost all SHPs in this region are being developed in run of the river (RoR) mode which is assumed to cause less/no submergence and less displacement of people as compared to large reservoir based hydropower production mode. However, RoR mode of power generation is causing ruthless tunnelling of hills, strangulation of streams due to improper muck disposal, conversion of streams into dry ditches, short term compensation gains and long term social cum environmental pains in the absence of proper planning and monitoring mechanism. This paper presents a SHP development study from hydro rich Beas river basin of Himachal Pradesh, a state nestled in western Himalayas region of India. In depth field studies and focus group discussions with the project affected people of some SHPs in this region suggest that sustainability issues with respect to SHPs are not small in proportion to their installed capacities. There is an urgent and strong need to revise the threshold limit of SHPs in this region and also include them under EIA process.

Keywords - Developers, Indian Himalayan Region,, Run of the river, Small Hydropower Projects,, Sustainability

*Centre for Energy and Environment, National Institute of Technology, Hamirpur, Himachal Pradesh, India

Introduction

In many parts of the world, large reservoir based hydropower projects have been in the line of fire for their multiple, large scale impacts such as submergence due to formation of reservoir and subsequent displacement and rehabilitation of native people. Hence, the focus is now on construction and development of small hydropower projects (SHPs). These projects can fulfil the technological, environmental, economic and social sustainability criteria in hilly regions of many developing countries [1]. It is the form of renewable energy technology which is considered to be economically viable, having long life (50 years or more), highly efficient (70 to 90%), largely carbon free, robust, flexible and having an attractive energy pay back ratio [2]. Due to these advantages, SHPs have become a favourite mode of power production all over the world in general and Himalayan countries in particular. However, in the absence of proper planning and monitoring, flouting of norms by developers and ever increasing public rage, sustainability of SHPs is under suspicion now.

This study is primarily aimed at assessing the sustainability of SHPs in Indian Himalayan Region (IHR) in general and western Indian Himalayan Region in particular. For assessing sustainability of SHPs in the real world, the paper presents field studies of 3 SHPs located in Beas basin of western Himalayan region of India.

Small Hydropower Development

Development of small hydropower is an important tool for sustainable development in mountainous regions of developing and underdeveloped world. Himalayan countries are particularly keen to develop SHPs due to availability of numerous glaciers and rain fed perennial streams and conducive topography. These projects are easy to install, having mature technology, publically more acceptable and suitable for sensitive mountain ecology particularly in run of the river mode. More than 90% hydropower projects (whether small or large) are now being designed and constructed in this mode only.

Scenario of small hydropower development in global, Asian and Indian perspective

Global small hydropower potential is about 173 GW. The installed small hydropower capacity (up to 10 MW) is estimated to be 75 GW in 2011/2012. More than half of the world's known hydropower potential is located in Asia. Southern Asia (Afghanistan, Bangladesh, Bhutan, India, Iran, Nepal, Pakistan and Sri Lanka) has the small hydropower potential estimated at 18,077 MW (for plants up to 10 MW), of which 3,563 MW has been developed. China ranks first in terms of an installed hydropower capacity of 249 GW. In this installed capacity, contribution of small hydropower is significant; with 45,000 stations nationwide and 65 GW installed capacity [3].

In India, hydropower projects having installed capacity > 2 MW but ≤ 25 MW are categorised and named as small hydropower projects (SHPs). An estimated potential of about 20,000 MW of SHPs exists in India. Ministry of New and Renewable Energy (MNRE) has created a database of potential sites of SHPs. 6,474 potential sites with an aggregate capacity of 19,749 MW for projects up to 25 MW capacity have been identified [4]. The ministry's aim is that the small hydropower installed capacity should be about 7,000 MW by the end of 12th five year plan (2012-17).

SHPs having cumulative installed capacity of 3763.15 MW were installed in India till 31st December, 2013 [5].

Scenario of small hydropower development in Indian Himalayan Region (IHR) perspective

The Himalayas are the world's highest, youngest and very fragile mountain ranges. The Indian part of Himalayas popularly known as Himalayan Region (IHR) includes 10 states, 95 districts, contributing about 16.2% of India's total geographic area and shares international border with 7 countries. With most of the part crowned with snow-covered peaks, presence of numerous glaciers, perennial streams and lakes, this region satisfies water needs of a large part of Indian sub-continent. This region is a house for three major river systems i.e. Indus, Ganga and Brahamputra [6, 7]. With the increase in demand of electricity due to population rise and industrial advancement, this area has been heavily targeted and at present under tremendous pressure for hydropower development. Western part of IHR includes three states Jammu and Kashmir, Himachal Pradesh and Uttrakhand having a hydropower potential of about 20000 MW, 23000 MW and 26215 MW respectively [8-10].

Fig. 1 shows the location of IHR in general and western Indian Himalayan region in particular.

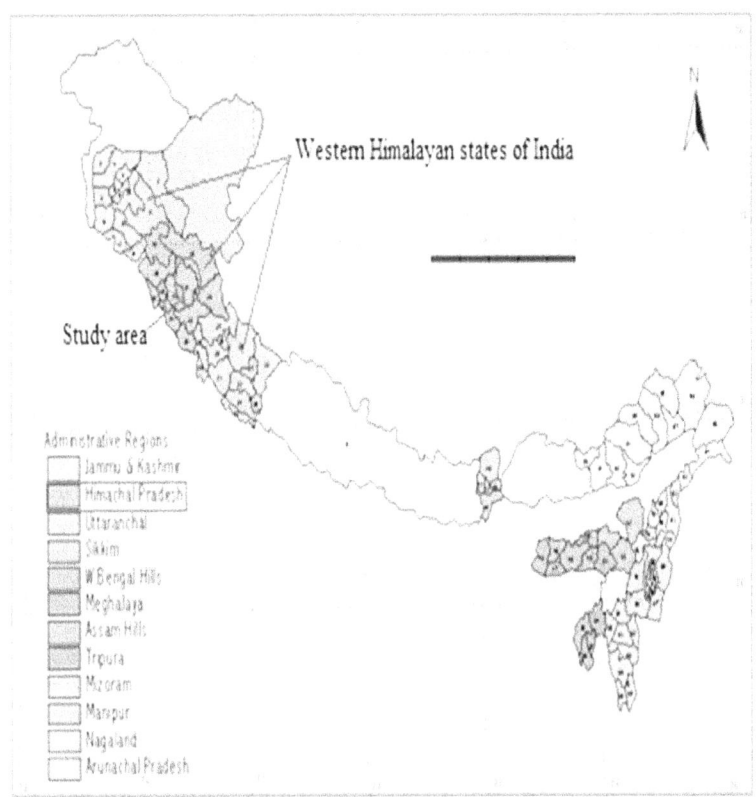

Figure 1   Indian Himalayan Region (IHR) states [6].

Sustainability of SHPs

SHPs often carry the tags such as "sustainable", "green", "environment friendly" etc. with them. These tags have been attributed to the fact that most of these projects are run of the river type with little or no storage. The water after being used for generation of electricity returns back to the same stream on downstream side. These are also of interest under the CDM (Clean Development Mechanism) because they directly displace greenhouse gas emissions while contributing to sustainable rural development [11]. Due to so called "sustainability" of small hydro projects, this type of projects has been exempted from environment clearance, environment management plan and public hearing in many countries (including India) no matter how severe their impacts maybe.

In the frenzy of tapping hydro potential for making profit/earn revenue, small projects are now coming up on the smaller streams also which sustain local livelihoods of remotely located poor communities. It disturbs the fragile but bio-diverse ecosystems in numerous ways. When numbers of projects are undertaken intensively and repeatedly over a large area, the nature is not able to absorb or dampen its adverse effects due to their recurrence and collective magnitude [12]. Same principle applies in case of extensive and unplanned development of SHPs in a particular region.

Factors creating the sustainability suspense about SHPs

Though almost all Himalayan states have formulated hydropower policies for development of small hydropower projects yet the implementation part is very poor. Due to lack of proper planning, inspection and monitoring, many factors have cropped up which are targeting all the three well known aspects (environmental, social and economic) of sustainability.

Environmental sustainability

Inadequate environmental flow, improper disposal of muck, lack of compensatory afforestation, climate change, cascade development etc. are some important factors which are affecting the overall environmental sustainability of SHPs.

Inadequate environmental flow

Streams are lifelines of people in Himalayan regions. Diversion of water for generation of power badly affects availability of water in the streams and ground water recharge of aquifers. Subsequently agriculture and/or fruit production, water mills, other vegetation, terrestrial animals and aquatic life which are all dependent upon stream water are badly affected. Although there are norms and guidelines for release of minimum flow in the streams for sustainability of ecosystem but these are hardly followed in the field.

Muck generation and improper disposal

RoR mode generally involves provision of tunnel (generally 1 to 2 km long, adits are additional) for diversion of water up to penstock. Many times, these tunnels cause diversion/interception or seepage of underground water.

Ruthless tunneling inside the hills (using blasting operation) produces large quantity of muck. Haphazard and unscientific dumping of this muck in nearby easily available sites (hill slopes, forest, along stream course without any protection or retaining works) spoils the common grass lands, causes permanent damage to affected vegetation, narrowing of stream path (or even blockage forming a small lake) and burying/diversion of outlets of water sources.

Compensatory afforestation

For restoring the environment back to its normal position after the construction of the project, compensatory afforestation (CA) is considered as an important step. However, in many regions, in spite of depositing necessary funds by the developers for compensatory afforestation, this process is not undertaken seriously by executing agencies (generally forest department).

Climate change

In the recent times, factor of climate change has also become important with respect to sustainability of hydropower sector. Excessive melting of glaciers, untimely and inadequate rain and/or snow and declining discharge in rivers and their tributaries have put a big question mark over the sustainability of small and large hydropower projects. Mapping of 224 glaciers of the river Beas basin during the period 1972-2006 had revealed that the glacier cover reduced from 419 km^2 to 371 km^2 thus, witnessing about 11.6% deglaciation in the basin [13].

Cascade development of projects

In order to tap maximum hydro potential from the same stream, elevation wise stretches are being allocated to small projects. In this process, mountainous streams are converted into cascades of power projects thus altering ecological conditions and leaving little space for original habitats [14] This process results in virtual death of steam in a comparatively longer stretch as compared to single project. It has already been highlighted by many researchers that the effect of more than one plant over a river is much greater than that of a single plant due to the cumulative impacts resulting from consecutive construction [15]

Social Sustainability

In the present scenario, social sustainability has gained prime importance. Any hydropower project cannot sustain without public support and co-operation. Lack of public acceptance and participation in decision making, false promises made by developers, inadequate and/or late compensation, impact on agriculture and/or horticulture, partiality in imparting project benefits etc. are some important issues challenging the social sustainability of SHPs.

Lack of public acceptance and participation in decision making

SHP affected people find it difficult to believe that their lives, streams and forests are being destroyed in the name of national development. In several areas across hilly states, news of local protests, formation of agitation groups, tirade of NGOs (Non-Government Organisations), cross filing (from both people and developer side) of police complaints, court cases have become common now. There is complete absence of mechanism to include participation of general villagers in decision making during different phases of project development.

False promises and flouting of norms by developers

In many regions, it is mandatory for the developer to seek NOC from the concerned Gram Panchayat (an elected village level institution in India) before proceeding for development of hydropower project. In order to get this NOC, developers make many promises like free electricity, employment to every project affected household, free LPG cylinder, construction of approach road or small bridge, free dispensary, scholarship to children etc. However, once NOC is granted, majority of promises are not kept. Further, in order to make easy and early profits, many times developers indulge in flouting the norms with impunity (like diverting whole water for power generation, dumping of muck at un-authorised sites, restrictions on movement of men and animals etc.)

Inadequate and/or late award of compensation

In majority of cases, project affected people do not receive the promised compensation and even if they get it any way, they get it quite late. Further, for any additional damage during project construction or after commissioning, it is very difficult to even talk of compensation. The people have started realising that one-time monetary compensation is inadequate in lieu of lost ancestral land, forestland and livelihoods [16]. Hence, they have now developed negative feelings about hydropower projects.

Impact on agriculture and/or horticulture

Diversion of water for power generation, less recharging of natural aquifers, seepage of water in the tunnels, air pollution, water pollution etc. directly or indirectly affects the agriculture crop and/or horticulture yield in the vicinity of project components. In many areas, apple and other fruit trees get damaged due to flying stones (as a result of open blasting) or laying of penstock through the orchards.

Partiality in imparting project benefits

While imparting project benefits, partiality is done. A vicious nexus between developers, authorities and public representatives work behind the curtains. The people who are pushing or relatives of influential people get priority in employment and award of good compensation. On the other hand, the people who are really needy are generally cheated. Sooner or later, they realise it and join the agitations against the projects.

Economic sustainability

This part of sustainability is inter-related with environmental and social sustainability. To make a project environmentally and socially sustainable, some extra cost may have to be incurred by the developer.

However, it will pave the way for un-interrupted project activities during construction and operation. This is a big factor for timely completion of construction and continuous flow of profit/revenue during operation. A project which is not environment friendly and socially acceptable cannot be economically sustainable.

Study region and area

State of Himachal Pradesh located in the western Himalayan region of India has been selected as study region. Beas basin in the Kullu district of the state forms the study area under selected region.

Study region

Himachal Pradesh is the land of snow, lofty peaks, cascading streams, alpine meadows and lush fruit-laden valleys). There are five river basins in state namely Satluj, Beas, Ravi, Chenab and Yamuna. Beas basin is the second largest basin in terms of hydropower potential (having about 20% of the total estimated potential) after Satluj [17]. With over 650 hydropower projects (of different capacities in different stages of development), this state is fast emerging as 'power state' of India. Table 1 shows the overall status of hydropower potential.

There are total 570 allotted SHPs (excluding cancelled and disputed projects) by Himurja (state nodal agency responsible for allotment of SHPs up to 5 MW installed capacity) and HPDoE having cumulative capacity of 2142 MW. However, only 15% projects (86 projects having cumulative capacity of about 420 MW) have been implemented till date. 12% SHPs (70 projects having cumulative capacity of 434 MW) are under construction, 25% SHPs (142 projects having cumulative capacity of 580 MW) are under the process of obtaining clearances and 48% SHPs (272 projects having an accumulated capacity of 708 MW) are under investigation stage. Fig. 2 shows the current status of SHPs (including mini hydropower projects, having installed capacity >100 kW but ≤2MW) in the state.

It can be deduced from the Fig. 2 that average implementation rate of SHPs in the state during the last 17 years (since start of private sector participation in 1996) had been only about 5 projects per year (or only about 25 MW per year in terms of installed capacity). Such a slow pace of SHP development is a matter of concern for planners and policy makers of the state. In view of these facts, importance of this study can be very well gauged.

Figure Showing Current status of SHPs (including mini hydropower projects) in Himachal Pradesh [9, 18]

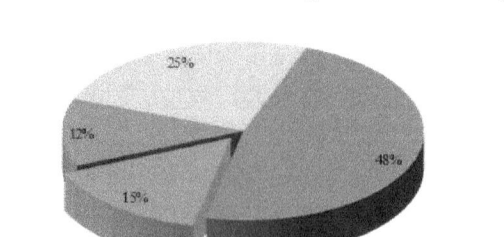

Table 1 Status of hydropower potential in Himachal Pradesh [9]

Sector		Commissioned		Under construction		Obtaining clearances		Under investigation		Others (dispute /cancelled /foregone)		Grand total	
		P	C	P	C	P	C	P	C	P	C	P	C
Him urja	State	10	2.37	0	0.00	15	61.55	1	1.50	0	0.00	26	65.42
	Private	58	219.25	51	182.60	109	303.87	256	508.29	0	0.00	474	1214.01
HPS EBL*	≤ 5 MW	11	21.10	0	0.00	0	0.00	0	0.00	0	0.00	11	21.10
	> 5 MW	11	456.45	2	110.00	0	0.00	4	70.50	1	6.00	18	642.95
HPP CL#	-	0	0.00	5	856.00	8	1285.00	7	963.00	1	20.00	21	3124.00
Central & Joint sector	-	9	5743.73	4	2532.00	1	66.00	1	588.00	0	0.00	15	8929.73
Yamuna projects (HP share)	-		131.57	-	-	-	-	-	-	-	-	-	131.57
Ranjeet Sagar dam (HP share)	-		27.60	-	-	-	-	-	-	-	-	-	27.60
Private	-	13	1829.40	24	765.50	24	865.50	30	3354.50	10	1721.50	101	8536.40
	Total	112	8431.47	86	4446.10	157	2581.89	299	5485.79	12	1747.50	666	22692.78

Balance potential under investigation	307.22	
Grand total	2300 0.00	
*Himachal Pradesh State Electricity Board Ltd.; # Himachal Pradesh Power Corporation Ltd.; P = No. of projects; C = Capacity in MW		

Study area

Beas river basin is an important basin of the Indus river system. Its basin is bounded between latitude 31°31′00″ to 32°45′00″ N and longitude 76°44′00″ to 77°52′00″ E. It originates in the Beas Rikhi at the Rohtang Pass in Himachal Pradesh and flows in almost north–south direction. At Larji, it takes a sharp turn towards the southwest up to the Pandoh Dam. Its major glacier fed tributaries are Parbati and Sainj. The river Parbati flows towards west and joins Beas at Bhuntar. Sarbari, Aleo, Duhangan, Tirthan, Garsa *Nallah*, Malana *Nallah,* Chhaki *Nallah* etc. are other tributaries which join river Beas at different places in the Kullu Valley. The catchment area is largely comprised of precipitous slopes and bare rocks. It joins the river Satluj at Harike Pattan, in Ferozpur district of Punjab [19, 20]. Fig. 3 shows Beas river basin and position of some of the large hydropower projects (commissioned and ongoing) in the basin.

Kullu district is known worldwide as 'Valley of Gods'. This district was chosen for case study as large numbers of SHPs have been planned here which are presently under various stages of development. At present 12 SHPs having total installed capacity of 58.4 MW are in operation and 6 SHPs having total installed capacity of 54.7 MW are under construction in the district. In addition, 10 projects (having installed capacity more than 5 MW and upto 25 MW) having total installed capacity 101.6 MW and 105 projects (having installed capacity less than 5 MW) having total installed capacity of about 210 MW are under various stages of clearance in different streams of Beas river basin in this district [18, 22]. Table 2 lists the SHPs under operation in district Kullu in river Beas basin.

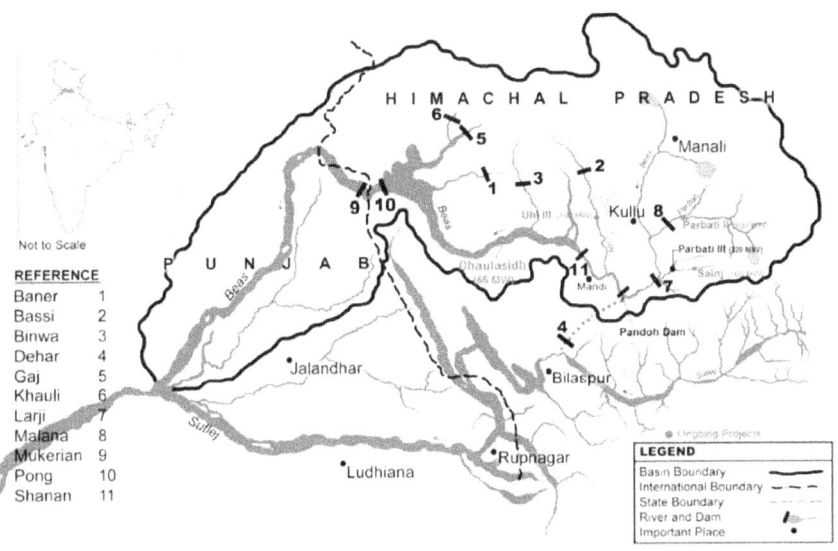

Figure 3   Basin map of river Beas showing some important hydropower projects [21]

Table 2   List of Small Hydropower Projects under Operation in River Beas Basin in District Kullu [18, 22].

S. No.	Firm Name	Project Name	Stream	Capacity (MW)	Commission Date
1.	K.K.K. Hydro Power Ltd.	Baragran	Sanjoin	4.90	05-08-2004
2.	Aleo Manali Hydro Power Pvt. Ltd.	Aleo	Allain	3.00	14-08-2005
3.	Chevron Hydel Pvt. Ltd.	Jiwa Kothari	Jiwa	1.00	23-12-2006
4.	Sai Engineering Foundation	Marhi	Beas	5.00	02-01-2007

5.	Harison Hydel Construction Co. Pvt. Ltd.	Brahm Ganga	Brahm Ganga	5.00	02-04-2008
6.	DSL Hydrowatt Ltd.	Sarbari-I	Sarbari	4.50	17-05-2008
7.	Sai Engineering Foundation	Toss-I	Toss	10.00	26-12-2008
8.	DSL Hydrowatt Ltd.	Sarbari-II	Sarbari	5.40	25-08-2010
9.	Kapil Mohan & Associates Hydro Power (P) Ltd.	Jirah	Jirah	4.00	31-01-2011
10.	Puri Oil Mills Ltd.	Chakshi	Chakshi	2.00	22-02-2012
11.	Kapil Mohan & Associates Hydro Power Pvt. Ltd.	Beas Kund *nallah*	Beas Kund	9.00	19-06-2012
12.	Usska Hydro power (P) Ltd.	Suman Sarbari	Sarbari	5.00	31-10-2012

Methodology

In order to substantiate and lay emphasis on the concerns raised in section 3 about sustainability of SHPs, case study approach has been selected. The research methodology included study of detail project reports (DPRs) and in depth field visits of projects under consideration. Hydropower policy of Himachal Pradesh, notifications of various departments related to hydropower projects, newspaper reports were combed. Interaction was done with project proponents, heads and villagers of project affected villages. Socio-economic detail of project affected villages was also collected. Focus group discussions were conducted in almost every project affected village to know villagers' views about pros and cons of the projects under study. Proponents were also interviewed to note their response to the points and concerns raised by the villagers during focus group discussions.

Projects under study

Three run of the river SHPs were selected for study in the Beas river basin. Out of these, 2 projects were under construction and one was in operation. Study includes more number of projects under construction as most of the impacts are clearly visible during this phase only. Figure 4 shows the location of these projects in district Kullu. Important salient features of these three projects have been listed in Table 3 and brief demographic profile of project affected area under each SHP has been given in Table 4.

Figure Showing Location map of SHPs under study [23]

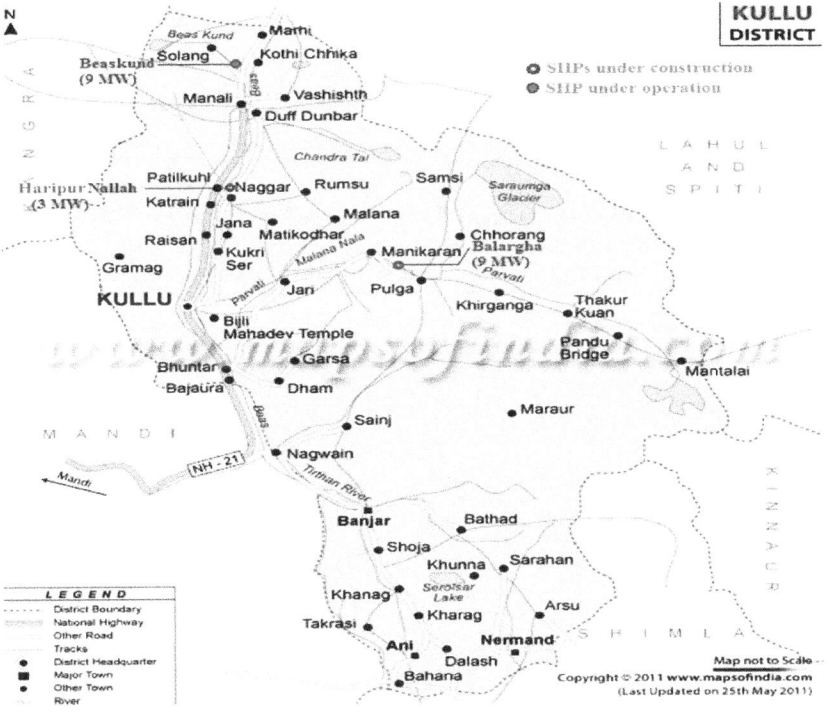

Table 3 Important Salient Features of SHPs under Study			
Salient features	Name of Small Hydropower project (SHP)		
	Balargha	Haripur Nallah	Beas kund
Installed capacity (MW)	9	3	9
Stream	Parbati	Pakhnoj Nallah	Beaskund Nallah
Current status	Under construction	Under construction	In-operation
Design discharge (cumec)	15.0	2.50	9.09
Net head (m)	84.0	141.8	119.0
Length of HRT (km)	1.56	No HRT	1.51
Penstock length and diameter	3 nos. each having: Length-111 Diameter- 1450 mm	Main penstock: Length – 1707 m Diameter- 1120 mm	Main penstock: Length – 435 m Diameter- 2000 mm
Turbines	Nos. – 3 (each 3 MW) Horizontal Axis Francis	Nos. – 2 (each 1.5 MW) Horizontal Axis Pelton	Nos. – 3 (each 3 MW) Horizontal Axis Francis
Source: DPRs of respective projects			

Balargha SHP (9 MW)

Balargha SHP is presently coming up on Parbati, a major tributary of river Beas. Site of this project is near the Manikaran town which is famous for its hot sulphur water springs. Structural design of this SHP's components also looks like a large project.

Views of project affected villagers

Villagers in the village Shillah are strongly against the project. They are agitated particularly against the way the blasting and muck disposal is being done by the proponent. Untimely blasts taken by the developer, flying stone pieces and dust causing damage to apple orchards on opposite bank, shifting of stream towards left bank due to muck dumping (from HRT and Power House site) on right bank, minor (like cracking of window panes, cracks in plaster, distortion of window/door frames etc.) and major (like movement of roofing stones, ground subsidence causing settlement/damage to retaining walls, foundations and floors, cracks in

Table Showing Brief Demographic Profile of Project Affected Area under Each SHP						
Name of SHP	Name of project affected Panchayat (s)	Name of project affected village (s)	Total number of households in the village	Male population	Female population	Name of the village (s) where focus group discussion held
Balargha (9 MW)	Barshaini	Shilla	123	241	243	Shilla and Oochhdhaar
		Oochhdhaar	40	126	119	
Haripur Nallah (3 MW)	Hallan-I	Batahar	117	221	225	Batahar and Dashaal
		Dashaal	102	224	218	
		Sarsai	102	230	198	
	Soyal	Haripur	160	312	321	Haripur
Beas kund (9 MW)	Palchan	Palchan	100	235	274	Palchan
		Ruaad	115	223	254	

Note: Population data is as on 31.12.2012
Source: Family registers of Gram Panchayat(s) related to respective
SHP

walls etc.) damage to houses due to impact and vibrations caused by blasting operations and noise pollution (due to drilling operations on hard rock at power house site), non-payment of compensation for damage caused to houses and/or orchards were major issues raised by the villagers. Operation of blasting was also said to be causing psychological impact on small kids.

The people rued that they had gained nothing from the project. The access road to their village was due to NHPC's Parvati-II hydropower project. The youth had got almost negligible employment in the project. Most of the Local Area Development Fund (LADF) was being spent in Pradhan's (Panchayat's headman) village only.

Oochhdhaar village is somewhat away from the direct noise and air pollution caused by the project. This village is smaller than Sillah. Land of some families had been acquired by the project and they were compensated for it. About 20 youth have also gained employment in the project. Village is near the HRT of the project. They felt minor vibrations during underground blasts taken during construction of HRT. However, no damage to any of the house was reported. People in this village had no major complained except inadequate compensation.

Views of project proponent

Most of the charges of the villagers are countered by the developer. It was told that only controlled blasts are taken at project site. It can be verified from the explosive consumption record being maintained at site. A joint inspection by the team comprising of administration, revenue, state PWD officials etc. had already been undertaken and the team had reported that the damage to houses was not caused due to project operations. The village is situated on a hill which is having many underground and over ground small water ways which is the main cause of subsidence.

For dust pollution, the bad condition of busy Mani Karan- Bahraini road (adjacent to project site) is major cause. The developer suggested deputing a local village man for ensuring taking blast between already agreed timings. The developer expressed his disappointment that local villagers now and then create hindrance in day to day working of project. Majority of local people, who have been given employment, want to earn the wages at their homes without doing any work. They are more or less a burden or liability on the developer.

Haripur Nallah SHP (3 MW)

This SHP is one of the most controversial SHPs in recent times. It is being constructed on Pakhnoj *Nallah*, a tributary of river Beas. This project is a classic example of fighting against a SHP due to failure of social sustainability in the form of strong public resistance. Since last few years, this project has been main local issue during all elections. Stay on construction work at the project site has been now and then imposed or lifted by Hon'ble High Court of Himachal Pradesh (a court case is being filed by a local NGO 'Jan Jaagran avam Vikas Sanstha' against the developer). Non-existence of HRT is unique feature of the project.

Opposition from project affected Panchayats

Villagers of two main project affected Panchayats are strongly crusading against the project right from the beginning as the project stream is the only source of water in the area for irrigation and drinking. Many resolutions had been passed and notices had been issued by the two Panchayats to developer for stopping the construction work. These Panchayats want that all MoUs signed by the state government for construction of all hydro projects on Pakhnoj stream should be cancelled as this stream feeds some small irrigation canals, drinking water schemes, 5 private trout fish farms, about 20 water mills, a fish hatchery farm, Indian Agricultural Research Institute (IARI) regional station etc.

Agriculture and horticulture of over 15000 people depend upon this stream.

Views of project affected villagers

During the focus group discussion held in village Haripur, people welcomed the hydropower projects in general but not at the cost of water availability for their agricultural fields and orchards. They favour the allocation of hydropower projects to local people or societies formed by local people (after imparting training in case they lack) as they can well understand their problems and will respect their own culture and traditions during project development. Developer got the NOC from the Pradhan without any resolution in Gram Panchayat or Gram Sabha (a meeting of all the adults living in a Panchayat area in India). People are also suspicious about the project due to large diameter of penstock. They suspect that this large size is more than enough to accommodate the discharge of whole Pakhnoj stream even in summer season when it flows full. They have no belief on developer that he will release mandatory environmental flow. Diversion of water for power generation will ruin village economy, fish farms, small irrigation canals and drinking water supply schemes.

Villagers of Dashaal village told that 8 resolutions had been passed by the Panchayat against the project. Local persons and their families, who are associated with the project developer, are being socially boycotted. Various memorandums against the implementation of the project had been given to local administration, state government, central government (Prime Minister, Environment Minister) and even to the President of India. They pointed out that most of the sufferings of the villagers due to projects are on account of poor knowledge of many clauses of project documents. The provisions under various minor clauses are not noticed/studied in detail by the village bodies/community leaders before signing of agreements/MoUs or imparting NoCs. In fact, in most of the cases, they don't have technical knowledge and expertise to understand the complex language of these documents. The developer/project proponents take advantage of this shortcoming of people. Hence it was suggested that they should take the help of an expert (for understanding each major and minor clause of document) before signing any agreement/deal/NoC/MoU etc. The villagers also told the stories of false cases by the developer against the local villagers (including women) during year 2010.

Views of project proponent

A meeting was held with the developer firm's officials. They pointed out that there is no consumptive use of stream water from weir to power house either for irrigation or drinking. There is only one fish hatchery farm and adjoining water mill downstream of the weir. For hatchery farm, MoU has already been signed with Fisheries department for continuous release of water @200 litres/s and even a security amount of Rs. 5 lac has been deposited by the developer. The developer is using the water for power generation which is just draining waste and almost un-utilised. All the irrigation kuhls (small canals) and drinking water schemes about which hue and cry is being made by the people are deriving water from upstream of the diversion weir of the project. Hence the use of water by the project will no way harm their interests. The people are having only false apprehensions.

As per their version, the project which is under clearance (Pakhnoj, 2.5 MW) on upstream of Haripur *Nallah* project will be actually affecting the people. However, there has been no agitation against that project due to vested interests of some local people. He disclosed that a sand mafia is active in the area near the power house and tail race site of the project. Actually, this mafia is against the project as their activities may be more noticed and disturbed due to presence of project in the area. This mafia is operating with the connivance of government officials. These mining mafias and government land encroachers are misleading other villagers also for opposing the project. Internal village rivalry of the opponents with the staff of the developer was also one factor.

Beas kund SHP (9 MW)

This SHP is located near world famous tourist hill station Manali. It was commissioned in year 2012. Same year, a cloud-burst occurred in Beas Kund *Nallah*. It caused damage to inlet trench weir and approach road of project inlet site. Switch yard of the project was completely damaged and had to be re-constructed and re-located. Flood slush had also entered the power house up to about half the height of turbines. The power house of the project is located in the heart of village Palchan and large penstock pipe runs through the beautiful hill and village. As the project is already commissioned, visible environmental impacts were not much except traces of cloudburst and extensive soil erosion near diversion weir.

Views of Project Affected villagers

Focus group discussion was held in Palchan village. The main problem raised by the people was noise pollution produced by moving of turbines and generators in the power house. Especially during night hours, the sound is felt more and disturb sleep of almost whole village. Village school is located very near the power house. Hence, sound of machinery disturbs the study of the students during school hours. On the issue of noise pollution, the Panchayat had even passed some resolutions against the project. Another point raised by the villagers was impact on a water source in the vicinity of the village due to seepage in HRT. Villagers also fear that any accidental bursting of penstock (running through the village) can be disastrous for the village people. However, the people were more or less satisfied with the disposal of muck and overall no effect on agriculture or fruit production due to project operation.

Views of Project Proponent

Discussion was held with project officials. They told that adequate measures have already been taken to contain noise pollution. A team of pollution control board had visited the power house and the noise pollution measured was found within permissible limit. They also denied impact on any water source and apprehension of any penstock failure.

Discussion

A case study comprising 3 SHPs situated in Beas basin in Kullu district has been presented in section 6. Views of both major stakeholders i.e. project affected people and project proponents have been included. The authors had tried to verify the facts at their best which were stated by both parties. More or less, version of both parties appeared to be true. Deteriorating environment due to SHPs in remote localities was witnessed by authors themselves. Numerous issues were raised and concerns were expressed by project affected people during focus group discussions with regard to sustainability of SHPs. Issues raised by the people and site observations with respect to SHPs under study have been compiled in Table 5.

Some of the impacts can be said to be short term or medium term like air pollution, water pollution, vibrations and noise due to blasting etc. as they appear during construction phase only. But, many impacts are long term like decreased/no flow in diverted stretch, impact on surface and/or underground sources of water, impact on agriculture and/or fruit production due to less water availability, impact on ecosystem dependent upon free flow of stream, permanent damage to vegetation due to improper muck disposal, impact on water mills, noise pollution from power house, fear in minds of villagers where large penstock pipes are crossing through the village etc.

False promise making and flouting the norms is quite rampant among project proponents. Nexus between the developer, public representatives and authorities is prevalent. In majority of cases, general villagers were not at all consulted before granting NOC. The facts discussed under section 3 (sustainability of SHPs) were practically verified to be more or less true. Overall, the study raises doubt over the so called sustainability of SHPs in the study area.

Suggestions and Recommendations

In a mad race to earn large and early revenue/profit, governments and developers are ignoring or compromising with many sustainability issues with respect to SHPs. There is a strong need to adopt judicious approach for sustainable development of SHPs and mitigate their long-term impacts on lives of native people. Present EIA regime is now being felt weak and insufficient to mitigate impacts of large number of small and large hydropower projects especially in the same river basin.

Many countries and organisations for example Norway, France, Greece, World Commission of Dams (WCM), European Small Hydropower Association (ESHA), International Energy Agency (IEA), etc. have been following the threshold limit of 10 MW with respect to SHPs [24, 25]. In some of the countries like Luxembourg, Sweden etc. threshold limit is just 1.5 MW and in countries like Poland, Austria, Netherlands, Germany etc., this limit is 5 MW [26]. Overall, 10 MW is the most acceptable threshold limit with respect to SHPs world-wide. This study also indicates that the environmental damage and social impacts of SHPs in a capacity range of about 10 MW and more are not worth ignoring and exempted from EIA process. Hence, it is the need of the hour that threshold limit for environmental clearance should be at least lowered to 10 MW with respect to SHPs in the Himalayan regions in general and India in particular.

Besides installed capacity, other factors such as extent of project area, quantity of muck to be generated, length of diverted reach, presence of other hydro project in the vicinity etc. should also be considered while granting environmental clearance. Allotment and development of SHPs in cascade fashion is especially required to be reviewed.

Mutual trust among three important stakeholders (project affected people, developer and authorities) is very important. Native people should be taken into full confidence before starting project work. The developer should make only those promises which he will be able to keep. Government should play the role of a facilitator between the developer and native people. It should act hard on certain mischievous elements with vested interests which misguide and mobilise the local people to oppose/stall the construction of projects on flimsy grounds. Avoidable conflicts between the developer and natives only escalate the project cost and delays revenue earning by the government. In addition, the government should take serious steps for periodic inspection and monitoring of SHPs. Capacity building and providing more teeth to controlling organisations are also required. Only then, the balance between the development and sustainability can be maintained.

Table 5 Concerns/Issues Raised or Observed with Respect to SHPs under Study				
Concerns/issues raised or observed	Duration of impact/ concern (whether short term/ medium term/ long term)	Name of the Small Hydropower Project		
		Balargha (9 MW)	Haripur Nallah (3 MW)	Beaskund (9 MW)
Inadequate environmental flow in the stream	Long term	N.A.	N.A.	Yes
Impact on agriculture and/or horticulture	Short term	Yes (blasting)	No	N.A.
	Long term (due to diversion of water)	N.A.	N.A.	No
Impact on water mills (if available)	Long term	N.A.	N.A.	Not Available
Improper muck disposal	Medium term	Yes	No	No
Impact on natural sources of water (other than main stream)	Long term	No	No	Yes
Noise pollution	Short term (during construction)	Yes	Yes	Yes
	Long term (during operation)	Not likely	Likely	Yes
Air pollution	Short term	Yes	Yes	Yes

Water pollution	Short term	Yes	Yes	Yes
Lack of public acceptance	Long term	Yes	Yes	Yes
False promises made by developer	Short term/long term	Yes	Yes	Yes
Flouting of norms by developer	Short term/long term	Yes	Yes	Yes
Inadequate and/or late award of compensation	Short term/medium term	Yes	Yes	Yes
Lack of public participation in decision making	Long term (during all stages)	Yes	Yes	Yes
Fear in mind of people due to project components (especially penstock)	Long term	No	Yes	Yes
Lack of satisfaction with respect to community works	Short term/medium term	Yes	Yes	No
Lack of employment generation	Long term	Yes	Yes	Yes
Minor damages due to blasting (flying stones/vibrations)	Short term	Yes	No	No
Nexus between developer, public representatives and authorities	-	Yes	Yes	Yes

Note:- Short term-up to 2 years; Medium term: >2 years but <10 years; Long term: > 10 years; N.A.- Not Applicable

Conclusion

The study indicates that sustainability issues with respect to SHPs are not small vis-a-vis size of their installed capacity. In fact, SHPs have been identified as one of the main pressure point in the development of Himalayan regions of India and neighbouring countries. SHPs could have an adverse impact on the degrading fragile mountain ecology if timely steps are not taken to ensure their sustainable growth with checks and balances. It is still time to take action as the majority of SHPs are in clearance stage. The timely and effective action can save the beautiful Himalayan regions from permanent wounds given by SHPs. Otherwise the suspense about the sustainability of SHPs will be no more a suspense. It will be a bitter truth that the future generations will be facing and cursing us for not envisaging future bad impacts of large scale development of SHPs.

References

[1] A. Gurung, I. Bryceson, J.H. Joo and S.E. Oh, Socio-economic impacts of a micro-ydropower plant on rural livelihoods, *Scientific Research and Essays, 6(19)*, 2011, 3964–3972.

[2] N.K. Sharma, P.K. Tiwari and Y.R. Sood, A comprehensive analysis of strategies, policies and development of hydropower in India: Special emphasis on small hydropower, *Renewable and Sustainable Energy Reviews, 18*, 2013, 460–470.

[3] H. Liu, D. Masera and EL. Esser, UNIDO (United Nations Industrial Development Organization); ICSHP (International Center on Small Hydro Power), *World small hydropower development report, 2013.*

[4] MNRE (Ministry of New and Renewable Energy); GoI (Government of India), *Annual report 2012-13*, http://mnre.gov.in/file-manager/annual-report/2012-2013/EN/chapter3.html#one (assessed 16.06.2014).

[5] MNRE (Ministry of New and Renewable Energy); GoI (Government of India), *Physical progress (achievements)*, 2014, http://mnre.gov.in/mission-and-vision-2/achievements/ (accessed 16.06.2014).

[6] GBPIHED (G. B. Pant Institute of Himalayan Environment and Development), *Indian Himalayan Region, 2014*, http://gbpihed.gov.in/main.htm (accessed 16.04.2014).

[7] M.K. Slariya. Development and water resources in Indian Himalayan Region: An invitation to disaster- a study of hydroelectric power developmental projects in Himachal Pradesh, *Scholarly Research Journal for Interdisciplinary Studies, 1(1)*, 2013, 1464–1475.

[8] JKSPDCL (Jammu & Kashmir State Power Development Corporation Ltd.). 2014. http://www.jkspdc.nic.in/ (accessed 17.06.2014).

[9] HPDoE (Himachal Pradesh Directorate of Energy), *Status of hydro potential in Himachal Pradesh, 2014*, http://admis.hp.nic.in/doe/DOEAuth/welcome.aspx (accessed 17.04.2014).

[10] UJVNL (Uttarakhand Jal Vidyut Nigam Ltd.), *Importance of small hydro projects, 2014*, http://uttarakhandjalvidyut.com (accessed 15.06.2014).

[11]   P. Purohit. Small hydro power projects under clean development mechanism in India: a preliminary assessment, *Energy Policy, 36,* 2008, 2000–2015.

[12]   S.A. Abbasi and N. Abbasi, The likely adverse environmental impacts of renewable energy sources, *Applied Energy, 65,* 2000, 121–144.

[13]   S. Dutta, A.L. Ramanathan and A. Linda, Glacier fluctuation using satellite data in Beas basin, 1972–2006, Himachal Pradesh, India, *Journal of Earth System Science 121(5),* 2012,1105–1112.

[14]   A. Erlewein, Disappearing rivers - The limits of environmental assessment for hydropower in India, *Environment Impact Assessment Review 43,* 2013,135–143.

[15]   S. Baskaya, E. Baskaya and A. Sari, The principal negative environmental impacts of small hydropower plants in Turkey, *African Journal of Agricultural Research 6(14),* 2011, 3284–3290.

[16]   A.P. Diduck, D. Pratap, A.J. Sinclair and S. Deane, Perceptions of the impacts, public participation and learning in the planning, assessment and mitigation of two hydroelectric projects in Uttarakhand, India, *Land Use Policy 33(1),* 2013,170–182.

[17]   DOEST (Department of Environment, Science and Technology), Govt. of Himachal Pradesh, *Environment master plan of Himachal Pradesh (Executive summary), 2013.*

[18]   Himurja, Himachal Pradesh Energy Development Agency, *District-wise/Steam-wise status of 472 Projects upto 5.00 MW capacity being developed under Private Sector Participation last updated on 31.10.2013,* http://himurja.nic.in/web470list.html (accessed 20.01.2014).

[19]   V.B.S. Chandel, K.K. Brar and S. Kahlon, Land use/cover change and its implications for Kullu District of Himachal Pradesh, India, *International Journal of Geomatics and Geosciences 3(3),* 2013, 538–551.

[20]   S. Sharma, J.C. Kuniyal and J.C. Sharma, Assessment of man-made and natural hazards in the surroundings of hydropower projects under construction in the Beas Valley of North-western Himalaya, *Journal of Mountain Science 4(3),* 2007, 221–236.

[21] SANDRP (South Asian Network on Dams, Rivers and People), *Map of Beas basin,* http://sandrp.in/basin_maps/Hydropower_Projects_in_ Beas_Basin.pdf (accessed 15.04.2014).

[22] HPDoE (Himachal Pradesh Directorate of Energy), *List of projects with detail,* 2014. http://admis.hp.nic.in/doe/ DOEAuth/welcome.aspx (accessed 20.04.2014).

[23] Map of District Kullu, Himachal Pradesh, India, http://www.mapsofindia.com/maps/ himachalpradesh/districts/kullu.htm (accessed 15.06.2014).

[24] C.S. Kaunda, C.Z. Kimambo and T.K. Nielsen, Hydropower in the context of sustainable energy supply: a review of technologies and challenges, *International Scholarly Research Network ISRN Renewable Energy, vol. 2012,* article ID 730631, 2012, 1–15.

[25] IPCC (Intergovernmental Panel on Climate change), *Special report on renewable energy sources and climate change mitigation,* 2011, Hydropower 5, 437–496.

[26] J. Zimny, P. Michalak, S. Bielik and K. Szczotka, Directions in development of hydropower in the world, in Europe and Poland in the period 1995–2011, *Renewable and Sustainable Energy Reviews, 21,* 2013,117–130.

Chapter- IV

Dams and Development in Sikkim: The Hidden Reality

Bipul Chhetri & Dr. Uttam Lal*

Abstract

Environmental degradation has always been the other face of development. Development always results in some form of negative consequences. In similar fashion, the rivers that are being used for the purpose of development have suffered adversely. The constructions of large dams have always hampered the environment. In fragile mountainous regions, the consequences of such development have been observed in the form of landslides, flash floods, and disturbance to the ecosystem. Besides this, it also threats the existing culture and society of the region. The development of such large dams in River Teesta has today become the issue of concern for the society at large. The developmental politics has the important role in distorting the environment. The voices of the masses are being suppressed by the government in several ways. Hence the development of rivers should take the issues like the fragility of the mountainous region, the society and their culture, the degrading environment and ecosystem etc. into consideration. Hence the paper would focus on the problems that the society in Sikkim today is facing as a result of construction of large dams in river Teesta. The focus group discussion has been made in some of the regions where such large dams have been constructed and efforts have been made to highlight the ground reality of development.

Keywords: Degradation, Development, Disaster, Fragility, Teesta,

*Department of Geography, Sikkim University, Gangtok, India

Introduction

The development of society in global era means the ability to modify the nature using the technology and exploit it till the voices are raised against it. Today the level development of any economy refers its ability to make use of nature and make the life as easy as possible. The need of human desire for luxurious, healthy and comfortable life have resulted in rapid degradation of natural resources of which the humans are less concerned of especially in the developing nations. The process of development have made the humans to make use of all the resources available like air, soil, water and every elements of nature which they are able to. The increasing population and the increasing need of goods and services have made the population to make use of every element that comes before them. In this process of so called 'development', the impacts brought by them are rather not seen. The development in similar fashion today has made the use of flow of water to generate electricity.

The electricity generation today though essential needs, has been compromised with several elements like nature, lives of the masses, and the environment of the existing landscape. The use of resources today has been the issue of political debate. The politics of development are played on the use of resources. Such use of resources when comes to the framework of political governance, its exploitation begins unless and until the visible impact are not felt. The voices that are made independently are never heard and that comes united are suppressed by the authority in power. Institution, state and social group enter into contingent interaction in complex situation to express power and exercise control over resources [1]. The development today has negative meaning when it comes in comparison with the nature and associated elements. The loss of such development are usually borne by the large section of the society whereas the benefits are acquired by such development gets concentrated in few hands. The politics of development thus gets mixes with the issue if equity.

The development of rivers for generating electricity in Sikkim today has been following the similar trend. The constructions of massive dams have resulted in large scale degradation of mountain environment. The populations have been raising the voices against the dam construction and to preserve their ethnic cultural landscape. The governments on the other hand have been trying their best in making use of the resources without understanding the sentiments and the cultural ideology of the population. The political ecology dimension of developing countries and the multiple utilitarian benefits provided by dams continue to favor the proliferation of these structures. Thus the problem arises in the developmental process when the motive of resource exploitation gets intertwined with the resource exploitation. These form of developmental activities always results in negative impacts on the environment because it lacks the idea of sustainable resource use.

Focusing on the development of dams and exploiting the available resource without being much concerned of the environment has been the common way of resource use today. The degradation of Himalayan ecosystem/environment is emerging as one of the major concern for ecologist and environmentalist across the country. It has been observed that creation of reservoir, fluctuation in natural river discharge and diversion through closed tunnel would completely change the ecological condition of the river systems [6]

The processes of development become questionable when the authority in power fails to keep the promises that they make before starting the projects. The voices comes to the forum when the development itself starts deteriorating the environmental conditions where the livelihood, culture and identity of the masses gets threatened. Same has been the cases in case of development of dams in Sikkim. The state justifies the reason for construction of such projects in Sikkim is to provide employment and economic benefits of the nation and the state through power generation. Thus the consequences of dam construction in Sikkim was felt among the masses only when they saw several dams being constructed ignoring several limiting factors and had just hidden motive in the name of developing the state.

Development in Sikkim

Sikkim is a small state situated in the Eastern Himalayas separated by

Singalila range from Nepal in the west, chola range from Tibet in the northeast and Bhutan in the south east. It has the total geographical of area of 7096 sq km. It shares its international border with three different nation like China, Bhutan and Nepal. 92% of its border is shared with neighboring countries [6] Sikkim has four district namely East district with Gangtok as its capital town, West District with Geyzing as the main town, South district with Namchi being the main town and North district. North district is the largest in terms of its Geographical area. The population of Sikkim comprises of Lepcha, Bhutia and Nepali and migrants from the plains. The population of Sikkim is predominantly Hindus (68%), Buddhist (27%) and Christians comprises of about (3%) of the total population. The North Sikkim has the majority of Lepchas and Bhutias population ie, region around Dzongu with Lepcha being in majority whereas Lachen and Lachung with Bhutias with their majority. Sikkim is primarily based on agricultural economy with more than 60% of its population directly engaged on agriculture sector. As a Special Category State, economically, Sikkim is largely dependent on preferential funding from the central government. The Special Category States receive substantial financial and non-financial support from the central government in the form of 90 per cent as grants and 10 per cent as loans [1] However the contribution of agriculture and allied activities on the gross domestic product (GDP) of Sikkim has drastically reduced over the years while that of secondary and tertiary sector has been on increase due to the upcoming of various industries and hydropower projects.

Power development as an economic growth model in Sikkim

Sikkim has large number of streams and rivers flowing which has its origin in the glaciers of Himalayas. Teesta and Rangit are the two major rivers of Sikkim which are fed by adjoining streams of various sizes on its way Besides this it has several other small rivers which also has the potential to generate power. The hydropower potential of these rivers is quite high due to the rapidity of the flow of these rivers. It is estimate that Sikkim has a potential to produce 8,000MW seasonally and about 3000 MW power during winter months (Annual report 2008-09, Govt. of Sikkim). The initial phase of power development in Sikkim had started in the Year 1927 in river Ranikhola with the installed capacity of 50 KW mainly to serve the Royal family and Gangtok town. There was further up gradation of this project in the year 1957, 1998. Till the end of 1975, the state was having a generation capacity of only 3MW from its small hydel projects (SHP) like Jali power house, Rimbi Micro Hydel, Manul Micro Hydel Power and Diesel Power House at Gangtok (Khawas V, et al 2013).

There was a huge transformation that took place in power generation after 1998 onwards when 60Mw Hydel project was commissioned in river Rangit in 1999. Besides these projects various small projects were commissioned in Sikkim like Kalez Khola Hydel Project (2Mw) in Dentam and Rabomochu power project (3 MW) in North Sikkim. The government then slowly started taking the initiatives of installing larger hydel power plants in Sikkim with the view of rural electrification and earning profit from these sectors. The state envisages that hydropower development will eventually lead to the overall infrastructural development here as hydropower generation involves construction of dams, tunnel, power station etc which involves developing transport linkages, opens up employment opportunities and generates income enhancing the socio- economic development of the population residing here [4] Sikkim, at present, has a total installed capacity of 100.7MW. This per capita consumption of electricity in the state is calculated a little over 182 KWh [6] Considering the capacity of these two mighty rivers along with their tributaries, the government awarded 26 projects to National Hydroelectric Power Corporation (NHPC) and other hydro power developers. the projects were under public, private and joint venture and was expected to fetch 12% free power for the first 15 years and 15% free power after that for the period of 35 years and after that the project would be handed over to the State government free of cost in its operating condition. The state visualizes prosperity by taping the enormous quantity of hydropower and earns the maximum benefits from it.

Debate on Dam construction in Sikkim

The dam construction in Sikkim faced a several form of critics from the people in which the sites were proposed for construction. The cause of concern and debate on the issue of dam construction was the problems related to environmental degradation and loss of sacred landscape of indigenous community. The construction of large dams on Teesta river basin had been opposed by larger section of the people in North Sikkim organization led by Affected Citizen of Teesta (ACT), Concerned Lepchas of Sikkim (CLOS) and Sangha of Dzongu. In many instances, the people concerned were not aware of scheduled public hearings, as those had not been publicized. Activists accuse the government of not sharing project information and explaining the purpose and impact of these projects on the affected people (Wangchuk 2007). The protestors wanted the dams that were constructed in Dzongu to be scrapped from their holy land which were constructed violating the impact factor assessment made by the central authority. Clearances have been issued without requisite studies being done and consulting the affected [1]. The protest made by ACT and CLOS were supported by the tribal communities and other environmentalists other than Sikkim i.e. from neighboring state of Bengal. The chief Minister of Sikkim decided to cancel the Teesta IV project, Lingza hydropower project, the Ringpi Hydropower project, The Rangyong hydropower project and the Rukel Hydropower project, all expected to affected the Lepchas of the Dzongu in North Sikkim in view of the constant protest. Several dams are still under the process of construction in North Sikkim and several dams are still under the process of construction. Some of the dams that have been completed are Teesta III in Chungthang (1,200 MW), Teesta V in Dikchu (510 MW), Teesta VI (500 MW) in Shirwani/Rangpo which has been handed over to LANCO. Thus the decision of construction of such mega dam in Sikkim had a motive hidden behind which was much larger in comparison to the cost of environment.

Dam construction and the issue of culture under threat

The construction of dams in Teesta besides being the concern of environment was also the issue of culture which the indigenous community felt as a threat. The Dzongu being the holy place reserved for the Lepchas were chosen the site for the dam construction. The government failed to see the hidden attachment and sentiments associated with the population in the view of dam construction. The clearances were presented before the masses brought from the Central authority and projects were started but these sentiments of the population that were hurt could not be stopped by the authority. The Lepchas in Dzongu had a fear that their population would be outnumbered by the population that would enter the region and contaminate their preserved culture. The fear of losing their identity and culture, the Lepchas of Dzongu protested against the authority and fought united.

Dams in Teesta: A Threat to Larger Masses

The dams that were constructed had no proper clearances from the higher authority and most of them were constructed without having proper Environmental Impact Assessment (EIA). Negative environmental impacts of dams can occur upstream, downstream, and in the reservoir. In addition to habitat degradation, dams induce significant barrier effects by blocking the downstream flow of sediments and nutrients and preventing the migration of fishes and other aquatic organisms (Meixer et al 2009). The population had hardly any idea of indirect impact of dam construction like degradation of river ecosystem. However the direct impact of dam construction was as such that they could hardly resist themselves from complaining and raising their voices. The drilling and blasting of the hills for the tunnels to divert water had an impact on the population and their households whereby the streams around had disappeared due to disturbance in the reservoir caused by blasting of the rocks. The disappearance of river was some of the major concern that was described by the people where they had to suffer the consequences of inadequate productivity due to drying of springs. Some argue that the biodiversity of the state would be lost due to the development of such dams in Teesta. The people around Dzongu expressed their views regarding blasting and complained that their houses had developed several cracks. The compensation was hardly paid by the government when they had approached with their petitions.

Dam construction in River Teesta: Critical assessment of government versus people's opinion

The government of Sikkim with its view of earning revenue from power generation had started the construction of massive dam under Public, private and joint ventures. The state started developing small, mini and micro projects to provide electricity to rural household as well as for urban lightings. The state present has a total installed capacity of 100.70 MW of its own. Some of the power house that the presently has are as follows:

Name of the Power House	Installed capacity in (MW)
Lower Lagyap Hydroelectric Project	12.00
Jali power House	2.10
Rimbi-I	0.60
Rongnichu-II	2.50
Chaten	0.10
Rimbi-II	1.00
Lachung	0.20
Meyonchu	4.00
Upper Rongnuchu	8.00
Diesel Power House	5.00
Rothak	0.20
Kalez Khola	2.00
Robumchu	3.00
Total Under State Sector	40.70
Rangit-III under NHPC	60.00
Total Installed capacity in the State	100.70

Source: Annual Report 2008-09, 2009. Energy and Power Department, Government of Sikkim

Besides the above mentioned hydro power projects, the government proposed the construction of number of other hydel power projects to the companies like Teesta I (280 MW), Teesta II (330 MW) Teesta III (1200 MW), Teesta IV (495 MW), Teesta V (510 MW), Teesta VI (500 MW). In addition to these number of other dams were constructed in the Tributaries of Teesta namely Lachen (210 MW), Panan (300), Rangyong

(117 MW), Ronginichu (96 MW), Sada Mangder (71 MW), Chugachen(99 MW), Bhasmey (32 MW), Rolep (36), Chakhungchu (50 MW), Raling (40 MW), Rangit II(40 MW), Rangit IV (120 MW), Dikchu (54 MW), Jorethang Loop (96 MW), Lingza (120 MW), Thankgichi (40 MW), Bimkyong (99 MW), Bop (90), Ting Ting (70 MW), Rateychu Bakchachu (40MW), Tashiding (60 MW).

The sum of all the values comes out be 5215 MW which itself reflects the ambition of the government to earn high revenue. The concern for environment related impacts were almost ignored. The above mentioned dams were constructed all over the state thereby neglecting the culture of indigenous community, the sacredness of lands of different ethnic groups, the degrading environment and threats to the masses due to associated landslides etc. However the people in North Sikkim initially favored the dam construction as they thought that there would be greater opportunity of employment for them and would be a source of livelihood in different ways. However in the later stage of development the negative impacts of dams were more felt by the population. The construction of dams posed them the threat to their lives instead. Thus they started opposing some of the dams in North Sikkim. They were afraid of the ill effects of dam construction in fragile lands. The people in North Sikkim formed the organizations like Affected Citizen of Teesta (ACT), concerned Lepchas of Sikkim (CLOS) and Sangha of Dzongu to oppose the dam construction and preserve their holy land which were meant for Lepcha Community. These organization protested against the government and demanded seven proposed dams in Dzongu to scrap. In May 2008, The chief Minister decided to cancel Teesta IV, Lingza, Ringpi, Rangyong and the Rukel Hydropower projects, all expected to affect the Lepchas of the Dzongu region in North Sikkim in the view of persistent protests [6]

Development at the cost of environmental degradation

Development in real sense is a qualitative change or the change for the betterment of the population or society at large. It must be appropriate and should not hamper the culture, environment and society in large

117

scale. Genuine development has an air of originality by virtue of being novel. In the strict sense of word genuine development is original because it has its origin in that society or community, and is not simply an imported copy or imitation of somebody else's [3]. However the development of hydro dams in Sikkim has not included the society and the community as a part of it. Justice and equity are the two important determinant of development. When the society or the communities are deprived of such justice and the community lack equity in terms of resource utilization and decision making, then it cannot be considered as a true development. When we talk of development in wide context, then it should include the issue of sustainability. The development made today should have its benefit tomorrow. The society should not suffer in future with the damages done in the name of development at present. However the development of hydro dams in North Sikkim had the impact on the society and culture in the region was in threat. Development itself has become a site of struggle and resistance, with people and social movements questioning a national development model which deprives them from livelihood, identity and dignity [5].

The construction of dams in River Teesta has been the issue of great concern for the environmentalist and activist as they argue that these dams have more environmental impacts then its economic prosperity. The negative impacts of dam construction have always been observed significantly over the globe and the developing nations suffer more than developed ones when the overall scenario of developmental activities is measured. The degradation of ecosystem services caused by dams has been quantified in several studies, but multiple institutional and economic barriers may prevent the implementation of safeguarding and protecting the environment [2].The government and other private profit making institutions do not consider the demands made by the population when they see a profit making resources at hand. Same has been the cases with the forms of development that has been taking place in Sikkim where the human values and their attachments with their territory did not find any significance. The degradation of environment and loss of livelihood by the people has constantly been complained by the people and government on the other hand has been trying their best to generate profits. The emergence of privately owned investment firm and increasing power of the local government have created a more flexible dam industry that is less constrained by bureaucratic limitation and under diminishing control by the central government. Thus the easy upcoming of privately owned firms and industries have accelerated the rate of environmental degradation in Sikkim where the voices made by the masses are paid very less attention by the government. According to noted environmentalist, Sunderlal Bahuguna, 'construction of several hydel projects in Sikkim amounted to "destructive act" against the ecology of the "greenest" state of the country. Besides this the planning of hydel dam projects in Sikkim in many cases had no proper assessment and environmental clearances. It was reported by CAG that there were many gaps in the proposed Environment management Plan (EMP). The CAG said that the EMPs for the projects had been prepared through assessment of secondary data without any diligent study or observation and no proper time series research of prevailing ground realities was done [6]. Thus the careless of the planners and policy makers on environment can easily be traced out in dam constructions which are itself linked with the lives and livelihoods of the people.

The construction of large dams on River Teesta in North Sikkim was restricted by large and the study conducted by CISMHE, had recommended that North Sikkim was not a favorable region for the construction of large dams (above 80 Mtrs). However such recommendation was paid less attention and the clearances were taken for the construction. Thus one can see the developmental politics of the government for extraction of the benefits. The state government had the clear vision of revenue generation rather than the welfare of the population and their lives under threat. Thus the real aspects of development lacked in case of construction of hydro dams in Sikkim. It was neither sustainable in nature as culture of the Lepchas and their identity was under threat.

Conclusion

The topic dams and development tries to reveal some of the critical issues of dam construction in River Teesta where the developmental model has always tried to play with the lives of the population at large. The negligence of the authority in power and its impact has been highlighted. But this has been the case not only in the State of Sikkim. Today most of the developmental activities in India have the inter linkages with the hidden politics where the benefits of such development gets concentrated in few hands while the sufferings are faced by the poorer section of the society. In the view of earning revenue and maximizing the profit the authority in power in most of the cases victimize the larger section of the society. The developmental activities beyond the carrying capacity of the resource always results with the negative impacts. The issues of culture, livelihood, and society are often ignored by the ruling class and the voices raised against such activities are penalized in different ways. Is this the development that society is in Need of? Is this the development where the environment gets distorted from its base to its apex? Is this the development where the people lament for their previous green natural environment in place of large concrete structures? When the culture, Identity, livelihood etc. has no place then how can it be a true development? The question raised above has been the critics of development that has been taking place in India today. Such question needs to be critically evaluated and examined in order to make masses aware of the activities so called "development".

The power lies in the hand of the masses and not among the higher authorities. Community participation, planning and decision making abilities can become effective measure to present the problems to the higher authorities. The authority in power should be made answerable to the population when such developmental activities become the part and parcel of their lives. Proper consultation of decision taken by the authority in power can help the process of development in most effective ways. The benefits acquired by such activities should have its share with the poorer section of the society and should not get accumulated in few hands. The overall development can only be achieved when such activities turn fruitful for the large masses, its sustainability can exist only when it has least impact on the environment and the reality not hidden.

References

Journal

[1] Arora V, 'They are all set to dam (n) our future': Contested development through Hydel power in Democratic Sikkim, *Indian Sociological Society, 58(1),* 2009, 94-114

[2] Marcus W Beck et al, Environmental and livelihood impacts of dams: common lessons across development gradients that challenge sustainability, *International Journal of River Basin Management, iFirst,* 2012, 1–20jn

[3] Slim H, What is development? *Development in practice, 5(2),* 1995,

[4] Subrata P, Hydro Power Development and the Lepchas: A case study of the Dzongu in Sikkim, India, *International Research Journal of Social Science, 2(8),* 2013, 19-24

[5] Arora V, Gandhigiri in Sikkim, *Economic and Political Weekly, 43(38),* 2008, 27-28

Chapter in Books

[6] Khawas V et al, Water for power: Debating new trends of water development in the Sikkim Himalayas, in S Somyaji and S Dasgupta (Ed), *Sociology of Displacement: policies and practice,* (New Delhi: Rawat Publication, 2013) 143-164

Chapter-V

Effect of Climate Change on Reservoir Inflow: A Case Study of Ukai Reservoir

Dr. S. M. Yadav & Utkarsh Nigam*

Abstract

Reservoir inflows are basically the runoff generated from precipitation or rainfall occurred in the river basin. Climate change causes variations in the meteorological and hydrological parameters such as rainfall, temperature, humidity etc. leads to the variation in reservoir inflow. Climate change is of global concern. Climate change studies aims to better understand the uncertainties involved in the system by analysing trend. The effect of climate change on reservoir inflow for Ukai reservoir has been studied. The paper presents the effect of changing climate on the reservoir inflow in which Ukai reservoir has been taken as a case study and also trend analysis has been done. Study aims to predict the future scenario by taking in consideration of the past variations of the data. The study is important from the flooding of Surat city as it is on the downstream side of Ukai dam and directly affected from the releases of Ukai dam.

Key-words: Reservoir Inflow, Climate change, Trend analysis, Ukai Reservoir

*Civil Engineering Department, SVNIT, Surat, Gujarat, India

Introduction

Any significant change in the measures of climate lasting for an extended period of time may be defined as climate change. In other words, climate change includes major changes in temperature, precipitation, wind patterns, weather and reservoir inflow, among other effects, that occur for longer time period from several decades or longer. It may be a change in average weather conditions, or in the distribution of weather around the average conditions (i.e., more or fewer extreme weather events). Reservoir inflow depends upon the hydrological parameter such as precipitation. Stochastic and non-linear variations are well availed and acclaimed in the hydrologic parameters being influenced by climate change. Climate change affects the inflows to reservoir system. Burn et al (1996) indicated that changing climatic change has potentially important implications for the operation of the reservoir system. Reservoir systems are considerably being affected by change in rainfall patterns, which in turn causes affect in reservoir inflow. The operation of reservoir systems are based on the operating rules derived using simulation and optimised methods (Labadie (2004). The predefined objectives and requirements of the reservoir can be achieved by revising the operating rules or planned policies. Impact of climate change on hydrology and water resources for peninsular malaysia was studied by Kavves M. L. et al (2006). McBean et al. (2008) carried out a long term analysis of the Great lakes of North America for the assessment of climate change. Xu and Tang (2009) depicted that change in inflow pattern may help in redefining the planned or operating strategies. Lund (1996) derived the optimised operating rules by analysing patterns of changes in inflow to facilitate the decision making for redefined strategies.

Hydrologic modelling employs the use of artificial intelligence in analysis. Zealand C. M. et al (1999) used artificial neural network in short term stream flow forecasting considering expected hydrological uncertainties. ASCE Task committee on application of artificial neural networks in hydrology (2000) analyse the river flow characteristics. Lischeid (2001) investigated trends of hydro chemical time series of small catchments. Guiller (2005) analysed stream flow prediction using artificial neural network for watershed modelling and water quality modelling. Jain and Kumar (2009) proposed dissection of trained neural network hydrologic architecture for knowledge extraction.

Earlier inflow trend analysis has been conducted using statistical methods. The Mann-Kendall (MK) test is popularly used to identify the trends in climatological time series (Zhang et al. 2001). Kumar et al. (2009) used four variations of the Mann-Kendall test to include both short-term and long-term serial correlation for analysing the streamflows and precipitation of Indiana state. Douglas et al. (2000) recommended a modified procedure to analyse the regional trends. Sawami A. W. (2011) carried out trend and reduction pattern analysis for assessment of impact of climate change on water resources of Jebba hydropower reservoir. Song et. al. (2012) studied analysing inflow trend of Indiana reservoirs using Self-organising maps (SOM).

In the present study effect of climate change due on reservoir inflow is done statistically using trend analysis methods i.e. Mann-Kendall's and Sen's slope method. The study area selected for the study is Ukai reservoir, Gujarat, India.

Study Area

Ukai Dam is situated on Tapi river at Ukai, Gujarat, India. The Ukai dam, situated on Tapi river, originally approved by the planning commission of government of India in 1969 and the construction of the dam was completed in 1973 (Figure 4.1). The Ukai reservoir at its FRL of 105.15 m (345 ft.) has a live storage capacity of 7369 MCM with water spread of about 600 km^2 and maximum length of about 112 km. The reservoir is expected to attain Maximum Water Level (MWL) of 106.99 m (351ft.) while passing the Probable Maximum Flood (PMF) of 59747 m^3/s (21.16 lakh cusecs). Ukai reservoir provides protection against heavy floods to an area of 827 km^2 on the downstream. Figure 1 shows the Ukai dam and reservoir. The salient features of the Ukai dam is shown in Table 1.

Figure 1: Ukai dam and Tapi basin

Methodology and Data Analysis

Data Collection

The reservoir inflow data were obtained from the Ukai Civil (Circle), Ukai dam authority. Reservoir inflow for 20 years i.e. 1992 to 2011 were obtained for the study and trend analysis.

Analysis of Data

The reservoir inflows for 20 years have been used to carry out trend analysis. Regression statistics, Mann-Kendall method and Sen's-slope estimator have been used for analysing trend of reservoir inflow.

Table 1: Salient Features of Ukai Dam and reservoir

State	Gujarat	Gross storage capacity at FRL	7414.29 MCM
District	Tapi (Vyara)	Dead storage below R.L.82.296 m	684.39 MCM
Taluka	Fort Songadh	Live storage	6729.9 MCM
Village	Ukai	Full Reservoir Level	105.15 m (345 Ft.)
River	Tapi	Water spread at R.L. 105.15 mt.	60095 ha.
Latitude	21'15'' N	(a) Cultivated land submerged (b) Other land submerged (c) Forest land submerged	30350 Ha. 7485 Ha. 22260 Ha.
Longitude	73'35'' E	Village affected by submergence	170 No
Crest level of spillway	91.135 mt. (299 ft.)	High Flood Level (HFL)	106.99 (351 Ft.)
Length of spillway	425.195 mt.	Length of reservoir	112 km. (70 miles)
Top of crest level	105.461 mt	Power capacity Installation of 4 units of 75 MW each	300 MW
Type of gates	Radial, 22 No.'s (15.545mt. x 14.783mt.)	Size of penstock	4 nos. 7.01 dia

Regression Statistics

The regression analysis can be carried out directly on the time series or on the anomalies (i.e. deviation from mean). A linear equation, $y = mx + c$, defined by c (the intercept) and trend m (the slope), can be fitted by regression. The linear trend value represented by the slope of the simple least-square regression line provided the rate of rise/fall in the variable. The method of linear regression requires the assumptions of normality of residuals, constant variance, and true linearity of relationship. The regression equation is of the form of equation (1).

$$Y = aX + C \qquad\qquad 1.$$

Where, X =time (year), a =slope coefficient, b = least square estimates of the intercept.

a and b can be computed using equations (2) and (3).

$$a = \frac{n \, \Sigma(x * y) - \Sigma x * \Sigma y}{n \, \Sigma \, (x * x) - (\Sigma x) * (\Sigma x)} \qquad\qquad 2.$$

$$b = \frac{\Sigma y - b * \Sigma x}{n} \qquad\qquad 3.$$

The sample correlation, r, is obtained from equation.

$$r = \frac{n \, \Sigma(x * y) - \Sigma x * \Sigma y}{\sqrt{[n \, \Sigma(x * x) - (\Sigma x) * (\Sigma x)] * [n \Sigma(y * y) - (\Sigma y) * (\Sigma y)]}} \qquad\qquad 4.$$

r ranges from -1 to 1. It measures the strength of the linear relationship between y and x, a correlation value close to 0 indicates no association between the variables. R-square ($R2$), or the square of the correlation coefficient, is a fraction between 0.0 and 1.0. A R^2 value of 0.0 means that there is no correlation between X and Y and no linear relationship exist between X and Y. On the other hand, when R^2 approaches to 1.0, the correlation becomes strong and with a value of 1.0 all points lie on a straight line. The regression analysis was carried out and presented in the Table 2, while the variation of reservoir inflow with time is presented in Figure 2.

Table 2: Results of Regression statistics

Variable	Regression Equation	Sample correlation	R-square	Whether Statistical significance
Reservoir Inflow	y = 57.133x - 105246	0.0754	$R^2 =$ 0.0057	NO

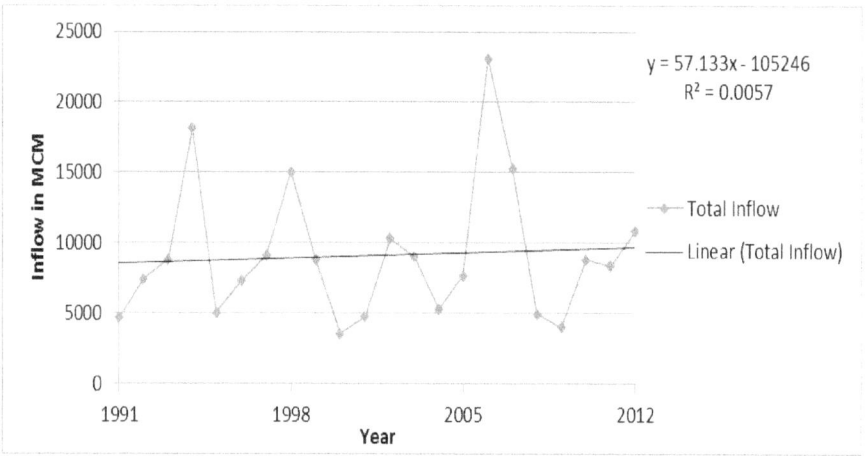

Figure 2: Reservoir Inflow variation with time

The statistical analysis of regression of reservoir inflow values shows that R-square and sample correlation are statistically insignificant. As the ranges of R-square value is quite low so it cannot be used in judgement of the value whether the increasing or decreasing trend is followed. However the formed trend line shows increasing trend.

Mann-Kendall Statistics

The most widely used method for trend analysis is the non-parametric Mann-Kendall trend test as indicated by recent studies of trend analysis. Mann originally derived the test and Kendall (1975) subsequently derived the test statistic commonly known as the Kendall's Tau statistic (Paulin and Xiaogang, 2005). It was reported to be an excellent tool for trend detection in different applications. The Mann-Kendall (MK) test is popularly used to identify the trends in climatological time series (Zhang et al. 2001). Kumar et al. (2009) used four variations of the Mann-Kendall test to include both short-term and long-term serial correlation for analysing the streamflows and precipitation of Indiana State. Douglas et al. (2000) recommended a modified procedure to analyse the regional trends. In this testing procedure, the hypothesis H of a two-sided test states that the distributions of Tj and Ti are not identical for all i, j $\leq$ n with i $\neq$ j (Zhang et al. 2001) The Mann-Kendall statistic (S) is given by

$$S = \sum_{i=1}^{n-1} \sum_{j=i+1}^{n} sign\ (Tj - Ti)$$
5.

$$sign\ (T) = \begin{cases} 1\ for\ Tj > Ti \\ 0\ for\ Tj = Ti \\ -1\ for\ Tj < Ti \end{cases}$$
6.

The time series consist of n data points and Ti and Tj are two sub-sets of data where $i = 1, 2, 3, \ldots, n - 1$ and $j = i + 1, i + 2, i + 3, \ldots, n$. Each data point Ti is used as a reference point and is compared with all the T_j data points as given in equations (5) and (6). A very high positive value of S is an indicator of an increasing trend, and a very low negative value indicates a decreasing trend. However, it is necessary to compute the probability associated with S and the sample size, n, to statistically quantify the significance of the trend. Prashanth (2005) estimated the variance of S as in equation 7.

$$\sigma^2 = \frac{1}{18}[n(n - 1)(2n + 5) - \sum_{p=1}^{g}(tp - 1)(2tp + 5)]$$
7.

In the above equation, n stands for number of data points, g is the number of tied groups (a tied group is a set of sample data having the same value), and tp is the number of data points in the pth group. The normalized test statistic Zs can be estimated using equation 8 as follows:

$$Zs = \begin{cases} \frac{S-1}{\sigma} & for\ S > 0 \\ 0 & for\ S = 0 \\ \frac{S+1}{\sigma} & for\ S < 0 \end{cases}$$
8.

The test statistic Zs is used as a measure of significance of trend. In fact,

129

this test statistic is used to test the null hypothesis, H_0: There is no monotonic trend in the data. If Zs is greater than $Z_{\alpha/2}$, where represents the chosen significance level (usually 5%, with Z0.025 = 1.96), then the null hypothesis is invalid, meaning that the trend is significant. Being significant implies the trend has a causative factor and did not occur by chance. McBean and Motiee (2008) indicated that the existence of positive autocorrelation in the data increases the probability of detecting statistically significant trends when actually none exist, and vice versa is a statistic used to measure the association between two measured quantities. A tau test is a non-parametric hypothesis test for statistical dependence based on the tau coefficient. Kendall's tau correlation coefficient (τ) is given by,

$$\tau = \frac{S}{n(n+1)/2}$$

9.

Equations 5, 6, 7, 8 and 9 were used in the present analysis. The analysis and results of the Mann-Kendall test for reservoir inflows are shown in Table 3.

Table 3. Mann-Kendall Trend Analysis Results for Annual Inflows of Ukai Reservoir

Paramet er	Kendall 's S	Kendal l's τ	Mann-Kendal l test Zs value	Natur e of trend	Identifie d trend (95% confiden ce level)	Statistica lly significa nt
Reservo ir Inflow	19	0.0822 5	0.5075	Positi ve	No trend	No

Sen's Slope Estimator

Sen's estimator has been widely used for determining the magnitude of trend in hydro-meteorological time series. In this method, the slopes (Ti) of all data pairs are first calculated by

$$T_i = (X_j - X_k)/(j - k) \quad i=1,2,3\ldots N$$

10.

Where X_j and X_k are data values at time j and k (j > k) respectively. The median of N values of T_i is Sen's estimator of slope which is calculated as

$$\beta = \begin{cases} T\frac{N+1}{2} & N \text{ is odd} \\ \frac{1}{2}\left(T\frac{N}{2} + \frac{N+2}{2}\right) & N \text{ is even} \end{cases} \qquad 11.$$

A positive value of β indicates an upward (increasing) trend and a negative value indicates a downward (decreasing) trend in the time series.

A 100 (1 - $\propto$) % two-sided confidence interval about the slope estimate is obtained by the non-parametric technique based on the normal distribution. The procedure in Man-Kendall's method computes the confidence interval at $\propto$ = 0.01 and $\propto$ = 0.05, resulting in two different confidence intervals.

At first $C_\propto$ is computed by equation 12,

$$C_\propto = Zs - \propto/2*((VAR\ (S))^{1/2} \qquad 12.$$

Where VAR (S) has been defined above in Man-Kendall's test and Zs - $\propto/2$ is obtained from the standard normal distribution. $M_1 = (N- C_\propto)/2$ and $M_2 = (N+ C_\propto)/2$ are computed. Lower and Upper limits of the confidence intervals $T_{max.}$ and $T_{min.}$ are the Mth largest and $(M_2 +1)^{th}$ largest of the N ordered slope estimate T_i. Sen's method is not affected greatly by gross data errors or outliers and it can be computed when data are missing.

The results of Sen's slope test and Man-Kendall's analysis shows positive or negative trend based on the Kendal's Tau (τ) value and varies between +1 and -1. The negative value shows decreasing trend and positive values shows the increasing trend. Kendalls Tau (τ) value gives significant information about trend of variable, reservoir inflow. Table 4 presents the analysis carried out for Estimated Sen's slope test.

Table 4: Estimated Sen's Slope value for Ukai Reservoir with Statistic values

Sr. No.	Parameters Name Sen's slope/ statistic	Value Number	Value
1	Minimum	1st	3568.363
2	Maximum	22nd	23091.052
3	Mean	-	9105.249
4	Standard Deviation	-	4918.884
5	Sen' slope (Median)	116th	60.087
6	Lower limit (Sen's slope estimator)	86.33rd	-127.69
7	Upper Limit (Sen's slope estimator)	145.66th	300.12
8	Kendall's Tau	-	0.08225

Discussion of Results

Regression Analysis

Regression statistics analysis is unable to give information about trend to be increasing or decreasing. As shown in Figure 2, there may be an increasing trend for the reservoir inflow in Ukai reservoir. The R-squared statistic indicates that the model, as fitted, explains only 0.57 % of the variability in reservoir inflow. The correlation coefficient equal to 0.0754 indicates a weak relationship between the variables and period as presented in Table 2.

Mann-Kendall

The value of S evaluated as positive demonstrates an existence of a positive trend. The value of Zs is 0.5075 (less than $Z_{0.05}$) which make it statistically insignificant as presented in Table 3. This is an indication that trend of increase or decrease in reservoir inflow would be insignificant. The evaluated value of Kendall's Tau ($\tau = 0.08225$) is very less to predict the agreement between two parameters. If τ is equal to zero or nearly equal to zero it means that the X (time) and Y (reservoir inflow) are independent. The same is occurring in our case resulting in blind trend.

Sen's Slope estimator

In case of regression statistical analysis, co-efficient of regression and sample correlation values obtained were less. Therefore, interpretation has been enhanced using Sen's slope estimator. The positive values of Kendall's Tau (τ) equal to 0.08225 shows an increasing trend of inflow in Ukai reservoir. The estimated Sen's slope value, Kendall's Tau and statistical values in the Sen's slope estimator is shown in Table 4. From analysis using non-parametric tests such as the Man-Kendall's test and Sen's slope estimator shows synonymous results that may be more conclusive than regression based simple trend analysis. The analysis by Sen's slope estimator gives an increasing trend which shows the increasing tendency of reservoir inflow to Ukai reservoir in future.

Conclusion

An attempt has been made to study effect of climate change on reservoir inflow using trend analysis for Ukai reservoir. The trend analysis is carried out using regression statistics method, Man-Kendall's test and Sen's slope estimator. The study indicates an increasing trend in the inflows to the Ukai reservoir. There were some notable changes in the hydro meteorological variables at Ukai dam/reservoir. However, the reservoir inflow exhibited positive trends, which indicate that the variability in inflow have tendency to increase and the rate of their changes are significantly positive. From the results of analysis, co-efficient of regression ($R^2 = 0.0057$) and sample correlation (R=0.0754) shows weaker statistics therefore analysis is enhanced by Man-Kendall's tst and Sen's slope estimator. The results from Man-Kendall's test and Sen's slope estimator shows positive trend with Kendal's Tau (τ) value equal to 0.08225. The kendall's Tau value (Sen;s slope estimator) give significant information about the identification of reservoir inflow trend as compared to regression analysis. A fairly good information to identify the reservoir inflow trend over Ukai reservoir is given by non-parametric statistical methods like Man-Kendall's test and Sen's slope estimator. It can be concluded that there is a positive impact of climate change on the water resources of the study area due to increase in reservoir inflow. Hence more water will be available at Ukai reservoir for irrigation, hydropower generation, water supply etc. in future. In trend analysis studies, the results significantly depend upon the period of data and the centre or stations whose data are used. There is another observation that most of the data used in trend detection pertain to the stations that are located in urban areas and these areas are a sort of heat islands. Thus, the study of trends using this data may not be the correct depiction of the reality and this aspect needs to be addressed. These concerns, in fact, highlight the importance of identifying a network of baseline stations for change detection studies.

References

Journal Papers

1. Burn, D. H., and Simonovic, S. P. (1996). "Sensitivity of reservoir operation performance to climate change." Water Resour. Manage., 10(6), 463–478
2. Labadie, J. W. (2004). "Optimal operation of multi-reservoir systems: State of the art review." J. Water Resour. Plann. Manage., 130(2), 93–111
3. Kavvas, M.L., Chen, Z.Q., Ohara, N., A.J. Amin, M.Z.M.(2006). "Impact of Climate Change on the Hydrology and Water resources of Peninsular Malaysia", International Congress on River Basin Management, 529-537
4. McBean, E. and Motiee, H (2008). "Assessment of Impact of Climate Change on Water Resources: A Long Term Analysis of the Great Lakes of North America", Hydrol. Earth Syst. Sci. Vol. 12, pp 239- 255.
5. Xu, Y. P., and Tang, Y. K. (2009). "Decision rules of water resources management under uncertainty." J. Water Resour. Plann. Manage., 135(3), 149–159.
6. Lund, J. R. (1996). "Operating rule optimization for Missouri River reservoir system." J. Water Resour. Plann. Manage., 122(4), 287–295.
7. Zealand C.M. , Burn D.H. and Simonovic S. P. (1999), "short term streamflow forecasting using artificial neural networks", Journol of hydrology, Volume 214, Issues 1–4, January 1999, Pages 32–48
8. ASCE Task Committee on Application of Artificial Neural Networks in Hydrology. (2000). "Artificial neural networks in hydrology. I: Preliminary concepts." J. Hydrol. Eng., 5(2), 115–123.
9. Lischeid, G. (2001). "Investigating trends of hydrochemical time series of small catchments by artificial neural networks." Phys. Chem. Earth, 26(1), 15–18.
10. Gueller, S. (2005). " Applied artificial intelligence to solve water resources and environmental problems." Proc., World Water and Environmental Resources Congress 2005, ASCE, Reston, VA.
11. Jain, A., and Kumar, S. (2009). "Dissection of trained neural

network hydrologic model architectures for knowledge extraction." Water Resour. Res., 45(7), W07420.

12. Paulin, C., and Xiaogang, S. (2005).   Identification of the Effect of Climate Change on Future Design Standards of Drainage Infrastructure in Ontario. Department of Civil Engineering, 1280 Main Street West Hamilton, Ontario, Canada.

13. Zhang, X., Harvey, K. D., Hogg,W. D., and Yuzyk, T. R. (2001). "Trends in Canadian streamflow." Water Resour. Res., 37(4), 987–998.

14. Kumar, S., Merwade, V., Kam, J., and Thurner, K. (2009). "Streamflow trends in Indiana: Effects of long term persistence, precipitation and subsurface drains." J. Hydrol. (Amsterdam, Neth.), 374(1), 171–183.

15. Douglas, E. M., Vogel, R. M., and Kroll, C. N. (2000). "Trends in floods and low flows in the United States: Impact of spatial correlation." J. Hydrol. (Amsterdam, Neth.), 240(1–2), 90–105.

16. Sawami A.W. (2011),   "Assesment of the impact of climate change on water resources of Jebba hydropower reservoir using trend and reduction pattern methods", 10th Anniversary conference of Fulbright held at Conference Centre, University of Ibadan, Ibadan.

17. Song A. N., Chandramouli V. M. ASCE, Gupta Nimisha (2012), " Analysing Inflow Trend of Indiana Reservoirs using SOM", Journal of Hydraulic Engineering @ ASCE/August/2012, DOI:10.1061 /(ASCE)HE.1943-5584.0000517.

18. Kendall, M. (1975). "Multivariate Analysis", Charles Griffin & Company, London

Chapter- VI

Environment Impact Assessment Process in India– Does it Deliver?

Shrawani Shagun*

Abstract

Rapid development by human is leading to swift deterioration in environmental conditions and human health, Impact assessment thus ensures that the potential problems are foreseen and addressed at an early stage in the projects planning and design. The International Association for Environment Impact Assessment (IAIA) defines an environmental impact assessment as "the process of identifying, predicting, evaluating and mitigating the biophysical, social, and other relevant effects of development proposals prior to major decisions being taken and commitments made. The purpose of the assessment is to ensure that decision makers consider the ensuing environmental impacts to decide whether to proceed with the project.

India is rapidly urbanizing, which lead to need of improvement and expansion of urban environmental infrastructure. In order to assure that infrastructure projects are planned, designed and implemented in an environmentally sustainable manner, it is important that comprehensive Environmental Impact Assessment[1] is undertaken during the project planning stage. EIA should address all relevant biological, physical and social issues associated with the planned project and make recommendations that avoid or minimize any adverse environmental impacts.

Keywords –EIA, pollution, development, India, environment degradation

---

[1] Used as EIA, herein after in the paper

*ICFAI University, Dehradun, India

Introduction

EIA is a planning tool that is now generally accepted as an integral component of sound decision-making. The purpose of EIA is to foresee and address potential environmental problems/concerns at an early stage of project planning and design. EIA/EMP[2] should assist planners and government authorities in the decision making process by identifying the key impacts/issues and formulating mitigation measures. Environmental Impact Assessment (EIA) methods consists five analytical functions "Identification, Prediction, Evaluation, Mitigation and Documentation"[3].

The Environmental Impact Assessment (EIA) is though not mandatory but directory as it helps in identifying and evaluating the potential impacts which can be beneficial or adverse, for development and projects on the environmental system. It acts as a useful aid for decision making based on understanding of the environment implications including social, cultural and aesthetic concerns which could be integrated with the analysis of the project costs and benefits. This exercise is to be undertaken in the planning stage itself of projects so that, selection of environmentally compatible sites, process technologies and such other environmental safeguards could be done without any abruption.

EIA is an important practice as it benefit to a group of people in making policy tool for decision makers, regulators and stakeholders to be aware of the possible environmental, social and economic costs of a proposed project and /or interventions. A proper EIA is also very essential for a sustainable and appropriate decision making process. As still all concerned person are less aware about the EIA and its benefits. So, there is a genuine need for capacity building in EIA processes and steps to conduct transparent public consultations and to evaluate EIA reports, especially after the new EIA notification by Government of India and need to develop awareness among community based organizations, ~~nongovernmental organizations,~~ corporate organization, academicians and ~~Environmental Management Planning~~ understand and review EIA reports as

[3]   As defined by International Association for Environment Impact Assessment

they are more or less technical in nature.

In the further sections of the paper basics of EIA has been dealt accordingly, EIA methodology, basic concepts, types of EIA, evolution of EIA in India, legal regime with respect to EIA in India and worldwide, misconception regarding EIA, what ideal EIA mean and how it should be reached, and further suggestion and conclusion.

Objectives of EIA

Before going in to the depth of EIA that how and when it evolved, the fundamental rules for ideal EIA, we need to understand nicely what should be and what the objectives of EIA are. Throughout the world EIA has following objectives:

- To ensure that the environmental considerations are explicitly addressed and incorporated into the development and decision-making process;
- To anticipate and avoid, minimize or offset the adverse significant biophysical, social and other relevant effects of development proposals;
- To protect the productivity and capacity of natural systems and the ecological processes which maintain their functions; and
- To promote development that is sustainable and optimizes resource use as well as management opportunities.

Basic EIA Principles

By integrating the environmental impacts of the development activities and their mitigation in early stages of project planning, the benefits of EIA could be realized in all the stages of a project, from exploration, planning, through construction, operations, decommissioning, and beyond site closure.

A properly-conducted-EIA also lessens conflicts by promoting community participation, informing decision-makers, and also helps in laying the base for environmentally sound projects. An EIA should meet

139

at least three core values:

Integrity: The EIA process should be fair, objective, unbiased and balanced

Utility: The EIA process should provide balanced, credible information for decision making

Sustainability: The EIA process should result in environmental safeguards   But except the basic principles, ideally an EIA process should have following traits to have better results:

Purposive- should inform decision-makers and result in appropriate levels of environmental protection and community well-being.

Rigorous- should apply 'best practicable' science, employing methodologies and techniques appropriate to address the problems being investigated.

Practical- should result in providing information and acceptable and implementable solutions for problems faced by the proponents.

Relevant- should provide sufficient, reliable and usable information for development planning and decision-making.

Cost-effective- should impose minimum cost burdens in terms of time and finance on proponents and participants consistent with meeting accepted requirements and objectives of EIA.

Efficient- should achieve the objectives of EIA within the limits of available information, time, resources and methodology.

Focused- should concentrate on significant environmental effects and key issues; *i.e.*, the matters that need to be considered while making decisions.

Adaptive- should be adjusted to the realities, issues and circumstances of the proposals under review without compromising the integrity of the process, and be iterative, incorporating lessons learnt throughout the project life cycle.

Participative - should provide appropriate opportunities to inform and involve the interested and affected public, and their inputs and concerns should be addressed explicitly in the documentation and decision-making.

Inter-disciplinary- should ensure that appropriate techniques and experts in relevant bio-physical and socio-economic disciplines are employed, including the use of traditional knowledge as relevant.

Credible- should be carried out with professionalism, rigor, fairness, objectivity, impartiality and balance, and be subject to independent checks and verification.

Integrated- should address the inter-relationships of social, economic and biophysical aspects.

Transparent- should have clear, easily understood requirements for EIA content; ensure public access to information; identify the factors that are to be taken into account in decision-making; and acknowledge limitations and difficulties.

Systematic- should result in full consideration of all relevant information on the affected environment, of proposed alternatives and their impacts, and of the measures necessary to monitor and investigate residual effects.

EIA Methodology

The term 'environmental impact assessment' is used to describe a wide range of activities whose purpose is examination of the environmental consequences of proposed projects. While EIA techniques use everything from very simple checklists of common environmental parameters to highly specialized testing regimes to quantify air or water quality, a basic methodology generally is observed. The EIA process includes:

Scoping to determine all potentially significant environmental impacts

Scoping should establish the spatial and temporal bounds of potential impacts and should be a participatory process. Participation from local communities in areas potentially affected by the project is best garnered through a combination of informal discussions, structured public meetings and meetings with NGOs and community-based organizations. Information gathered through public participation should be a vital part of subsequent decision making.

Identifying the affected environment and creating a basic inventory of biological, geophysical and cultural resources located within the spatial bounds of the proposed project.

Examining potentially significant environmental impacts

Generally field work is undertaken to gather qualitative and quantitative data sufficient to make a judgment about the impacts of the proposed project. Meeting with local residents is a critical part of this process because their knowledge of the local environment is unique.

Considering a range of alternatives to the proposed project

Alternatives analysis includes looking at alternative sites for proposed facilities (e.g. a manufacturing plant project), alternative routes (e.g. a road building project), alternative means of achieving the same project objectives (i.e. constructing a run of river hydropower plant rather than creating a reservoir) and not undertaking the project at all ("the no action alternative").

Developing an environmental management plan to mitigate or eliminate significant impacts and monitor future impacts

Mitigation generally includes structural and non-structural interventions that reduce the impact of the proposed project (i.e. plants grasses along steep side slopes to prevent erosion). Monitoring requires establishing baseline conditions for key environmental parameters prior to project implementation and collection of additional data for the same parameters

at some point(s) after implementation. The parameters examined during the course of the EIA should include:

• Biological resources (e.g. wildlife habitat, plant and animal species present)

• Physical/chemical aspects (e.g. air, water or soil quality); and

• Human-interest related factors (e.g. religious sites, schools, homes)

When designing a monitoring plan, it is important to isolate measured parameters to the maximum extent possible to minimize the effect that factors external to the project have on measured parameters. For example, a point at which water quality is measured downstream of a new manufacturing facility should not be in the downstream path of any other new effluent source.

Figure Showing flowchart showing the EIA process

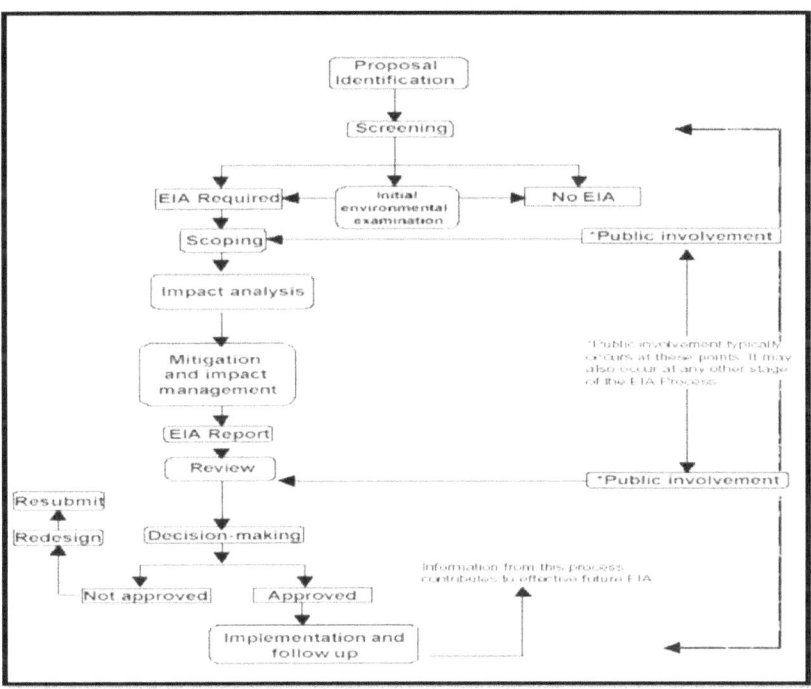

Explanation of the above figure and meaning thereby -

1. Screening: First stage of EIA, which determines whether the proposed project, requires an EIA and if it requires EIA, then the level of assessment required.

2. Scoping: This stage identifies the key issues and impact that should be further investigated. This stage also defines the boundary and time limit of the study.

3. Impact analysis: This stage of EIA identifies and predicts likely environmental and social impact of the proposed project and evaluates the significance.

4. Mitigation: This step in EIA recommends the actions to reduce and avoid the potential adverse environmental consequences of development activities.

5. Reporting: This stage presents the result of EIA in a form of a report to the decision-making body and other interested parties.

6. Review of EIA: It examines the adequacy and effectiveness of the EIA report and provides information necessary for the decision-making.

7. Decision-making: It decides whether the project is rejected, approved or needs further change.

8. Post monitoring: This stage comes into play once the project is commissioned. It checks whether the impacts of the project do not exceed the legal standards and implementation of the mitigation measures are in the manner as described in the EIA report.

Types of EIA

Environmental assessments could be classified into four types which are precisely discussed below:

Strategic environmental assessment

Strategic Environmental Assessment (SEA) refers to systematic analysis of the environmental effects of development policies, plans, programmes and other proposed strategic actions. SEA represents a proactive approach to integrating environmental considerations into the higher levels of decision-making – beyond the project level, when major alternatives are still open.

Regional EIA

EIA in the context of regional planning integrates environmental concerns into development planning for a geographic region, normally at the sub-country level. Such an approach is referred to as the economic-cum-environmental (EcE) development planning. This approach facilitates adequate integration of economic development with management of renewable natural resources within the carrying capacity limitation to achieve sustainable development. It fulfills the need for macro-level environmental integration, which the project-oriented EIA is unable to address effectively. Regional EIA addresses the environmental impacts of regional development plans and thus, the context for project-level EIA of the subsequent projects, within the region. In addition, if environmental effects are considered at regional level, then the cumulative environmental effects of all the projects within the region can be accounted.

Sectoral EIA

Instead of project-level-EIA, an EIA should take place in the context of regional and sectoral level planning. Once sectoral level development plans have the integrated sectoral environmental concerns addressed, the scope of project-level EIA will be quite minimal. Sectoral EIA will helps in to addressing specific environmental problems that may be encountered in planning and implementing sectoral development projects.

Project level EIA

Project level EIA refers to the developmental activity in isolation and the impacts that it exerts on the receiving environment. Thus, it may not effectively integrate the cumulative effects of the development in a region.

From the above discussion, it is clear that the EIA shall be integrated at all levels *i.e.*, strategic, regional, sectoral and project level. Whereas, the strategic EIA is a structural change in the way the things are evaluated for decision-making, the regional EIA refers to substantial information processing and drawing complex inferences. The project-level EIA is relatively simple and reaches to meaningful conclusions. Therefore in India, project-level EIA studies take place on an large-scale and are being considered.

However, in the re-engineered Notification, provisions are incorporated for giving a single clearance for the entire industrial estate for *e.g.*, Leather parks, pharma cities, *etc.*, which is a step towards the regional approach. As we progress and the resource planning concepts emerge in our decision-making process, the integration of overall regional issues will become part of the impact assessment studies.

Evolution of EIA in India

The 1987 World Commission on Environment and Development report Our Common Future, also known as the "Brundtland Report", was the first significant document to identify the importance of EIA as a tool. The Report recommended that, "A broader environmental assessment should be applied not only to products and projects, but also to policies and programmes, especially major macroeconomic, finance, and sectoral policies that induce significant impacts on the environment".

In India, EIAs of development projects were first started in 1977-78 when the Department of Science and Technology took up environmental appraisal of river valley projects. Subsequently, various other projects were brought under the purview of EIA. It was, however, with the enactment of the Environment Protection Act. 1986, that there was a broad move towards institutionalizing environmental procedures. The Central Government, under S. 3(1) and S. 3(2) of the Environment Protection Act, 1986, and under Rule 5(3) (a) of the Environment Protection Rules, 1986 issued a draft notification in 1992 laying down norms and procedures for impact assessment. This was followed by a final notification in 1994 and two other notifications amending it. Environmental Impact Assessment has been formally introduced in 1994.

It relied on the institutional framework that has a strong supporting legislative, administrative and procedural set-up. Both central and state authorities together are sharing the responsibility of its development and management. This broadly constitutes the law relating to EIAs in India. The procedure established by these notifications, and the alterations that these procedures have undergone in a short time have been examined further in paper.

Legal Regime for EIA in India

The Legal and Policy Framework in India EIA practice in India is relatively well established, though its application is not universal. The central government in India has created a foundation for environmental protection over the past two decades, beginning in 1974 with the enactment of the Water Prevention and Control of Pollution Act. A similar act addressing air pollution, the Air Prevention and Control of Pollution Act was passed in 1977. These laws established baseline thresholds for water and air quality.

In 1986, a more comprehensive Environmental Protection Act was promulgated which established a framework for environmental clearance, requiring that EIAs be conducted for development projects with a cost of Rs. 50 crore or more. To rectify ambiguity regarding exactly what type of projects were subject to the Act, specific project types were enumerated in a 1994 EIA Notification issued by the Ministry of Environment and Forests. The Notification identified 29 categories of projects for which proponents must conduct EIAs and receive a clearance from the central government. These include a range of manufacturing facilities, power plants, high ways, ports, airports, dams and tourist development in coastal areas.

The Notification does not require EIAs for urban environmental infrastructure projects (UEIP) because these are assumed to result in positive environmental impacts. However, this assumption neglects two important facts characteristic of large scale infrastructure development projects:

1. Most create significant short term disruptions to the physical and social environment during and just after completion of construction activities; and

2. Many create localized, long term environmental impacts. Proper EIA practice does *not* weigh project positive environmental impacts against negative environmental impacts; rather, any significant negative impacts should be clearly identified and mitigated to acceptable levels.

In addition to central government requirements, some states, regional development authorities and municipal corporations have established their own EIA requirements for projects under their jurisdiction. These requirements vary widely from one jurisdiction to another. Environmental clearance generally falls under the jurisdiction of the State Pollution Control Boards in each state. Some states require EIAs for certain types of UEIPs, others do not. Those that do require environmental clearance for UEIPs, generally specify sewage treatment and solid waste disposal. The situation is similarly mixed at the regional and municipal levels.

The initiatives on environmental protection including policy in India dates back to the fourth Five Year Plan (1969-74) subsequent to which an initial legislation was promulgated in 1974 with the goal of protecting water quality. This legislation, referred to as the Water (Pollution, Prevention and Control) Act, was followed in 1981 by the Air (Pollution Prevention and Control) Act and the Environment (Protection) Act of 1986, an umbrella act that covered all the aspects of the environment and several others following this.

Currently, the MoEF is the nodal agency at the central level responsible for planning, promoting, and coordinating environmental programs and formulating environmental policies. At the center, responsibilities for industrial pollution prevention and control are primarily executed by the CPCB, a statutory authority attached to the MoEF. The CPCB was constituted in September 1974 for implementing provisions of the Water Act and, in 1981, the Air Act. The State Department of Environment and Forests (SDEF) and the State Pollution Control Board (SPCB) are the designated agencies to perform these functions at the state level.

Environment Protection Act, 1986

This is an umbrella legislation to provide for the protection and improvement of environment and for matters connected therewith. This act gives specific definitions, which are to be used in all rules enacted under this act. It provides power to the Central Government to take all such measures as it deems necessary in protecting and improving the quality of environment and preventing and abating environmental pollution. The central government also has to lay down standards for emission or discharge of environmental pollutants from various sources giving regards to the quality or composition of the emission or discharge of environmental pollutants from such sources. Industries operating in India have to meet the following requirements to remain in compliance with the Environment Protection Act.

Comply with the directions issued in writing by the Central Government within in a specified time as mentioned in the order. The directions may include:

1. Closure, prohibition or regulation of any industry, operation or process; or

2. Stoppage or regulation of the supply of electricity, water or any other service

3. Prevention discharges or emissions of environmental pollutants exceeding the prescribed standards

4. Furnishing of information to the prescribed agencies of any accidental or unforeseen event in which environmental pollutant(s) not conforming to the prescribed standards are being discharged, or are likely to be discharged, into the environment.

5. Allow Central Government or any official empowered by it, to take samples of air, water, soil or any other substance from the industrial establishment for the purpose of analysis.

6. Submit an "Environmental Statement" every year, before 30th September, to the PCB.

7. Obtain prior "Environmental Clearance" from MoEF, in case of a new project or for modernization/expansion of the existing project.

The penalties set under this act are imprisonment, which may extend up to 5 months and/or fines up to rupees hundred thousand. In case of continuing offenses, fines of Rs. 5000 per day may be charged.

Minimum National Standards (MINAS)

The rules under the Environment Protection Act provide specific standards for industry (total of 79 industry sectors) and general standards of discharge of environmental pollutants in Inland Surface water i.e. like lakes and rivers, public sewers, land for irrigation and coastal areas. Minimum National Standards for thermal power plants have been formulated for pollution control in India.

The Environmental Impact Assessment Notification, 1994

The Ministry of Environment and Forests, Government of India notified the Impact (EIA) Notification, 1994 under the Environment (Protection) Act, 1986. As per the notification, 30 types of industries scheduled therein have to obtain the environmental clearance from the Government of India. Any organization, which desires to undertake any new project or expansion or modernization of any existing industry or project, with investment of more than Rs.5 crores, requires conducting an environmental impact assessment. These projects require an environmental clearance from the central government. The clearance granted is valid for a period of five years from commencement of the construction or operation of the project. No construction work, preliminary or otherwise, relating to the set up of the project may be undertaken till the environmental and/or site clearance is obtained.

The Water (Prevention and Control of Pollution) Act, 1974

The Water Act established the general standards for effluent discharge into receiving water in order to prevent water pollution. The major responsibilities of SPCBs under the Act include granting consent to establish and operate facilities, restricting areas of operation, conducting surveys, and determining the use and misuse of streams and wells within its jurisdiction.

The Air (Prevention and Control of Pollution) Act, 1981

The general legislative conditions of this act are similar to the Water Act in terms of obligations, responsibilities and penalties. The primary responsibility for controlling air pollution resides with the SPCB. Under the Air Act, the state governments are authorized to designate any area or areas within the state as an air pollution control area, after consulting with the SPCB and notifying the official gazette. Depending upon the quality of air in the designated area(s), the SPCB may set air emission standards in the notified area. The standards set by the SPCBs shall not be more lenient than the ambient air standards set by the CPCB. Any industry to be established in the air pollution control area must acquire the consent to establish and consent to operate from the state.

Noise Pollution (Control and Regulations) Rules, 1999

This rule is to reduce the noise pollution from various sources, inter-alia, industrial activities, public address systems, generator sets, construction activity, that may affects the physical and psychological well-being of the people. Ambient noise standards for different areas have been specified in Annexure of these rules. The Central Government or its designated authorities may categorize areas into industrial, commercial, residential or silence zones for the purpose of implementation of noise standards for different areas. An area up to 100 meters around hospitals, educational institutions and courts and sensitive areas (i.e. forests) shall be declared as a silence zone for the purpose of these rules.

Other rules, which may be applicable depending on the nature of the case, are as follows:

1. The Hazardous Waste (Management & Handling) Rules, 1989;
2. The Manufacture, Storage and Import of Hazardous Chemical Rules (MSIHC), 1989 (amended in October 1994 and January 2000);
3. Public Liability Insurance Act, 1991;
4. The National Environmental Tribunal Act, 1995;
5. Chemical Accidents (Emergency Planning, Preparedness & Response) Rules, 1996;
6. The Factories Act, 1948, (amendment in 1976 and 1987);
7. The Petroleum Act, 1934 and rules framed there under;
8. The Motor Vehicles Act (amended in 1988);
9. Gas Cylinder Rules, 1981;
10. International agreements on environmental issues
11. India is signatory to a number of multilateral environment agreements (MEA) and conventions. An overview of some of the major MEAs and India's obligations under these is presented below. These are discussed at length in the respective chapters.

Convention on International Trade in Endangered Species of wild fauna and flora (CITES), 1973

The aim of CITES is to control or prevent international commercial trade in endangered species or products derived from them. CITES does not seek to directly protect endangered species or curtail development practices that destroy their habitats. Rather, it seeks to reduce the economic incentive to poach endangered species and destroy their habitat by closing off the international market. India became a party to the CITES in 1976. International trade in all wild flora and fauna in general and species covered under CITES is regulated jointly through the provisions of The Wildlife (Protection) Act 1972, the Import/Export policy of Government of India and the Customs Act 1962 .

Montreal Protocol on Substances that deplete the Ozone Layer (to the Vienna Convention for the Protection of the Ozone Layer), 1987

The Montreal Protocol to the Vienna Convention on Substances that deplete the Ozone Layer, came into force in 1989. The protocol set targets for reducing the consumption and production of a range of ozone depleting substances (ODS). In a major innovation the Protocol recognized that all nations should not be treated equally. The agreement acknowledges that certain countries have contributed to ozone depletion more than others. It also recognizes that a nation's obligation to reduce current emissions should reflect its technological and financial ability to do so. Because of this, the agreement sets more stringent standards and accelerated phase-out timetables to countries that have contributed most to ozone depletion (Divan and Rosencrantz, 2001).

India acceded to the Montreal Protocol along with its London Amendment in September 1992. The MoEF has established an Ozone Cell and a steering committee on the Montreal Protocol to facilitate implementation of the India Country Program, for phasing out ODS production by 2010.

To meet India's commitments under the Montreal Protocol, the Government of India has also taken certain policy decisions. Goods required to implement ODS phase-out projects funded by the Multilateral Fund are fully exempt from duties. This benefit has been also extended to new investments with non-ODS technologies. Commercial banks are prohibited from financing or refinancing investments with ODS technologies.

The Gazette of India on 19 July 2000 notified rules for regulation of ODS phase-out called the *Ozone Depleting Substances (Regulation and Control) Rules, 2000*. They were notified under the Environment (Protection) Act, 1986. These rules were drafted by the MoEF following consultations with industries and related government departments.

Basel Convention on Trans boundary Movement of Hazardous Wastes, 1989. Basel Convention, which entered into force in 1992, has three key objectives:

1. To reduce trans boundary movements of hazardous wastes;

2. To minimize the creation of such wastes; and

3. To prohibit their shipment to countries lacking the capacity to dispose hazardous wastes in an environmentally sound manner.

India ratified the Basel Convention in 1992, shortly after it came into force. The Indian Hazardous Wastes Management Rules Act 1989 encompasses some of the Basel provisions related to the notification of import and export of hazardous waste, illegal traffic, and liability.

UN Framework Conventions on Climate Change (UNFCCC), 1992

The primary goals of the UNFCCC were to stabilize greenhouse gas emissions at levels that would prevent dangerous anthropogenic interference with the global climate. The convention embraced the principle of common but differentiated responsibilities which has guided the adoption of a regulatory structure.

India signed the agreement in June 1992, which was ratified in November 1993. As per the convention the reduction/limitation requirements apply only to developed countries. The only reporting obligation for developing countries relates to the construction of a GHG inventory. India has initiated the preparation of its First National Communication (base year 1994) that includes an inventory of GHG sources and sinks, potential vulnerability to climate change, adaptation measures and other steps being taken in the country to address climate change. The further details on UNFCC and the Kyoto Protocol are provided in Atmosphere and climate chapter.

Convention on Biological Diversity, 1992

The Convention on Biological Diversity (CBD) is a legally binding, framework treaty that has been ratified until now by 180 countries. The CBD has three main thrust areas: conservation of biodiversity, sustainable use of biological resources and equitable sharing of benefits arising from their sustainable use. The Convention on Biological Diversity came into force in 1993. Many biodiversity issues are addressed in the convention, including habitat preservation, intellectual property rights, biosafety, and indigenous peoples' rights.

India's initiatives under the Convention are detailed in the chapter on Biodiversity. These include the promulgation of the Wildlife (Protection) Act of 1972, amended in 1991; and participation in several international conventions such as CITES.

UN Convention on Desertification, 1994

Delegates to the 1992 UN Conference on Environment and Development (UNCED) recommended establishment of an intergovernmental negotiating committee for the elaboration of an international convention to combat desertification in countries experiencing serious drought and/or desertification. The UN General Assembly established such a committee in 1992 that later helped formulation of Convention on Desertification in 1994.

The convention is distinctive as it endorses and employs a bottom-up approach to international environmental cooperation. Under the terms of the convention, activities related to the control and alleviation of desertification and its effects are to be closely linked to the needs and participation of local land users and non-governmental organizations. Seven countries in the South Asian region are signatories to the Convention, which aims at tackling desertification through national, regional and sub-regional action programmes. The Regional Action Programme has six Thematic Programme Networks (TPN's) for the Asian region, each headed by a country task manager. India hosts the network on agroforestry and soil conservation. For details refer to the land resource chapter.

International Tropical Timber Agreement and the International Tropical Timber Organisation (ITTO), 1983

The ITTO established by the International Tropical Timber Agreement (ITTA), 1983, came into force in 1985 and became operational in 1987. The ITTO facilitates discussion, consultation and international cooperation on issues relating to the international trade and utilization of tropical timber and the sustainable management of its resource base. The successor agreement to the ITTA (1983) was negotiated in 1994, and came into force on 1 January 1997. The organization has 57 member countries. India ratified the ITTA in 1996.

Comparison between EIA notification 1994 and 2006 with reference to latest provisions

As per the notification of "The Environmental Impact Assessment of Development Projects Notification, 1994":

1. All projects listed under Schedule I require environmental clearance from the MoEF.

2. Projects under the delicensed category of the New Industrial Policy also require clearance from the MoEF.

3. All developmental projects whether or not under the Schedule I, if located in fragile regions must obtain MoEF clearance.

4. Industrial projects with investments above Rs. 500 million must obtain MoEF clearance and are further required to obtain a LOI (Letter of Intent) from the Ministry of Industry, and an NoC (No Objection Certificate) from the SPCB and the State Forest Department if the location involves forestland. Once the NoC is obtained, the LoI is converted into an industrial license by the state authority.

5. The notification also stipulated procedural requirements for the establishment and operation of new power plants. As

per this notification, two-stage clearance for site-specific projects such as pithead thermal power plants and valley projects is required. Site clearance is given in the first stage and final environmental clearance in the second.

6. A public hearing has been made mandatory for projects covered by this notification. This is an important step in providing transparency and a greater role to local communities.

Despite of the strict rules made, there were certain obvious loopholes visible in EC Process under EIA Notification, 1994, which are:

1. It laid down very Cumbersome Procedure which was quite uneasy to handle.

2. Disproportionate details sought with application

3. The process itself was the main reason to cause the delay in appraisal meetings

4. Then , the overall procedure was time consuming and requiring undue effort

5. Reopening of technical issues during various stages of appraisal

6. Though there was stringent process, then also it did not helped in reaching the desirable quality of EIA reports

7. Procedure laid down was quite evident enough which was the main reason for the delays by other concerned agencies

Unlike 1994 notification, EIA Notification, 2006, has brought with the aim "to formulate a transparent decentralized and efficient regulatory mechanism" to:

1. Incorporate necessary environmental safeguards at planning stage;

2. Involve stakeholders in the Public Consultation Process;

3. Identify Developmental Projects based on Impact Potential instead of the investment criteria.

4. Categorization of projects into 'A and 'B' Category based on impact potential

5. Scoping of projects for prescribing TORs

6. Decentralization of Appraisal Process

7. More structured Public consultation

8. Time limits prescribed for each step

9. NOC from other Regulatory Agencies not a pre-requisite.

In the 2006 notification there is time frame for Appraisal of Projects so as to avoid any kind of undue delay in the effective implementation of EIA and such time frame are given below along with the cases in which it will be applicable -

1. 60 days for prescribing Time of references

2. 45 days for completing Public Hearing

3. 105 days for Environmental Appraisal and communicating the decision

The Rationale for EIA – Does it deliver??

This misconception regarding EIA practice sometimes leads to a "balance sheet" approach to evaluating a project's environmental impacts, in which projects judged to have an overall positive impact are not subjected to rigorous EIA, despite prediction of some significant negative environmental impacts. Environmental Impact Assessment is a project development tool which, when properly applied, improves the long term sustainability of infrastructure activities. While EIA often is viewed narrowly as a regulatory hurdle that must be crossed before finalizing project design, it is actually a tool that should be part of the project planning and design process. Conducting comprehensive EIA is an opportunity to look systematically at the way a potential project will affect the surrounding natural and built environment, allowing consideration of alternatives to the proposed project and seeking out participation by affected communities in decision making.

Using EIA as a mechanism to assure community participation is increasingly important. Local residents generally have intimate historical knowledge about local environmental conditions and cultural resources. The prioritisation of development and the dilution of regulation have had predictable consequences. Today, after many years of the EIA notification, NGOs and communities continue to struggle with fraudulent EIA reports, staged public hearings, and unscrupulous environmental clearances. In the process, the positions taken by various stakeholders in this process have become intense and extremely polarised, with the government and industries on one side, and the NGOs and local communities on the other. As public opposition to specific projects has become increasingly intense - leading to such incidents as police firing on demonstrators - it is growing more evident that the questions that were passed by too quickly in the beginning must be asked and answered again.

Therefore, their active participation often leads to design solutions that are better suited to local conditions, socially acceptable, more effective and long lasting. The delay or cancellation of some high profile infrastructure projects in the last few years demonstrates that social acceptance is crucial to project success in India and so EIA process is not that much effective as it was supposed to be.

Improving EIA

The purpose of Environmental Impact Assessment (EIA) is to identify and evaluate the potential impacts (beneficial and adverse) of development and projects on the environmental system. It is a useful aid for decision making based on understanding of the environment implications including social, cultural and aesthetic concerns which could be integrated with the analysis of the project costs and benefits. This exercise should be undertaken early enough in the planning stage of projects for selection of environmentally compatible sites, process technologies and such other environmental safeguards. However, it's worth mentioning here that despite of the many attempts and the process lay down and notified / amended time to time, and then also it does not give the expected results. Certain Steps that should be considered if implemented properly to Improve EIA Process are :

1. Constitution of Sector specific Expert Appraisal Committees (EACs) and Holding of regular and longer duration EAC Meetings
2. State Level Environment Impact Assessment Authorities and Committees focus to bring changes and help to all and work in the direction of spreading awareness
3. Display of project status and minutes on website without any undue delay
4. Issue of administrative instructions for clarity and uniformity in implementation of EIA Notification time to time
5. Initiated scheme for accreditation of consultants should be implemented without any hurdle and Accreditation of consultants should be done through Quality Council of India
6. Timely review of the monitoring mechanism should be done
7. Regional approach to EIA should be taken in to consideration
8. An Independent Oversight Committee should be established as the binding authority over the MoEF. As it presently stands, the MoEF can be easily threatened by government pressure and seek out loopholes to grant environmental clearances.
9. The EIA process should be free from political agendas and manipulative gestures and instead concentrate on the task it was enacted to do.
10. Second, public consultations should be required for all development projects and occur at various stages of the EIA process. Many projects, therefore, are strategically labeled as one of the allowed exemptions to avoid public participation. Such exemptions should be eradicated from the EIA Notification, and it should be mandatory that all projects be subject to public consultations.

Conclusion

The extent of the environmental legislation network is evident from the above discussion but the enforcement of the laws has been a matter of concern. One commonly cited reason is the prevailing command and control nature of the environmental regime. Coupled with this is the prevalence of the all-or–nothing approach of the law; they do not consider the extent of violation. Fines are levied on a flat basis and in addition, there are no incentives to lower the discharges below prescribed levels.

The major problem with the environment impact assessment process is too much concentration of powers in the hands of the MoEF. Even a cursory look at the structure overseeing the EIA process would reveal that it's the Government, in one form or the other, controlling the EIA process, with little accountability towards the common man. The entire EIA discourse/mechanism is top-down rather than bottoms-up public consultation is a farce, industry driven rather than being community driven public consultation has little relevance and autocratic rather than democratic which only pays lip service to the lofty ideals of environmental protection as enshrined in the Constitution and plethora of environmental legislations and policy documents. Unless we have speration of powers/responsibilities and have independent and impartial and empowered regulators and adjudicators with clear accountability there is little that can be achieved through the current 'impacted' EIA process.

References

1. *"Principle of Environmental Impact Assessment Best Practice."* International Association for Impact Assessment. 1999.
2. Divan S and Rosencranz A. 2001 *Environmental law and policy in India, cases, materials and statutes*, 2nd Edition New York: Oxford University Press. 837 pp
3. *CITES and the wildlife trade in India*, New Delhi: Centre for Environmental Law, WWF-India. 182 pp.
4. Holder, J., (2004), *Environmental Assessment: The Regulation of Decision Making*, Oxford University Press, and New York; for a comparative discussion of the elements of various domestic EIA systems, see Christopher Wood Environmental Impact Assessment: A Comparative Review (2 ed, Prentice Hall, Harlow, 2002).
5. Daniel, S., Tsoulfas, G., Pappis, C., & Rachaniotis, N. (2004) *Aggregating and evaluating the results of different Environmental Impact Assessment methods Ecological indicators* 4:125-138
6. Hitzschky, K., & Silviera, J. (2009) *A proposed impact assessment method for genetically modified plants (As-GMP method) Environmental Impact Assessment review* 29: 348-368
7. R., & Rodriguez, E., (2009) *Environmental impact Assessment procedure: A new approach based on Fuzzy logic Environmental Impact Assessment review* 29:275-283
8. Wilson, L., (1998), *A Practical Method for Environmental Impact Assessment Audits Environ Impact Assess* Rev 18: 59-71
9. Bandyopadhyay, J., and V. Shiva. 1985. The conflict over limestone quarrying in Doon Valley, Dehradun, India.ENVIRONMENTAL CONSERVATION 12 (2):133–142.
10. FIRE (D) Project Technical Report *Guidelines for EIA for Urban Environmental Infrastructure Projects* by ENC Consulting Engineers, New Delhi.

11. *Status of EIA in India* – Country Report, Regional Workshop on Environmental Impact, Assessment in Asia: Good Practices and Capacity Needs, *JUNE 9-10, 2010 DR. S.K. AGGARWAL, Ministry of Environment & Forests*

12. Biswas, H. S. 1983, Environmental impact analysis of Panchpatmali bauxite mine. MTech thesis. Indian School of Mines, Dhanbad.

13. Chakraborthy, P. K. 1988. Socio-economic study of Jharia coalfield. Department of Industrial Engineering and Management, Indian School of Mines, Dhanbad.

14. Chattopadhyay, S. 1984. Environmental impact statement of Singrauli coalfield till 2000 A.D. MTech thesis. Indian School of Mines, Dhanbad.

15. Technical EIA guidance manual for thermal power plants prepared for the ministry of Environment and forest Department by IL and FS Ecosmart, Hyderabad

16. Biswas, A. K. 1988. Effectiveness of environmental impact assessment in developing countries. International conference on environmental impact assessment for developing countries, New Delhi. 28 Nov.–2 Dec.

17. Bhattacharya, J., P. Singh, P. De, and D. Dutt. 1987. Adoption of environmental strategies in the planning and operational phase of mine development. IN S. C. Ray, G. B. Misra, S. D. Barve, M. N. Biswas, and N. Mukherjee (eds.), Proceedings of the national seminar on environmental pollution and control in mining, coal and mineral based industries. Indian Institute of Technology, Kharagpur. 13–15 February, pp. 61–70.

18. Bissett, R. 1988. Devising an effective EIA system for developing countries. International conference on environmental impact analysis for developing countries, New Delhi. 28 Nov.–2 Dec.

19. Dhar, B. B., S. Ratan, and R. Mehta. 1987. A suggestive approach for developing an environmental management plan for mining operations. IN B. B. Dhar (ed.), National workshop on environmental management of mining operations in India—a status paper. Department of Mining and

Engineering, Institute of Technology, Banaras Hindu University, Varanasi, pp. 109–120.

20. Fedra, K. 1988. Simulation modelling in environmental impact assessment. International conference on environmental impact analysis for developing countries, New Delhi. 28 Nov.–2 Dec.

21. Jha, M. 1987. Environmental management of mining operations in Singrauli coalfields, NCL. IN B. B. Dhar (ed.), National workshop on environmental management of mining operations in India—a status paper. Department of Mining Engineering, Institute of Technology, Banaras Hindu University, Varanasi, pp. 47–53.

22. MoEF, http://envfor.nic.in,Ministry of Environment & Forests, Government of India,

23. International Tropical Timber Organisation, www.itto.or.jp /Index.html.

24. World Commission on Environment and Development 1987

25. http://envfor.nic.in

Chapter- VII

Vulnerability and Adaptation to Flood Disaster: A Case Study on Chilmari Upazila under Kurigram District of Bangladesh

Asib Ahmed*

Abstract

The study attempts to expand knowledge on the lives and livelihood of the people affected by major floods in Chilmari upazila of Kurigram district. People in the study area have suffered a lot due to their agricultural production and lives and livelihood badly affected by major floods and flash floods. The study prepared profiles of most affected areas among various unions of Chilmari Upazila and vulnerable livelihood groups in the area. It was found that all livelihood groups were affected by flood but three groups were vulnerable. The damages of crops and the occurrence of related factors (e.g. most of the house were partially damaged, high price of food, agricultural input and financial crisis etc.) remained as the major form of vulnerability for the farmers in the study area. The wage laborers faced unemployment, low wage rate and lack of health facilities. The study found various types of mitigation strategies and some local adaptive practices in the study area. Some national and international organization helped the vulnerable people to cope with the situation. Credit was also an important coping mechanism in the flood situations, but insufficient access to credit, high interest rate and failure of repay loan by poor households at that time adversely affected their lives and livelihood. The major floods and flash floods created immediate vulnerabilities in the area but lack of various forms of assets created long term vulnerabilities. As a result vulnerable people lost various types of assets and are losing yet in the study area.

Key Words: Adaptation, disaster, flood, mitigation, vulnerability

---

* Department of Geography and Environment, University of Dhaka, Dhaka, Bangladesh

Introduction

Bangladesh as a South Asian country is prone to natural disaster like flood due to its location on the Ganges-Brahmaputra-Meghna basin where many tributaries & distributaries flow into the Bay of Bengal. About seventy five percent of Bangladesh is less than 10m above sea level and 80 percent is flood plain, therefore Bangladesh is at risk of severe flood. At least 50 to 70 percent of the country's territory is exposed to intermittent extreme flooding that has far-reaching negative impacts on the national economy. Bangladesh is also a small country of 147,570 sq. km area with a huge population. The density of population is 964 per sq. km. It has a low per capita income of US $ 755 per annum [1]. Kurigram District is located in the northern region of Bangladesh along the border of India. The area of the district is 2,296.10 km² and population is 1,782,277 [1]. Weather of Kurigram district is bit different from the middle or southern part of Bangladesh. During summer, temperature is higher and during winter is lower than middle or southern part of Bangladesh. The average maximum temperature is about 32-33 degree Celsius when average minimum temperature is about 10-11 degrees. Heavy rainfall is usually observed during the rainy season like other parts of Bangladesh and the average annual rainfall is about 3000 mm. Several rivers are flowing through the heart of this district. The major rivers are Brahmaputra, Dharla and Tista with minors Dudhkumar, Phulkumar, Gangadhar, Jinjiram etc. It is evident that flood in Kurigram district occurre almost every year for which communities are not well prepared [2]. Flash floods in most of the upazila of Kurigram are very common which cause damage of property and infrastructure [3]. Chilmari, the study area is one of the upazilas which is prone to severe riverine and flash flood. The study area was most adversely affected during 1998 flood which was long lasting comparing with other floods [4]

The Study Area

Chilmari is located at 25.5667°N 89.6917°E . It has 20129 units of house hold and total area 224.97 km². The study area is located in the northwest region of Bangladesh spreading over Kurigram district (Fig. 1). The area is bounded in the north-west by the Lalmonirhat district, in the south-east by the Tista river, in the southern area is bounded by Gaibandha and Jamalpur district. The other part of the area is bounded by India. Situated in the northern part of Bangladesh, it is located by the Indo-Bangladesh frontier. Chilmari Upazila is intersected by the mighty Brahmaputra River. The total area of this Chilmari is 224.97 km² and the total number of population is 100,516 [5]. Chilmari has 6 unions. Most of the area is low lying. This area is situated at the bank of the Brahmaputra river. Most of the people are engazed in agricultural activities in the study area [6]. Various kinds of flood such as flash flood, river-induced flood, rainfall flood occurs this area almost every year. But at the interval of 5-7 years a colossal flood occurs in this area.

Figure 1: Location of the study area.

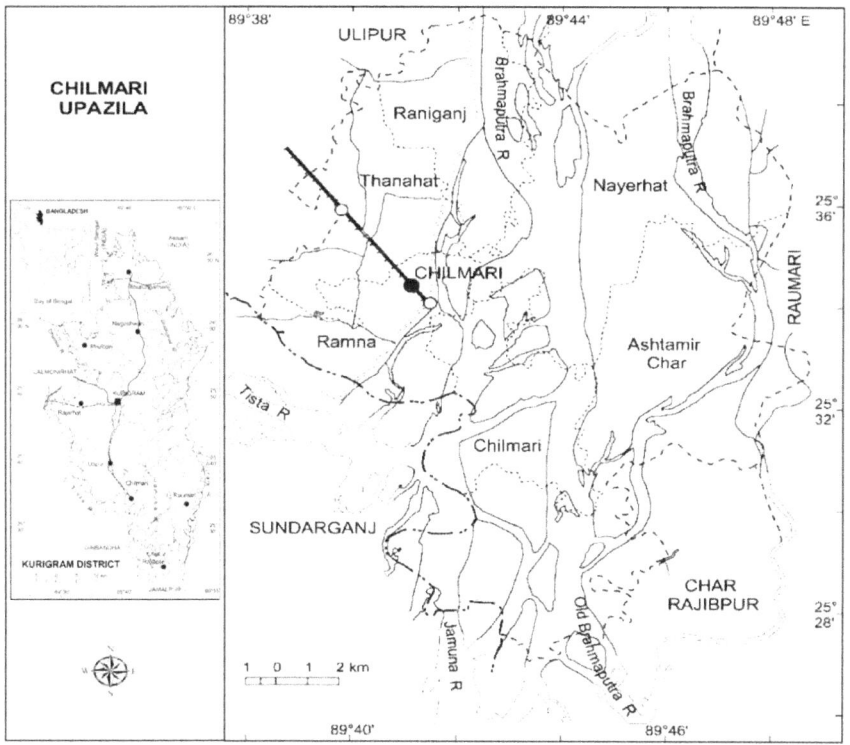

Source: Compiled from Banglapedia (2012) and redrawn by the authors

Objectives of the Study

The study aims at investigating the scenario of lives and livelihood of the flood affected people of Chilmari Upazilla of Kurigram district of Bangladesh. The specific objectives of the study are:

1. to observe the flood vulnerability in the study area
2. to examine the consequences of the floods on the livelihood of the people
3. to give light on the mitigation strategies of the flood vulnerable people of the study area

Methodology of the Study

The methodology adopted for the present study has been made extensive use of primary and secondary materials to build up and support the objectives of the study. The methods used for this research were a combination of physical and human parameters. Relevant data for this research were collected directly from the field through Focused Group Discussions (FGD) and questionnaire survey from May to July, 2012. Six separate Focused Group Discussions (FGD) were undertaken comprising of 10 people in each FGD in six unions of Chilmari through chosen randomly from among households irrespective of those being affected by flood. Data processing and analysis was completed by using relevant statistical method. The sample size for household interviews was 120 households in six unions of Chilmari (20 x 6). The household was the unit of the sample and each questionnaire was used for one household. The method of framing questionnaire is exclusively purposive. The key part of the questionnaire inquires the flood disaster scenario and the coping strategies at the household level response. They included all types of households regardless of profession, nature of work, academic attainment, social status, political attitude, land ownership, gender perspective and other components to get a respective opinion.

Secondary data were used to understand the background of the study area and to evaluate the adjustment process. A broad outline of different issues of flood disaster in the study area has been gained through reviewing available literature. Collection of map, data and information about study area has been gained from satellite image, BBS office, atlas, reports, chapter of books, journal articles, books, IWM office, newspaper, DMB office, and internet. Data on affected areas during major floods in Chilmari have been collected from Disaster Management Bureau (DMB) of Bangladesh where data on physiographic condition of study area has been acquired from Institute of Water Modeling (IWM), Dhaka. Population census data have been collected from Bangladesh Bureau of Statistics (BBS).

Results and discussion

Flood vulnerability of Chilmari

The flood season in Chilmari generally begins with flash floods occurring as early as in late April and early May. Generally observed in the villages of the riverbank of Chilmari, flash floods usually occur after a heavy downpour in the neighboring hills and mountains of India and are characterized by a very sharp rise in the water level in rivers and subsequent overbank spillage with a high flow velocity. With the onset of monsoon Brahmaputra river swelling to the brim and bring flood water from upstream. The river cannot smoothly drain all the waters and the water level begins to rise sharply during the peak flow periods. When rising water levels cross riverbanks, spillage occurs. Such events are common in the study area in every hydrological year. However, if certain conditions arise, riverine overbank spillages frequently trigger the most devastating floods in the area. High intensity of riverine floods continues for months, as it was observed during 1988 and 1998.

Floods in Chilmari are often triggered by heavy rainfall episodes, either within the sub-basin or in upper catchment areas. Local excessive rainfall often generates high volume of runoff in the Brahmaputra river and creeks in excess of their drainage capacity. Kurigram district of Bangladesh receives, on an average, some 2931 mm rainfall annually [7]. The above average and long period of heavy rain which causes Brahmaputra river to have their peak flows. Rainfall, considered as a climatic factor, is the main cause of flood in the study area. Apart from the factors mentioned above, there are several other factors, although not directly induced by climatic factors, which influence occurrences of floods in study area are the non-climatic factors. The non-climatic factors responsible for causing flood variation in Chilmari are deforestation, siltation of principal distributaries, synchronization of flood peaks of the major river, and unplanned infrastructure development.

Among six unions of the study area Chilmari, Ramna, Nayerhat and Ashtamir Char are highly vulnerable to flood disaster. About 85 to 90 percent areas of these four unions are under 'Very Risky' and 'Risky' categories of flood vulnerability [8]. Raniganj and Thanahat unions are comparatively less vulnerable (60 to 65 percent) to flood disaster in Chilmari upazila (Fig. 2). Since the danger level of water set by Bangladesh Water Development Board for Chilmari station is 24 mPWD the recorded highest water level of 25.20 mPWD was observed during the flood occurred in 2004.

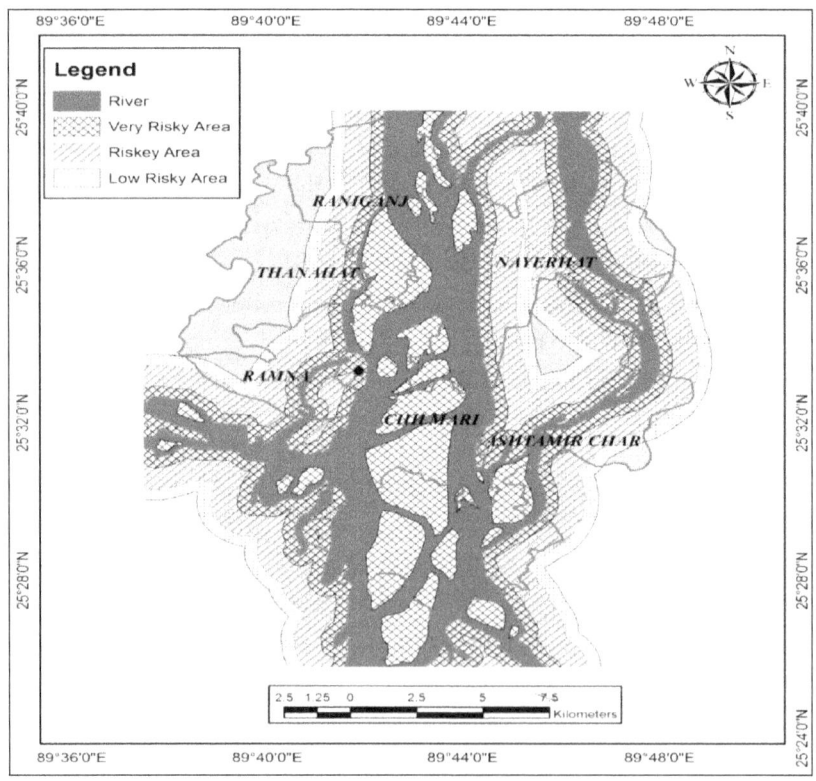

Figure 2: Flood vulnerability of the study area. *Source:* IWM (2011)

Profile of Vulnerable group

The selection of the more vulnerable livelihood groups and the least vulnerable livelihood groups has been identified through reviewing of data sets of latest available national population census 2011 and different research works of Disaster Management Bureau (DMB). Marginal farmers, wage laborers and small businessman are identified as most vulnerable livelihood groups where large farmer and large businessman are under least vulnerable livelihood groups [1]. In general terms, the women are facing a higher degree of vulnerability comparing to the men in the study area (Table 1). However, in flood time where the villages have a limited access to sanitation, drinking water, food and migration opportunities etc, often face some degree of vulnerabilities as well.

Table 1: Gender and age specific flood vulnerabilities in Chilmari Upazila

Gender and age	Types of Vulnerabilities
Women	Lack of sanitation access Lack of food and drinking water Pregnancy Increased working loads Social insecurity in absence of male household head (while migrate out)
Old and Child	Difficult migration in flood time More dependency Lack of medical facilities Lack of food

Source: Field Study, 2012.

Effects of major floods in Chilmari

Chilmari Upazila is intersected by the mighty River Brahmaputra. Among the major floods maximum area (198.25 sq km) of Chilmari was

171

affected during 1988 flood. The long lasting flood was occurred in 1998 flood which covered more than 79.18% of total area. Depending upon the severity of flood a general assessment of damages and destruction caused by flood disaster is shown in the table (Table 2). In 1988 food the study area is mostly affected (88.12%) comparing other floods. But the total amount of damage of crops and others was high in 1998 flood.

Table 2: Type of destructions in the study area due to major floods.

Flood occurring years	Flood Affected Area in percentage	No. of affected unions	No. of affected people	Affected cropped area (sq. km)	No. of affected homesteads	No. of dead persons	No. of dead cattle	Affected road in km	No. of affected institutions
2007	62.23	06	113650	636	904	01	11	40	17
2004	58.83	05	92786	610	820	01	15	36	15
1998	79.18	05	78492	724	1010	04	19	58	19
1988	88.12	06	65921	820	734	07	16	27	07
1987	75.67	05	52350	423	420	02	09	24	04

Source: Disaster Management Bureau (DMB), 2012.

Flood Mitigation in Chilmari

There are a number of ways of flood management intervention in the study area. Flood mitigation in Chilmari mostly implies the use of some structural as well as non-structural measure or methods to avoid, prevent, minimize or reduce the impact of flood disasters. It is also focused on the susceptibility to flood damage through a variety of intervention. Construction of embankment is very essential for flood protection in Chilmari [9]. In the study area a 16.1 km long embankment has been constructed. Most of the portions of the embankment are used by the residence of poor people. As a result the condition of the embankment is going to be worsened. The constructed embankment is not enough for flood protection in the study area. Hence, the length of the embankment should have to be increased and proper management of the embankment is needed. Another way of flood mitigation in the study area is the improvement of existing drainage and channels. Drainage congestion in the major streams results from silting up of river channels making them shallower with inadequate conveyance capacity during the flood season. This is especially true in this study area. Improvement of channel to facilitate drainage can be accomplished through loop cutting dredging in Brahmaputra river. In the 1985, river traininig activities in Chilmari were confined to temporary measures like bamboo and timber pilling in smaller rivers and bank revetments with stones, cement blocks and brick mattresses in Brahmaputra river. Currently river training works which are implemented in the study area are Guide banks for bridges, weirs, Groynes and spurs for deflecting the river course in major rivers and bank protection structures like planned forest cover and bamboo porcupines for small rivers, revetments for medium Brahmaputra river [4].

In the study area flood forecasting and warning is recognized as one of the most effective non-structural methods for flood damage mitigation. The present flood forecasting and warning system is composed of four main elements such as meteorological forecasting, flood forecasting, real time rainfall and water level data collection and flood warning dissemination. On the basis of real time observed data obtain from Chilmari station and the result of model forecast, various bulletins are issued by Flood Forecasting and Warning Center (FFWC) of Bangladesh Water Development Board (BWDB) predicting the likely rise or fall of river stages in Chilmari. Data transmission occurs from India only when the water level reaches the warning stage, i.e., one meter below the danger level. At present actual and forecast level data are transferred to FFWC from only three stations in India, viz., Dhubri and Goalpara on the Brahmpatura, Domohani on the Teesta. Regional cooperation with India in flood forecasting and warning could immensely benefit Bangladesh in achieving greater flood preparedness. Public education is considered as both mitigation and preparedness measures in Chilmari. Some projects designed to educate the public may include one or more like awareness of the flood risk, pre flood preparedness behavior, post flood response behavior and post flood recovery behavior.

Adaptation strategy with flood

Adaptation strategies of flood affected respondents have been grouped under two headings (Table 3). Both household and community level strategies play significant role to cope with flood in the study area.

Table 3: Household and Community level coping strategies.

Strategy	Particulars
Household level	
Borrow money	From local money lenders
	From relatives or neighbors
	From a nongovernmental organization
	Purchase rice on credit from a farmer
	From a bank
	From local money lenders
Sell Assets	Sell livestock (cattle, buffalo, cow, chicken etc)
	Sell or mortgage land
	Sell means of transport
	Sell jewellery
	Sell rice stocks to buy other essential needs
Change eating habits	Reduce food consumption
Consume assets	Eat reserve seeds
Migration	Flood time
Others	Defer monthly installments on loans
	Deplete savings
	Sell of higher ground
Community level	
Community Level Strategies	Increase income through access to common property
	Reduce threats via community based initiatives
	Share cropping
	Help cropping
	Help each-other in flood and after flood time

Source: Disaster Management Bureau (DMB), 2012.

Institutional Response

Several types of stakeholders have been consulted extensively in the study area to evaluate the institutional responses to flood damage mitigation. They are representatives and members of different Government and non-government organization. Most of the government departments in the study area have an operational structure up to the upazila level. It was found during the data collection from various sources that the government line agencies have upazila officers and representatives posted in their respective upazila. During flood various types of government organization were helping (such as flood shelter, food supply, agriculture input etc) the flood affected people in the study area. The government of Bangladesh implemented numerous programs in order to meet the immediate needs of flood-affected households. They began with immediate relief efforts involving the provision of shelter, clothing, food, and clean water while the flood waters still covered much of the study area.

A good number of non-government agencies working in this area. Some national NGOs such as BRAC, GRAMEEN BANK, RDRS, CHHINNOMUKUL and PROSHIKA have relatively grater operation and establishment in the study area but the presence of local level or even the district level NGOs are highest in number. The activities of NGOs are microcredit distribution for poultry, agriculture, and small business purposes, intensively relief works during flood and after period etc. Some international organization such as Action AID, Relief WEB, Red Cross, OXFAM and CARE are also implementing different programmes during and after flood in the study area like relief works, development works and awareness building.

Shelter during Flood

During flood in this area normally people take shelter on the road and embankment. But when the severity of the flood is high then the people of flood affected area take shelter in the school cum sheltered house. Among the major floods the sufferings were more in 1988 flood because during this flood almost 80% of the total area was submerged. As a result people took shelter on roads and embankments. But when roads are also submerged then the people took shelter again in school cum shelter house. A total of 321 people took sheltered in this sheltered house in 1988 flood. These people stayed there almost 2 months. As a result their income sources were seriously affected and they had to live on very hardship. It is evident that the people of the study area usually did not take shelter at a greater rate because of lack of shelter houses. Most people of the vulnerable area such as Astamir char and Chilmari unions use embankment for shelter. This is due not only to its easy accessibility but also to insufficient accommodation in the flood shelters.

Conclusion

The study area is located at the bank of Brahmaputra river. As a result, flood is easily occurred due to overtopping of the banks. Livelihood of most of the people is directly and indirectly related with agriculture. These people are mostly vulnerable to flood. Among major flood, 1988 flood was the most devastating which occurred in the study area, responsible for the greatest damage of this area. Chimari is low-lying area compared to other upazilas of Kurigarm district. For these reasons this area is flooded every year. Most of the people are illiterate in the study area. Women, children and older are mainly vulnerable to flood. Most of homesteads are made of bamboo and tin which are most vulnerable to flood. Most part of this study area is char land which are flooded every year. Some-time flash floods are occurred due to its location. During flood most affected people take shelter on embankment.

Relief from government and NGOs are not enough during flood and post-flood and the distribution of relief is not properly maintained. The people of this study area are very unconscious about the devastating effects of flood. The deterioration in the economic situation and the health environment had a major negative impact on food consumption, food insecurity, and health outcomes. A substantial increase in illness, especially diarrhea and respiratory illness were noticed during flood and in the immediate post-flood period. The floods also led to increase vulnerability for both older and children. Most of the households borrowed money heavily form NGOs, friends, neighbors and local money lenders for food and other expenditures. This additional money and credit programs could have enhanced households ability to cope with the vulnerable flood situation and helped them to improve for short term period. In the long run, these factors have increased vulnerability of the people in the study area and vulnerability households can never achieve their previous condition.

References

[1] *Bangladesh Population Census 2011* (Bangladesh Bureau of Statistics, Statistical Divisions, Ministry of Planning, Government of People's Republic of Bangladesh, Dhaka, 2011).

[2] *Cash for book*, (Flood Rehabilitation Programme, Oxfam, Dhaka, Bangladesh, 2001).

[3] K. Nizamuddin, *Disaster in Bangladesh* (Disaster Research Training and Management Center, Dhaka, Bangladesh, 2001).

[4] *Flood in Kurigram* (Disaster management Bureau, Dhaka, 2012).

[5] *Bangladesh Population Census 1991* (Bangladesh Bureau of Statistics, Statistical Divisions, Ministry of Planning, Government of People's Republic of Bangladesh, Dhaka, 1991).

[6] CARE-Bangladesh, *Bangladesh Emergency Response on flood 1998,* Final report on CARE, Dhaka, Bangladesh, 2000. Banglapedia, Retrieved from: http://www.banglapedia. org/HT/K_0322.HTM dated on 25 June, 2012.

[8] IWM, *Topographic survey and Detail Irrigation Using Mathematical Modeling Technique Kurigram Irrigation Project(South Unit),* Institute of Water Modeling, A H Development publishing House, Dhaka, Bangladesh, 2011.

[9] K.B.S. Rasheed (ed), *Bangladesh: resource and Environmental Profile* (A. H. Development Publishing House, Dhaka, Bangladesh, 2008).

Chapter- VIII

Earthquake Disaster and Vernacular Construction- A Case Study of Traditional Building Technology in Mitigating the Impact of 2011 Earthquake Disaster in Sikkim Himalaya

Pribat Rai, Vimal Khawas*

Abstract

Sikkim Himalaya covering the area of 7,096 sq km is one of the ecologically sensitive and earthquake prone area. It lies under seismic zone IV, which is known as very high risk zone. Though vulnerable to earthquake hazards the state still doesn't have any appropriate building code which has resulted in unplanned building structure with no regard for seismic safety. During 2011 earthquake more than 60 people lost their lives and thousands of building structures were damaged. During the post disaster survey vernacular building structure was seen least effected and remained stand still with minimum loss of lives and property damage. Therefore the paper attempts to document the cost effective traditional building skill and practices used by the indigenous traditional people of Sikkim Himalaya in mitigating the impact of 2011 earthquake disaster. The study will be based upon the available literature review, extensive field survey and focus group discussion with the experts in traditional building technology. Exploration and documentation of these knowledge and skill can be vital in helping the policy makers and planners to incorporate the methods needed for modern scientific building code in improving the building design towards seismic safety.

Key words: Earthquake, Disaster, Traditional Buildings, Mitigation, Sikkim Himalayas

---

*Department of Geography, Sikkim University, Gangtok, India

Introduction

Sikkim is a part of huge and elongated Himalaya which is moving northward against the Eurasian plate. Therefore it is obvious that earthquake has been a common natural phenomenon in Sikkim. Sikkim has experienced 18 earthquakes of magnitude 5 or greater over the past 35 years within the 100 km of epicentre of September 18, 2011 events [1] including the events of 1980 Sikkim, 1988 Bihar-Nepal and 2006 Sikkim.

On 18 September 2011, 18:11 hours IST a strong earthquake of magnitude 6.8 shock Sikkim and Darjeeling areas and adjoining Nepal [2]. The epicentre of the quake was near the Nepal-Sikkim Border about 68 km from Gangtok along the junction point of Teesta lineament and Kanchenjunga fault in the northern district of Sikkim. Earthquake was such a great that it was felt not only around its epicentre area but also in Rajasthan in India, Northeast state of India and neighbouring country of India-Nepal, Bangladesh and Bhutan.

The tremor triggered various types of natural calamities in the form of landslides, road blocks, falling debris, flash floods etc causing severe damage to the life and property. High level of stress through seismic forces caused huge destruction to the building structure especially in and around the urban area of Gangtok. The most affected areas with the highest level of ground shaking were *Chungthang* and *Lachung* with the maximum intensity of VIII in North Sikkim and the greater area of *Gangtok* with an intensity of VI on MSK scale [3].

In Sikkim the loss and damages to public infrastructure by the earthquake adversely affected the economy of the state, thereby leading to reduction in employment activities, loss in revenue generation and slowdown in investment in the industrial sector. According to preliminary feasibility study report prepared by *Engineering Private India Limited*, the estimated cost for reconstruction of damaged infrastructure works out to Rs 1471 crores [4]. Besides the earthquake occurred in the monsoon season so heavy rain and landslides added to the woes of the affected community and made the rescue work extremely difficult.

History of earthquake in Sikkim above magnitude 5 (from 1990-2011)

Year	Latitude	Longitude	Magnitude	Region
1990	28.2	88.1	5.7	Sikkim
1996	28	87	5.2	Sikkim
1996	27.8	87.6	5.2	Sikkim
06-01-2000	27.18	88.31	5.1	Singtam, Geyzing, Jorethang
06-02-2000	27.2	88.48	5.1	Singtam, Mangan, Jorethang
13/6/2000	27.5	88.36	5.3	Singtam, Geyzing, Mangan
16/6/2000	27.68	88.29	5.2	Singtam, Geyzing, Mangan
30/4/2002	27.91	88.54	5.2	Singtam, Jorethang, Melli
25/4/2002	27.24	88.78	5.3	Singtam, Mangan, Aritar
2/05/2002	27.97	88.87	5.3	Mangan, gangtok, Jorethang
30/04/2002	27.35	88.8	6	Mangan, Gangtok, Aritar
26/03/2005	27.7	88.0	5.1	India (Sikkim)-Nepal border
3/02/20006	27.4	86.7	5.3	Nepal (close to Sikkim-Bihar
14/02/2006	27.7	88.8	5.7	Sikkim
18/09/2011	27.7	88.2	6.8	Sikkim (IMD)
18/09/2011	27.723	88.064	6.9	Sikkim (USGS)

Source: compiled from various sources.

18th September, 2011 Earthquake in Sikkim

Earthquake and its impact on building structures in Sikkim

During 2011 earthquake more than 60 people lost their lives and thousands of building structure was damaged and collapsed. Modern construction around the town area of Gangtok was severely affected by the earthquake resulting in heavy loss of lives and properties. Faulty construction practices and poor compliance with seismic codes was considered as the chief cause of damage. Many unique and inherently poor construction features such as weak and very slender partition walls in brick (block masonry or in lightly reinforced/plain concrete, construction on sloped ground, unstable slopes, weak retaining walls, etc.) significantly added to the seismic vulnerability of structure [5]. The walls of such type of construction in Gangtok have varying thicknesses like 450, 600, 750 mm, with no earthquake resistant features – no bands, no through stones, and no vertical reinforcement at corners and around openings [6]. Therefore unchecked and unplanned urbanization was the chief reasons for the numerous damage of buildings structure in Sikkim especially in Gangtok area. The shaking of the ground is not what killed most of the people but the falling buildings in Sikkim was the reason of vast casualties and dead.

Brief list of structural damages caused by the 2011 earthquake in Sikkim

Structure	No. of Damage
Hospitals/PHCs centre	*377*
ICD (Aganwadi)	*875*
Government Building	*1255*
Bridges	*8135*
Gram Panchayat	*60*
Houses	*34,159*

Houses damaged (Sikkim)

District	Full damaged	Severe	Partial damage	Minor Damage
North	6000	-	-	-
South	820	-	446	1582
East	6000	-	9000	-
West	1679	5327	8342	-
Total	14499	5327	17788	1582

During the post disaster survey vernacular building structure was seen least effected and was later revealed that the traditional Sikkimese architecture had an earthquake resistant element made from the available natural resources. In most of the rural area of Sikkim where the aged old traditional building structure dominates remained stand still with minimum loss of lives and property damage. *Traditi*onal houses like Ekra performed well as expected as they evenly distributed the deformation in which adds to energy dissipation capacity of the system [5].

Evidence of Seismic resistance Vernacular construction

The reports of seismic resistance traditional houses are mentioned in many literatures. For example *Langinlach* [7] has reported the resistance of timber and masonry houses during Marmara and Duzee earthquake in Turkey. According to the report, of the 25,000 or more who died in the Marmara earthquake, very few of those were trapped in traditionally build infill-structure. Therefore the report has pointed out the sustenance and capability of traditional old timber and masonry building to resist the earthquakes as they remained standing next to the collapsed modern building.

Similarly, *Papadopoulos, M.L.* (2013) [8] has also highlighted the effective resistance and significant resilience of local historical structural system during the time of earthquake in the old city of Xanthi, in Northern Greece. The structure not only performed well in terms of services but also shown an impressive resilience, deformation capacity and strength to earthquake load. He reports that historical structure rarely had a catastrophic collapse than the other concrete structure

Dixit, Amod Mani et al. (2004) [9] has reported that even today centuries old building structure in Nepal has stand still irrespective of number of earthquakes occurred. Recent Earthquake Safety Program ensuring the awareness in using right earthquake resistant features for the construction of houses and building under the program conducted by National Society for Earthquake Technology-Nepal (NSET) has found the evidence of seismic-resistant elements in those traditional building structure in Nepal. Systematic exploration of those traditional wisdom and skill of earthquake-resistant technologies is needed in the Nepal Himalaya which is disappearing due to change brought by the modern society to reduce the earthquake risk, death and injuries.

Similarly, *Khan (2008)* [10] has highlighted the significance of traditionally build structure in Jammu and Kashmir in mitigating earthquake disaster. He has reported that, on October 8, 2005, the magnitude of 7.6 earthquake had a severe impact in the state of Jammu and Kashmir where about 90,000 household in Kashmir division and 8,000 household in Jammu division were greatly affected. Regardless of this destruction and devastation, traditionally constructed building having the *Taq* and *Dhajji-Dewari* system helped to save the lives of many individual as it sustained the shock of the earthquake, even when the portion without such system had given away.

A century earlier *Auther Neve* [7], a British visitor to Kashmir earthquake had observed and has reported in 1912- *Part of the Palace and some other massive old buildings collapsed ... [but] it was remarkable how few houses fell.... The general construction in the city of Srinagar is suitable for an earthquake country; wood is freely used, and well jointed; clay is employed instead of mortar, and gives a somewhat elastic bonding to the bricks, which are often arranged in thick square pillars, with thinner filling in. If well built in this style, the whole house, even if three or four stories high, sways together, whereas more heavy rigid buildings would split and fall."*

Purpose of the study

The main purpose of the study is to document the cost effective traditional building skill and practices used by the indigenous traditional people of Sikkim Himalaya in mitigating the earthquake disaster. Good performance of traditional earthquake-resistant constructions in regions where modern construction technologies have performed unsatisfactorily provide important lessons for seismic safety of the economically weaker sections of the society [11]. Therefore exploration and documentation of these knowledge and skill can be vital in helping the policy makers and planners to incorporate the methods needed for modern scientific building code in improving the building design towards seismic safety.

Vernacular Structure

Vernacular structure refers to the traditional houses or buildings build from the available natural resources like bamboos, stone, mud or timber. Scientifically they are non-engineered construction as they are built without professional assistance from architects or engineers. Therefore the said structure lacks building safety codes authorised by government agency. However traditional vernacular structures have some specific qualities in terms of others non engineered structure i.e. this structure actually emerged in terms of changing environmental phenomenon [12]. They are the result of ancient traditions, improved by time as a response to requirement of their social and physical environment. In consequence, vernacular construction have been praised by architects, engineers and cultural anthropologists as being extremely effective solutions to the needs of their dwellers and to the physical requirements posed by their environment [12].

Almost all the vernacular traditional houses are made from the natural resources available near the settlement. The use of stone, bamboo, mud, timber is normally seen. Depth of the foundation is normally not so deep but depth can be increased according to the size or increase in storeys. From structural behavior consideration, these technologies can be divided into the following general categories [11]:

1. Construction technologies using ductile construction materials – *such as building made of timber and bamboo.*
2. Construction technologies using robust architectural forms – *such as buildings with symmetric plan and elevation.*
3. Construction technologies using resilient structural configuration – *such as buildings with bands and braces.*
4. Construction technologies reducing seismic forces – *such as through use of light-weight non-structural members.*

Building Structure in Sikkim Himalaya

Urbanization in Sikkim is taking place rapidly with impressive building and other infrastructural development. The skyline of Gangtok and other urban town of Sikkim are mainly dominated by modern multi-storied buildings. The building are observed to have either flat or sloping roofs made up of different materials that include GI sheet, thatch, RCC, RBC and wood [2]. However in most of the rural areas of Sikkim we find semi pucca *(Ekra or Assam type)* houses. It is a wooden structure house where thin tin roof are applied. Walls are normally built with bamboos which are plastered with mud or cement. In upper altitude where wood and bamboos are scare in numbers, people normally uses stone to construct the houses.

Classification of building in Sikkim (According to material used) [2]

Category A	Building in field-stone, rural structure, unburnt brick houses, clay house
Category B	Ordinary brick building: building of the large block and prefabricated type, half-timbered structures, building in natural hewn stone
Category C	Reinforced building, well-built wooden structure
Category X	Other types not covered in A, B, C. These are generally light

Vernacular structure in Sikkim

In Sikkim most of the traditional houses are built with bamboo, timber, stone, mud and cement plastered. Mainly three types of traditional building structure are seen in the study region. Namely, Chaukat house, Ekra house and Chitra house.

Chaukat house

It is a traditional house found in most part of the Sikkim. It is normally two-four stored house which are built normally from the locally available building material. Wooden logs, stones and soil materials are generally used to construct Chaukat. A typical Chaukat stands 10 to 20 m high from the ground level and has 5-6 floors with at aleast 4 rooms on each floor [13]. The foundation for the stability of such high structure is normally dugged 2-3 m deep and filled with dressed stone. The building raised above the ground level-up to height of 2.30 m, to form a rectangle platform (with the help of flat stone and clay and stone filling) rested the main structure of the Chaukat Constructed [13]. Wooden logs are normally used or placed from the floor to support the upper storey of the front structure. Whereas well-dressed flat stone are raised as a wall from both the left, right and backside of the house to support the upper storey.

Fig. 1

A.   B.

A. Front face of Chaukat
B. Side face of Chaukat

Ekra House

Ekra house are traditional building structure made up of stone foundation normally plastered with cement, bamboo wall plasterd with mud or cement and thin roof sheet. These are single or two storied house built with a wood frame as main structural features along with columns and roof beams. Light metal sheets like asbestos are used as roofing material supported by the wooden frame. The infills between wooden columns are bamboo spilts matting which are plastered with mud or cement. Ekra house normally have 1 or 2 storeys because the material used for its construction is not much strong to support higher storeys construction. Such houses are much stable during the event of earthquake and even if such houses collapse they do not result in loss of lives. Therefore inspite of being non-engineered structure, these houses have a proper system of bamboo/wooden beam-column and fulfil most of the earthquake safety requirement of having a proper connection between different elements [14].

Fig.2

Two storey Ekra house

Chitra house

Chitra is a traditional name given to a house made up of bamboo mat. Wall of this house are firstly made by cutting bamboo into thinner parts i.e. bamboo is fabricated into sheets which later raised along the wood beams and fixed with the help of nails. No mud thatching is used on the wall like Ekra house. To keep roof light weighted and sustained by wood beams the house is covered by light weight tine sheets. Even if these houses collapse no major casualties will be seen.

Fig. 3

Chitra House in Chungthang (North Sikkim)

Seismic performance of modern and vernacular building structure during 2011 earthquake in Sikkim

The earthquake caused severe damaged to lives and properties in Sikkim. Unexpected severe damage to buildings was seen in towns of Gangtok, Chungthang, Lachen and Lachung. Around 40,000 houses have been reported to be fully, partially and severely damaged. Among fully damaged buildings, about 20% was comprised of RC frame whereas 5% buildings consist of traditional construction. Cause of damage to the urban building was due to the lack of engineered planning. Wrong site selection especially along the downhill side of the road suffered severe damaged. This building basically appears to have only 2-3 storeys from the road but when seen from the base has another additional of 3-4 storeys. Out of the 779 schools in the state, 682 schools building collapsed/damaged, this means that 80 % of school building were affected [16].

In urban town of Gangtok must of the building are closely packed with high elevation ignoring the building code. As a result many adjacent building, which were in close proximity to each other, had an improper and undesirable separation between them in upper floors. This has resulted in structural vulnerability to earthquake [17]. In addition most of these buildings are not engineered and normally built on steep slopes. The buildings are upto 8 storied in Gangtok, wherein 3-4 storeys are below ground level. Mostly the building are constructed for gravity loads and no provision is made to resist lateral loads [6]. Chungthang (North Sikkim) was one of the main centre where 2011 earthquake had severe damage to properties and lives. Almost every modern construction even the government buildings has been severely damaged in Chungthang and even today 40 % of building are deserted i.e. not a single person lives in it because of the severe cracks formed along the joints and walls of the building.

During 2011 earthquake not the shaking or tremor killed the people but the collapse of the building did. Unplanned construction and illegal increase of building storeys to gain maximum profit during the tourism season by allocating tourist and other non-residential Sikkimese people was one of the main reason in collapse and destruction of many concert building in Gangtok urban area. Since most of the building doesn't follow any regulation and are built by local mason, often these structure turns out to be vulnerable to earthquake and 2011 earthquake did not left its chance for this types of construction. Many RC buildings in Gangtok and most of them in Chungthang (North Sikkim) suffered severe damages, the most common being shear and/or flexure failure at column end region, failure of beam–column joints, inplane failure of weak infills and out-of-plane failure of slender walls. Many unique and inherently poor construction features such as weak and very slender partition walls in brick/block masonry or in lightly reinforced/plain concrete, extended floor plans in upper stories supported on cantilevered beams and slabs, construction on sloped ground, unstable slopes, weak retaining walls, poor construction material etc., significantly added to the seismic vulnerability of structures [6].

In Sikkim neither engineers nor architects design most of the building nor are most of the buildings approved by the state authorities before construction. Even though building is only planned for few floors in the initial stages, years later more floors are added to the same building which makes the structure weak and more vulnerable. This was the chief reason why most of the modern concert structure was collapsed or damaged not only in urban area of Gangtok but also in many areas of Mangan, Chungthang and Lachung. In Chungthang (North Sikkim) where the destruction of 2011 earthquake was the most, witnessed the highest number of people killed on being trapped under the debris. The observation shows that basic requirement for good seismic performance of RC buildings viz. planning, design, configuration, load path, reinforcement detailing etc., were not followed [6].

However impact of earthquake was also seen in many traditional house but the casualties and damage was far less than the concert structure in Sikkim. According to South Sikkim Earthquake report 54,000 of the total 92,000 rural houses suffered various degrees of damage, but very few casualties. There was only few death due to these house. Wooden framed houses with traditional Ekra walling and light iron sheet roof was mostly intact. The traditional houses like Ekra performed significantly better compared to RC frame / masonry buildings and suffered only minor damages at ground story level, mainly due to damage to plinth masonry. Presence of wooden frames at close intervals resulted as excellent braced, light weight structural system performed well during earthquake for traditional houses [6].

Shri Arun Rai, resident of Assamlengy (East Sikkim), has described about the effect of 2011 earthquake as most destructive event ever he have seen in Sikkim. He has two houses, one is made up of cement concrete and the other is Ekra house made up of bamboo and timber. He build his cement concert house in 1990 whereas his Ekra house was built on 1980 but when the earthquake came about 60 % of his concrete house was damaged though he and his family had minor injuries. However his Ekra house did not show any damaged or neither had it collapsed. According to him it just shakes but never falls.

Several traditional building exist in Lachung which are mostly low rise-single storey, light weight, timber with sheet roof. Local mason or builder informed that these types of house has a long history and has been constructing from ages. By looking at the lesser impact of these houses during earthquake one can observe that the earlier generation was aware of the severity of earthquake and therefore, they have explored and adopted earthquakes resistant building construction [18]. In most of the rural area of Sikkim traditional houses dominates the area. Built by the local natural resources like bamboo, stone, mud etc available near the settlement, this house area are very light weight. Therefore even if the houses collapse during the earthquake no major injuries can occur to the people living inside the house. The house constructed by using light weighted material could resist high magnitude of earthquake. This practice is considered as the environmental friendly and cost effective [18].

Many modern building developed cracks and clipped off concretes appeared on almost all houses. Central Govt. provided ten pre-fabricated bamboo houses for the needy person in North Sikkim [4]. This pre-fabricated bamboo house has almost similar building make up with the traditional Ekra house. The level of foundation, material used, size, shape, weight, cost effectiveness and environmental friendly every aspect is almost similar with the traditional Ekra structure. Only thing different is that pre-fabricated bamboo house has an integration of modern and traditional building technology.

Fig. 4

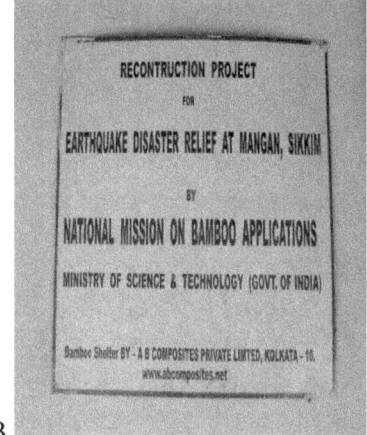

A. Pre-fabricated bamboo house provided by Central Govt. in Chungthang (North Sikkim).
B. Wall post attached on the wall of the pre-fabricated bamboo house.

Fig. 5

C.   D.

A. Destruction of concert cement building by 2011 earthquake in Chungthang (North Sikkim),
B. Formation of cracks on the walls of government building in Chungthang (North Sikkim),
C. Deserted building in Chungthang (North Sikkim) due to the impact of earthquake,
D. Formation of cracks in the inner part of the building in Chungthang (North Sikkim).

Fig. 6

Performance of RC Buildings in Gangtok [19]

A.   B.

Source: Rai, Durgesh et al (2011), Effects on Built Environment and A Pespective on Growing Seismic Risk

A. Pan-caking failure of two stories of a 9-storey building at Gangtok
B. Collapsed building colliding with adjacent building at Gangtok

Fig. 7

A. Ekra house in Chungthang (North Sikkim) which resisted the impact of 2011 earthquake
B. Two Storey Ekra house in Chungthang (North Sikkim) standing still even after the earthquake

Conclusion

It is generally found that the owners of buildings constructed with modern materials and technology in developing countries belong to the socially and economically more affluent classes. On the other hand, the economically weaker sections of the society are more likely to use traditional construction materials due to its lower cost. Since most indigenous earthquake-resistant construction technologies have relatively low cost, the use of these provide an exciting opportunity for safer housing for the economically weaker sections of society who are otherwise forced to live in weak constructions [11].

Disaster Risk Reduction is today a vital process to eliminate the future suffering but the cost incurred in disaster reduction process is too high and still the result in management of this efforts is not satisfactory. The societies and communities who are much affected by earthquake disaster normally belong to underdeveloped or transitional groups. Financial investment for these groups in reducing the disaster is burdensome. Therefore a complete working balanced or integration between traditional technology and scientific technology can present a viable option in the face of financial concerns for disaster reduction work as traditional knowledge offers a very coast effective approach to Disaster Risk Reduction.

References

[1] India Disaster Report, 2011,National Institute of Disaster Management, *June, 2012,* http://nidm.gov. in/PDF/pubs/India%20Disaster%20Report% 2020-11.pdf, *accessed on 23-11-2013.*

[2] Sikkim Earthquake of 18th September, 2011 A Report, *Disaster Mitigation and Management Centre, Dehradun, Uttarakhand, India, 2012.*

[3] INTACH, Architectural Heritage Division, 71 Lodhi Estate, New Delhi, 2012.

[4] Land Revenue and Disaster Management Department, White Paper on the High Intensity earthquake of 18th September 2011 in Sikkim, Govt. of Sikkim, Dec 2012.

[5] Building Back Better: A more Resilient Sikkim Post 2011 earthquake-Issues, *No 98, Oct 2013.*

[6] Bhattacharya and Chourasia, Experience on 2011 Sikkim post earthquake damage assessment: strategies for risk reduction, *ISET Golden Jubilee Symposium, 2012.*

[7] Langinlach, Randolph, Earthquake Resistant Traditional Construction is Not an Oxymoron: The Resilience of Timber and Masonry Structures in the Himalayan Region and Beyond, and its Relevance to Heritage Preservation in Bhutan, The Royal Government of Bhutan, *International Conference on Disaster Management and Cultural Heritage, 2010*

[8] Papadopoulos, M.L., Seismic Assessment of Traditional House in the Balkans-Case studies in Xanthi, *Journal of Civil Engineering and Science, 2[3], 2013, 131-143.*

[9]Dixit, Amod Mani et al., Indigenous Skills and Practices of Earthquake Resistant construction in Nepal, *13th World Conference on Earthquake Engineering, Vancouver, Canada, Paper no 2971, August 2004.*

[10] Khan, Amir Ali, Earthquake Safe Traditional House construction Practices in Kashmir, in Shaw, Rajib et al. (Ed.), *Indigenous Knowledge for Disaster Risk Reduction: Good Practices and Lesson Learned from Experience in the Asia-Pacific Region,* (Bangkok: Kyoto University, 2008) 5-8.

[11] Sinha, Ravi et al. (2004) Indigenous Earthquake-Resistant Technologies-an overview, *13ᵗʰ World Conference on Earthquake Engineering Vancouver, B.C., Canada, Paper no 5053*

[12] Gutierry, Notes on the Seismic adequacy of Vernacular Building, *13ᵗʰ World Conference in Earthquake Engineering, Vancouver, Canada, Paper No 5011, 2004.*

[13] Joshi et al, Traditional Knowledge of Natural Disaster mitigation and Ethnic medicine practices in Himalaya with Special reference to Sikkim, *Indian Journal of Traditional Knowledge, 10 (1)*, 2011, 198-206.

[14] Tambe et al., How safe are our rural structure? Lessons from the 2011 Sikkim earthquake, *Current Science, Vol 102[10], 2012, 1394-1395.*

[15] A brief report on damage survey for Sikkim earthquake of 2011.

[16] Khanna, Nina et al., Sikkim Earthquake: Perils of Poor Preparedness, *Focus, Vol 6[1], 2012.*

[17] Sinvhal, Amita et al., A Brief Report on Damage survey for Sikkim Earthquake of 2011, *ISET Golden Jubilee Symposium, Paper No. A022, 2012.*

[18] Joshi et al, Traditional Knowledge of Natural Disaster mitigation and Ethnic medicine practices in Himalaya with Special reference to Sikkim, *Indian Journal of Traditional Knowledge, 10 (1)*, 2011, 198-206.

[19] Rai, Durgesh et al., 2011 Sikkim Earthquake Effects on Built Environment and Perspective on Growing Seismic Risk, *Department of Civil Engineering, Indian Institute of Technology, Kanpur, 2011.*

Chapter- IX

Impact of Climate Change and Natural Hazards on Industries: Key Mitigation and Adaptation Measures

Amit Tuteja*

Abstract

This paper will elucidate the impact of climate change and natural hazards on the industries, followed by key mitigation and adaptation measures. As the industries are also vulnerable to impacts of climate change, and particularly to the impacts of extreme weather. The industries can adapt these potential impacts by designing facilities that are resistant to projected changes in weather and climate, and diversifying raw material sources, especially forestry or agricultural inputs. Industries can respond to these by mitigating their own emissions and developing lower emission products. The direct impact of rise in temperature on industrial processes is to be tackled by taking appropriate precautions while designing the manufacturing process adopted in the industry. However the impact of climate change induced natural hazards on various elements of industries, needs to be considered carefully and suitable action for their mitigation should be taken. All the concerned industries should take necessary mitigation measures by making changes in process operations, safety of machines, power sources, secured storage & transportation etc. to avoid the adverse impacts of climate induced natural hazards (including sea level rise, flooding, cyclonic storm, drought condition and other extreme weather events) on the industries as well as on the communities.

Keywords: Adaptation, Chemical, Climate change, Industries, Major Accident Hazard (MAH) Units, Mitigation

*National Disaster Management Authority (NDMA), Government of India

Introduction

When we talk about the climate change and emissions of Green House Gases (GHGs), usually the industries are held responsible to a large extent, various national and international reports also address the same. Here it is very important to first understand the concept of climate change, especially in context of the industries. In simple terms, Climate is the average weather of particular location/ area/ region, over a long period of time. It helps to better understand the weather of the area/ region, and also provides assistance in carrying out the subsequent analysis and forecasting. Climate change may refer to a change in weather conditions or the frequent occurrence of extreme events, over a longer period of time. Climate change can also be referred as increase in the average global temperatures due to warming across the globe. This phenomenon of global warming and climate change is primarily based on the increase in Green House Gases (GHGs) such as Carbon Dioxide (CO2), Methane (CH4) and other industrial gases including Hydro Fluoro Carbons (HFCs), Per Fluoro Carbons (PFCs) etc. In the current scenario of industrialization and development, there are a wide variety of industrial activities that cause Green House Gas (GHG) emissions. These GHGs lead to the Green House Effect, which results into the rise in earth's average temperature. The earth may become less habitable for humans, plants and animals, in case of rise in earth's temperature. Therefore a lot of efforts are going on worldwide, to reduce the green house gas emissions such as construction of energy efficient buildings, use of alternative energy sources, effective urban planning, promote renewal energy and reforestation. Industries are also committed to reduce the GHG emissions. This aspect has been addressed separately in detail, in the climate change mitigation section of this article.

In recent years it has been observed that the occurrence of extreme events have increased exponentially, especially in context of India. The country has faced a number of extreme climatic events in less than a decade. Incidents like Mumbai floods (944mm rainfall on 26th July 2005), unprecedented floods in drought prone Rajasthan (Barmer flood in August 2006), Leh cloudburst (250 mm rain in 30 minutes on 6th

August 2010), Uttarakhand cloudburst (440% excess rainfall in Kedarnath region, 16-17 June 2013) and now Jammu & Kashmir Floods (aprox. 400% excess rainfall in 10 Districts during 1st week of Sept, 2014) are the live examples of extreme climatic events, occurred in recent years in India. The IPCC (Intergovernmental Panel on Climate Change) Fifth Assessment Report: Climate Change 2014, also projects the drastic increase in heavy precipitation/ extreme rainfall in India, on the basis of all the models and scenarios. The industries are vulnerable to impacts of extreme weather (due to climate change) as well. The climate change is expected to have direct implications on the industrial performance, including the associated machinery, infrastructure, transport, storages and wastewater systems. Primarily, the climate change will have the direct impact on certain elements of industrial processes that are sensitive to temperature. It will also affect the heating and cooling demand of the industries (depending on the nature of operations). Further, there will be huge financial implications in case of infrastructure damage including buildings, piping system, storage of chemicals & gases, source of power generation, waste disposal and induced effect to the surroundings. Therefore, to address the pertinent issue of extreme climatic events (induced by climate change), the key mitigation and adaptation measures are required to be taken on priority, at the industrial level.

Impact of Climate Change and Natural Hazards on Industries

Industries are vulnerable to the impacts of climate change, particularly to the impacts of extreme weather. In Indian context, especially in the recent years, a number of extreme events have been observed quite frequently, such as urban floods, cyclone, landslide, cloudburst and earthquake. Industries can adapt to these potential hazards and subsequent impacts by designing facilities that are resistant to projected changes in weather and climate, relocating plants to less vulnerable locations, and diversifying the raw material sources.

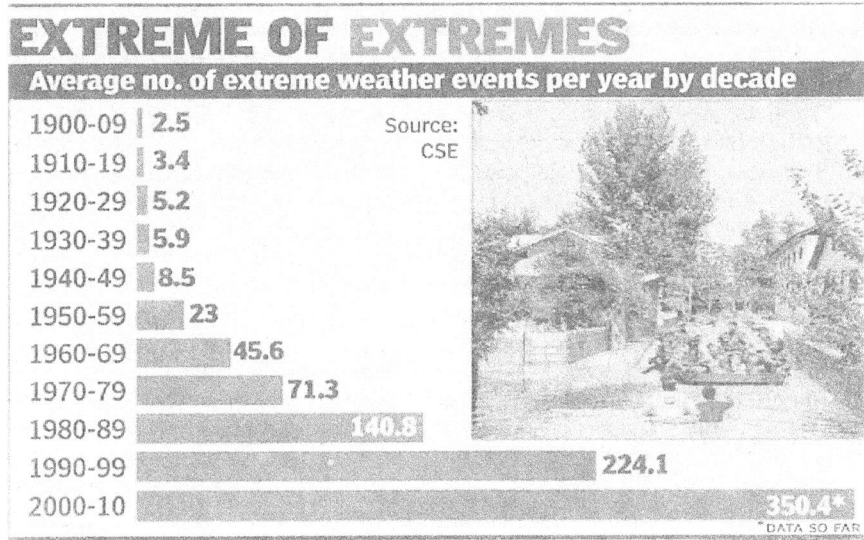

EXTREME OF EXTREMES

Average no. of extreme weather events per year by decade

1900-09	2.5
1910-19	3.4
1920-29	5.2
1930-39	5.9
1940-49	8.5
1950-59	23
1960-69	45.6
1970-79	71.3
1980-89	140.8
1990-99	224.1
2000-10	350.4*

Source: CSE

*DATA SO FAR

Fig.1 – Summary of extreme events recorded globally in last 110 years *(Source – CSE, EM-DAT Database)*

The above figure shows exponential rise, particularly in last decade, in the occurrence of extreme events globally. This is a major cause of concern for the industries as well as for all concerned stakeholders. Till now the industries were not much concerned about the extreme events or natural calamities, as the frequency of such events was quite less. But in the changing scenario of steep rise in extreme events, now the industries are left with no option but to take it very seriously, as these incidents are directly hampering the industrial performance, their business continuity as well as goodwill in the sector.

According to the study carried out by World Bank, the direct economic losses from natural hazards induced disasters have been estimated to amount up to 2% of India's GDP. It also shows the serious repercussions of natural disasters to the industries, particularly in context of India. The example of extreme events such as Mumbai 2005 urban floods and its effects to industrial sector is in front of us. The city is considered to be the business capital of India, but everything came to a halt, when number of corporate offices, belonging to various industries, got submerged for days and destroyed all vital records, also including servers and backups

201

of various industries. It is also evident from the history that many industrial disasters in the past were triggered by natural disasters.

Gujarat cyclone 1998 highlighted the unpreparedness also destroyed the industrial compounds, structures, windmills in the region. Orissa super cyclone in 1999 had resulted in damage to phosphoric acid sludge containment, in 2001 (Bhuj earthquake), acrylonitrile was released at Kandla Port. There are many more similar cases of extreme events/ natural hazards, which not only hampered the established industrial processes but also led to vast devastation. Jamnagar, after Bhuj (Guajrat) Earthquake, Jan. 2001 also affected the nearby phosphate and other industrial plants.

Fig. 2 Toppled electrical panels at Tata Chemicals Plant,   Fig.3 Orissa Super cyclone (1999) destroyed the Paradip Port

It has been observed that the selection of an industrial site involves a complex array of critical factors involving economic, social, technical, and environmental issues. Besides it is important to look into the existing and emerging risks during the siting of industries. At global level, the notable examples of nature induced incidents are (i) Storms on December 1999 in France - damaged thermal power plant, nuclear plant and waste treatment plant (ii) Earthquake in Kocaeli, Turkey in August 17, 1999 (magnitude 7.4) - triggered large fires, toxic air releases of dangerous substances and oil spills at several industrial facilities. (iii) A dam broke at the Aurul Mine Tailings Recovery Plant near BaiaMare, 2000 -

Industrial waste water with high cyanides concentration. A breach of about 25 m in the ponds dam was produced. (iv) August, 2005, Hurricane Katrina, caught the United States unprepared, it was one of the costliest nature induced incident occurred so far (aprox. Loss of $150 billion) in the history, it impacted the most of the industries. (v) Japan Earthquake (6.8-magnitude) July 16, 2007 - triggered fire at the seven-reactor, 8,212-megawatt Kashiwazaki-Kariwa nuclear power plant that burned a transformer, spilled several hundred barrels containing radioactive waste and vented radioactive waste and (vi) Sichuan earthquake, August 30, 2008 - In the city of Shifang, the collapse of two chemical plants led to leakage of some 80 tons of liquid ammonia. (vii) March 2011, Japan multiple disasters (Earthquake, followed by Tsunami also led to Fukushima Nuclear disaster) hit the Japan (one of the most developed countries across the globe) hardest. It was a major setback for industries in Japan. (viii) In 2011, Urban Floods in Bangkok, took Thailand by surprise, the industries got hampered, and it affected the global market, as the flood water inundated in most of the industrial estates.

Figure: 4

Figure:5

Fig. 4 March 2011 Earthquake-Tsunami Multi Disaster and Fig.5 Bangkok urban flood (2011) hit hard the global damaged Fukushiman nuclear and other industrial plants industrial market, as flood water inundated in most areas

Industries are also vulnerable to the impacts of changes in consumer preference and government regulation in response to the threat of climate change. Industries can respond to these by mitigating their own emissions and developing lower-emission products. The direct impact of rise in temperature on the industrial process is to be tackled by taking appropriate precautions while designing the manufacturing process adopted in the industry. However, the impact of climate change induced natural hazards on various elements of the industry needs to be considered carefully and suitable action for its mitigation should be taken. This is very important in case of Major Accident Hazard (MAH) units/ industries. All concerned industries should take necessary mitigation measures for avoiding adverse impacts due to natural hazards on the industry as well as on the communities.

Natural Hazards in India

India is prone to various natural hazards due to the geographic and environmental settings. Out of 35 States and Union Territories in the country, 27 of them are disaster prone. Almost 58.6 % of landmass is prone to earthquakes of moderate to very high intensity; over 40 million hectares (12% of land) is prone to floods and river erosion; of the 7516 km long coastline, close to 5700 km is prone to cyclones and tsunamis; 68% of cultivable area is vulnerable to drought and hilly area at risk from landslides and avalanches.

The Govt. of India had initiated the process of risk assessment all over the country, long ago. 241 Districts were identified as multi hazard prone, as per the Vulnerability Atlas of India (2006), published by Building Material Technology Promotion Council (BMTPC). The Atlas has taken into consideration all the major hazards including flood, earthquake, landslides and wind hazards.

Utility of Vulnerability Atlas

The Vulnerability Atlas of India presents the earthquake hazard map, cyclone and wind hazard map, and the flood prone area map for each State and Union Territory of India. These maps not only show the boundaries of the hazard zones of various intensities but also indicate district-wise areas lying in the different intensities. For each of the districts, the classification of houses based on their wall material and roof type, area of district lying in a particular hazard intensity zone and the risk to house types according to the intensity of the hazards, is presented in tabular form in Vulnerability Atlas. The landslide prone area maps are also presented by BMTPC on macro scale.

The Vulnerability Atlas of India can be used as follows (from mitigation, prevention and adaptation point of view):

> i. Prior to set up the industrial unit, interested party will get a very broad idea from vulnerability atlas – the intensity of earthquake or wind hazard applicable to locality. The owner

interested in setting up the industry, can also find if the location is prone to floods or storm surge from the sea. From district table, the interested party will also come to know the level of risk that exists, to the type of existing set up they want to own. If the location is found to be risky, appropriate action to strengthen or upgrade the existing set up, can be taken to meet the threat of the hazard.

ii. The Disaster Manager of the district can easily determine the location and percent of area most susceptible to hazard occurrences, the probable maximum hazard intensities, the type and number of units existing in the district and risk from the hazards. Knowing the extent of problems of future disasters, the district authorities can formulate development plans for (a) preventive actions required for hazard resistant construction, retrofitting and upgrading of existing buildings, (b) reducing the impact of different types of hazards, (c) installation of a warning system and required drills for its use, (d) setting up of a hierarchical structure for preparedness down to the village level, (e) training of various task forces for emergency response, (f) implementation of land zoning regulations in flood plains and coastal areas and (g) building byelaws with disaster resistant features in various cities and towns, etc.

iii. Members of State Legislatures and National Parliament can study the hazard problems in their constituencies, propose the safer locations for installations of industrial set ups and also recommend and institutionalize the disaster mitigation programmes for their districts and the whole State in respective State Plans and National Five Year Plan.

iv. The State and National Authorities and Planning Commission may identify the districts highly prone to disaster situations and those with multi-hazard situations requiring priority action in planning, formulating integrated mitigation policies covering awareness, education and training, preventive and preparedness measures, improvement in warning systems, etc.

Development projects will need to include mitigation measures against the disaster impacts at the initial plan formulation as well as execution stage, so that the existing industrial development work should not suffer any damage at later stage.

v. MAH (Major Accident Hazard) Units may be able to use Vulnerability Atlas to identify natural hazards, the location is exposed to, and to take the relevant mitigation measures accordingly.

MAH Units/ Installations

As per Manufacture, Storage and Import of Hazardous Chemical Rules (MSIHC)1989, the major accident means as occurrence including any particular major emission, fire or explosion involving one or more hazardous chemicals and resulting from uncontrolled developments in the course of an industrial activity or due to natural events leading to serious effects both immediate and delayed, inside or outside the installation, likely to cause substantial loss of life and property, including adverse effect on the environments.

Major Accident Hazard (MAH) Units means isolated storage and industrial activity at a site handling (including transportation through carrier or pipeline) of hazardous chemicals equal to, or in excess of the threshold quantities specified in Column 3 of Schedule 2 and Schedule 3 of Environment Protection Act (EPA) 1986, respectively.

Districts with MAH Installations

The MAH Units are highly hazard prone, and also sensitive to natural hazards. There are 1861 active MAH (Major Accident Hazard) Units, spread across 301 Districts and 28 States & Union Territories, in all zones of the country.

Apart from it, the other small and medium sized industries and new industries are also establishing at a rapid rate. All the concerned industries will have to take necessary mitigation and adaptation measures by making changes in process operations, safety of machines, power sources, secured storage & transportation etc. for avoiding adverse impacts of climate induced extreme events and natural hazards.

Sr. No	States, UTs	No. of MAH Units	No. of Districts with MAH Units	Sr. No	States, UTs	No. of MAH Units	No. of Districts with MAH Units
1	A&N	3	1	15	M.P.	77	23
2	A.P.	157	21	16	Maharashtra	379	27
3	Assam	26	10	17	Manipur	2	2
4	Bihar	13	5	18	Meghalaya	2	1
5	Chhattisgarh	19	4	19	Nagaland	2	1
6	Delhi	18	7	20	Orissa	23	13
7	Goa	17	2	21	Pondicherry	3	2
8	Gujarat	381	23	22	Punjab	58	14
9	Haryana	56	13	23	Rajasthan	109	14
10	H.P.	8	4	24	Tamil Nadu	115	22
11	J&K	13	6	25	Tripura	2	2
12	Jharkhand	13	5	26	Uttar Pradesh	120	38
13	Karnataka	73	16	27	Uttarakhand	41	4
14	Kerala	46	9	28	West Bengal	85	12
	Sub Total	843	126		Total	1861	301

Table 1: State wise List of MAH Industries including No. of Districts (Source MOEF Database as on 31.03.13)

Impact of climate change induced extreme events and natural hazards on industries. The following extreme events and natural hazards have been considered in this section, can affect the various elements pertaining to industries:

(i)   Urban Flooding/ Flooding
(ii) Cyclonic storm
(iii) Drought
(iv) Tsunami
(v)   Sea level rise
(vi) Earthquake
(vii) Extreme weather change (cloudburst/ heavy rain/snow fall/ severe heat)

The following elements in the industry may be affected by these extreme events and natural hazards:

(a)   Power source
(b)   Process operations
(c)   Machines and equipments
(d)   Industrial building/ compound
(e)   Storage of chemicals and gases
(f)   Conveyor and piping system
(g)   Waste disposal
(h)   Transportation by road and rail
(i)   Induced effect to surroundings

The impacts of various hazards on the industry related elements are discussed below:

(a) Impact on power source

Sr. No	Hazard	Impact
(i)	Urban Flooding/ Flooding	There are direct and indirect impacts of urban flooding/ flooding on the power source. Inundation of power source - be it transformers to draw electricity from grid or power plants - may lead to total disruption of power supply, in turn leading to disruption of industrial functioning. Secondly unsafe or damaged electric wiring during floods may increase chances of electrocution. Short circuits may also lead to fires.
(ii)	Extreme weather change	Climate change induced extreme weather will ultimately affect the heating and cooling demand of the industries. Temperature rise will reduce power production efficiency of captive power plants owned by industries. To achieve the same level of productivity, the power plants will have to increase their water intake.
(iii)	Tsunami	Unsafe or damaged electric wiring due to seismic sea waves may increase the chances of electrocution. It can also disrupt the entire power supply.
(iv)	Drought	In some cases, the in-built power plants use water, and in case of drought (water scarcity), it can hamper the functioning of power plants.
(v)	Cyclonic storm	Cyclonic storms accompanying high speed winds are capable of damaging any loose installation on the top or on the outside of the building. Apart from it, oil spill caused in the transformers may lead to a bigger tragedy. It could lead to snapping of power lines and collapse of poles and pylons.
(vi)	Sea level rise	No impact, unless the power source or electrical poles are located too close to the sea. Precautionary measures need to be taken to combat high tide and land submergence.
(vii)	Earthquake	During earthquake, the collapse of any unsafe structure may not only cause disruption of normal functioning of the power source but it

		can also lead to major life casualties.

(b) Impact on the process operations:

Sr. No	Hazard	Impact
(i)	Urban Flooding/ Flooding	Due to urban flooding/ flooding, the chemicals can get mixed with flood waters and spread over to various parts of factory premises. Inundation of factory premises can hamper access to and from the industry premises. It could also lead to disruption of services. Sometimes it may affect the whole Lube Oil console, which is a huge loss.
(ii)	Cyclonic storm	Cyclonic storm can damage any loose items of the plant. It can directly affect the ongoing work at open site. The power supply may be disrupted affecting the industrial processes. It can also lead to secondary accidents such as fires and gas leaks.
(iii)	Drought	Drought conditions would reduce availability of water, impacting the industrial process directly. Example: In a number of industries, ground water is used as a source for Cooling Towers. And in case of water scarcity, this will directly hamper the processes.
(iv)	Tsunami	It affects the industrial plants located in the coastal belt. Seawater can spread over to entire industry premises, and may drastically hamper the process operations through saline water.
(v)	Sea level rise	Salty water of sea can affect the processes, but the probability is very low in terms of occurrence.
(vi)	Earthquake	Earthquake can induce leakage in pipelines (due to breaking of rigid joints). The leakage of stored gases may be catastrophic during earthquake.
(vii)	Extreme weather change	Heavy rain, additional snow load may damage/ affect the vital installations of the plant. Heavy rain may overwhelm the drainage system and flood the premises leading to secondary disasters. Extreme heat can affect the ambient

| | | temperature, thus affecting the process. |

(c) Impact on machines and equipments

Sr. No	Hazard	Impact
(i)	Urban Flooding/ Flooding	Flood water inundation of machines and equipments may lead to complex situations of direct and indirect damages like oil spill, damage to machines, rusting etc.
(ii)	Cyclonic storm	Cyclones generally can't cause much damage to machines or equipments directly, but if the machines and equipments are installed in open, and are directly exposed to the outside environment then definitely cyclonic storm can damage the machines and allied equipments.
(iii)	Drought	No direct impact of drought on instruments, machine parts.
(iv)	Tsunami	Inundation is the major problem in case of Tsunami. The affected machines and equipments may stop functioning in post Tsunami scenario.
(v)	Sea level rise	Unless machines are installed too close to the sea level or are completely unprotected, sea level rise may not have a direct impact on machines and equipments.
(vi)	Earthquake	The machinery fixtures and placement of the same matter a lot in case of earthquake. Especially the heavy machineries are under direct threat of earthquake damage, unless mitigated properly as per requirements.
(vii)	Extreme weather change	Heavy rain fall or snow fall can damage machines in more than one way. Apart from the damages by inundation heavy rainfall increases humidity in the surrounding atmosphere, leading to chances of corrosion of machine parts.

(d) Impact on the industrial building/ compound

Sr. No	Hazard	Impact
(i)	Urban Flooding/ Flooding	Inundation of industrial building may be dangerous, it can cause not only disruption of normal functioning of the industrial activities, but also impart heavy loss to electrical and other telecommunication lines, vital installations like cooling plants etc. Flooding may damage structural parts like foundation, floors, lower parts of the wall etc.
(ii)	Cyclonic storm	Cyclonic storms accompanying high speed winds are capable of damaging any loose installation on the top or on the outside of the building. Apart from it, these broken industrial components may damage vital parts under the influence of high cyclonic winds exposing the inner installations vulnerable to rain. The roof and light weight structures are under extreme threat during cyclonic conditions, leading to collapse of trees.
(iii)	Drought	Except reducing the availability of water for proper functioning of the industry, drought may not have direct impact on the building.
(iv)	Tsunami	Seismic sea waves can drastically hamper the industrial building (primarily located in coastal region), due to the lateral force and acceleration from behind (seaside).
(v)	Sea level rise	No impact, unless the industry is located too close to the sea. In case the industry is located close to the sea shore, it may need to relocate or take appropriate steps from recurrent sea water flooding during high tide.
(vi)	Earthquake	During the earthquake any unsafe structure may collapse which will not only lead to disruption of normal functioning of industry but also the major life casualties.
(vii)	Extreme weather change	Heavy downpour or snow fall can disrupt normal operations by clogging drainage system, water seepage on vital installations and even inundation

| | | of low lying areas. Heavy rainfall may lead to failure of structural systems due to excess loads. |

(e) Impact on storage (chemicals, gases)

Sr. No	Hazard	Impact
(i)	Urban Flooding/ Flooding	Flooding can cause chemical pollution from the storage, leading to a larger disaster. Pollutants can contaminate flood water and reach to the far end, with flow of water. Depending on the nature of pollutant, consequential health and safety hazards may arise.
(ii)	Cyclonic storm	Similar to damages caused by flooding in the storage of chemicals and gases, cyclonic conditions can cause large scale damage with high wind velocity and flowing water.
(iii)	Drought	No impact of drought on storage of chemicals and gases.
(iv)	Tsunami	Tsunami effect can induce the leakage of stored gases and spillage of hazardous chemicals. Apart from affecting the humans it can also pollute the environment.
(v)	Sea level rise	Similar to urban flooding/ flooding.
(vi)	Earthquake	Storage (chemical, gas) can lead to huge damage due to the earthquake. Leakage of stored gases may be catastrophic. Leakage of hazardous material may also cause secondary disasters like fire.
(vii)	Extreme weather change	Similar to damages caused by urban flooding and cyclonic conditions

(f) Impact on conveyor and piping system

Sr. No	Hazard	Impact
(i)	Urban Flooding/ Flooding	Urban flooding/ flooding may be most damaging for low level conveyor and piping systems. Any damage to piping system may cause contamination of the flood water that may

		lead to health and safety hazards.
(ii)	Cyclonic storm	Cyclones may cause major damages to the piping system and conveyor belts. Any damage to the piping system may cause contamination of the flood water and that may lead to health and safety hazards.
(iii)	Drought	No impact of drought on conveyors and piping systems.
(iv)	Tsunami	Seismic sea waves can be very dangerous to existing conveyors and piping system. High velocity sea water can damage the existing supports to the laid pipelines and also the conveyor base, supporting electrical motors and allied pulleys.
(v)	Sea level rise	In worst case scenario, impacts will be similar to flooding.
(vi)	Earthquake	The piping infrastructure, primarily carrying the hazardous material (chemicals, gases) can lead to huge damages during earthquakes. Also the leakage of hazardous material may cause secondary disasters like fire.
(vii)	Extreme weather change	May not be that damaging to the piping infrastructure in a short span of time but can lead to a major disaster in case of persistent climatic changes and subsequent impacts.

Impact on waste disposal

Sr. No	Hazard	Impact
(i)	Urban Flooding/ Flooding	Flooding may cause water logging of waste disposal sites. This would further cause decomposition of waste and spread of waste to other areas through water. Waste may also percolate into the ground water sources and contaminate them.
(ii)	Cyclonic storm	Cyclonic storms may lead to dispersal/ spreading of industrial waste over large areas. Spread of hazardous industrial waste may have the catastrophic consequences. It

		can also lead to land pollution.
(iii)	Drought	No direct impact of drought on the waste disposal process.
(iv)	Tsunami	Similar to urban flooding/ flooding.
(v)	Sea level rise	Same as flooding. In addition it would also cause the loss of disposal sites due to the submergence. Oil and dangerous chemicals may spread over a large area through water.
(vi)	Earthquake	Earthquake can also hamper the hazardous waste disposal process by affecting the weaker installations.
(vii)	Extreme weather change	Same as flooding.

(g) Impact on transportation (by road, rail)

Sr. No	Hazard	Impact
(i)	Urban Flooding/ Flooding	Option of transportation of goods and people are limited during flooding conditions. Floods may lead to the damage of existing roads and rail tracks. Hence it may restrict the transportation of relief or urgent repairs necessary to avert a major disaster. Transportation may resume after clearance of debris and carcass.
(ii)	Cyclonic storm	Cyclonic storms tend to uproot trees, electric poles or small constructions that may block the roads and rail tracks (though temporarily). The cyclonic storm is a short duration hazard and all transportation shall be suspended during the course of storm.
(iii)	Drought	No impact of drought on transportation of goods.
(iv)	Tsunami	Tsunami may hamper the means of transportation along the coastal belt, depending upon the intensity. It may damage the road and rail network.
(v)	Sea level rise	Similar to urban flooding/ flooding
(vi)	Earthquake	Major Earthquakes may lead to road blockage with debris of the falling structures. Transportation may resume after clearing the debris.
(vii)	Extreme weather change	Extreme weather conditions can disrupt the processing of incoming and outgoing of goods etc.

(I) Induced effect to surroundings

Sr. No	Hazard	Impact
(i)	Urban Flooding/ Flooding	Urban flooding/ flooding can hamper the entire flora and fauna of the surroundings. It can lead to structural damages like damage to foundation, walls, flooring, roads, etc. The housing for industrial workers especially at the lower levels can also be disturbed with water inundation. It can also damage the electrical and telecommunication lines.
(ii)	Cyclonic storm	Similar to flooding, cyclonic storms can damage the environment, including housing for workers. Loose installations on the roof, light weight structures may bear the force of the hazard. In case of high cyclonic wind speed even the roofs of the structure may get damaged.
(iii)	Drought	Drought conditions may not impact structure of the housing directly but it can reduce the availability of water both surface and ground.
(iv)	Tsunami	Tsunami (Seismic sea waves) can devastate the seaside industries where it makes landfall as well as the community residing nearby.
(v)	Sea level rise	In worst case scenario, the consequences will be quite similar to flood, but impacts will be low.
(vi)	Earthquake	During an earthquake the collapse of any unsafe structure may not only disrupt the normal functioning of industry but can also lead to the major life casualties.
(vii)	Extreme weather change	Heavy downpour or snow fall can disrupt normal operations by clogging drainage system and causing water seepage to the housing. It may even cause sudden inundation of low lying areas. Heavy rainfall, snowfall, hailstorm may lead to failure of existing structure due to the excess loads as well.

Climate Change Mitigation

Mitigation of climate change and global warming primarily involves taking actions to reduce the greenhouse gas emissions and to enhance sinks aimed at reducing the potential extent of global warming. This is in distinction to the adaptation to global warming which involves taking action to minimize the effects of global warming. Mitigation is effective at avoiding warming, but not at rapidly reversing it. Scientific consensus on global warming, together with the precautionary principle and the fear of abrupt climate change is leading to increased effort to develop new technologies and sciences and carefully manage others in an attempt to mitigate global warming. The Stern Review on the economics of climate change identifies several ways of mitigating climate change. These include reducing demand for emissions-intensive goods and services, increasing efficiency gains, increasing use and development of low-carbon technologies, switching to cleaner energy sources and reducing non-fossil fuel emissions.

Climate Change Mitigation by Industries to Reduce Emission

Industrial sector emissions of greenhouse gases (GHGs) include carbon dioxide (CO_2) from energy use, from non-energy uses of fossil fuels and from non-fossil fuel sources (e.g. cement manufacture); as well as non-CO_2 gases.

Many options exist for mitigating GHG emissions from the industrial sector. These options can be divided into three broad categories:

1. Sector-wide options, for example more efficient electric motors and motor-driven systems; high efficiency boilers and process heaters; fuel switching, including the use of waste materials; and recycling.

2. Process-specific options, for example the use of bio-energy contained in food and pulp & paper industry wastes, turbines to recover the energy contained in pressurized blast furnace gas, and control strategies to minimize PFC emissions from aluminum manufacture.

3. Operating procedures, for example control of steam and compressed air leaks, reduction of air leaks into furnaces, optimum use of insulation, and optimization of equipment size to ensure high capacity utilization.

Management tools are available to reduce GHG emissions, often without capital investment or increased operating costs. Staff training to reduce GHG emissions and the company's general approach to energy efficiency for use in their day-to-day practices has proved quite beneficial. Programmes, for example reward systems that provide regular feedback on staff behaviour, have paid good results. Even when energy is a significant cost for an industry, the opportunities for improvement may be missed because of organizational barriers. The energy audit and management programmes create a foundation for improvement and also provide guidance for managing energy throughout an organization.

Several countries have instituted voluntary corporate energy management standards, for example Canada, Denmark and USA. Others, for example India, has promoted energy audits through Bureau of Energy Efficiency. Integration of energy management systems into broader industrial management systems (allowing the energy use for continuous improvement in the same manner as labour, waste and other inputs are managed), is highly beneficial. The documentation of existing practices and planned improvements is essential in order to achieve a transition from energy efficiency programmes and projects dependent on individuals, to processes and practices that are part of the corporate culture. Software tools are also available to help identify energy saving opportunities. Further, the Government of India is institutionalizing National Action Plan on Climate Change(NAPCC). The action plan (NAPCC) includes provisions to reduce disaster risk induced by climate change. NAPCC is composed of 8 National Missions It lays emphasis on vulnerability assessments, incorporating Disaster Risk Reduction (DRR) concerns into development practices and building capacities. It also acknowledges the importance of upgrading forecasting, tracking early warning systems for cyclones, flood, tsunamis and storm surge and building resilience of community through appropriate training against events such as natural disasters.

Key Prevention and Adaptation Measures for Industry

To minimize or avoid the impacts of climate change induced extreme events and natural hazards on the industries, the key prevention and mitigations are listed here. However, these measures are only indicative; the detailed measures for specific industry should be decided based on its characteristics and other constraints.

Process operations

i. Institutionalize the GIS based Decision Support System (DSS), properly aligned with the existing industrial setups, preferably in MAH installations for efficient communication system.

ii. Preparation and rehearsal of the On-site & Off-site emergency plan through conducting periodic mock drills.

iii. Devise the mechanism for early warning and emergency situations, dissemination of alerts and response, regular checking of the same.

iv. Ensure all emergency safety equipment and protective gears are in place.

v. Roles and responsibilities of various stakeholders (SOP) in the industry should include decision making function of whether to run a particular machine or not in the event of a hazardous event.

vi. Ensure continuous presence of medical supplies and medical personnel in the in-plant safety room.

vii. Carry out annual health check up of the employees; ensure rotation of workers based on their health condition.

viii. Periodic training and retraining should be conducted.

ix. Ensure safety of data and documents; store them in proper place that is not affected by flood, cyclone or earthquake.

x. Provide windsocks in visible locations for the benefit of workers as well as the general public.

xi. Business Continuity Planning should be done to meet the situation of disruption of specific inputs due to hazard event.

xii. Hazards Operatibility (HAZOP) Study should be carried out at the industrial level, taking into account the probable hazards.

Storage of chemicals and gases

i. Material Safety Data Sheets (MSDS) of the chemicals and gases should be available and adhered at the industrial level.
ii. Appropriate sensors should be installed for sensing the leakages of chemicals and gases. The inventory limit of the same should also be maintained.
iii. Gas cylinders should be kept in vertical position; firmly secured using chains put around them.
iv. Proper system for securing cylinders should be used moving them on hand trolleys or forklifts.
v. Workers should be trained in proper handling of chemicals and gases, including checking of gas pressure. They should use personal protective gear.
vi. Proper distance between different types of gases should be maintained. For example, oxygen and dry acetylene should be stored at least 5 m apart.
vii. Drums storing used chemicals should be kept in an area such that any leaked liquid is collected in a pit.
viii. Storage of chemicals and gases should be away from critical installations.
ix. Periodic inspection of chains, gauges should be done.
x. Foundation supports of the storage tanks of chemicals and gases should be able to withstand any eventuality.

Power source

Foundation of the electrical poles and piles should be structurally strong and safe with adequate plinth level, to   withstand firmly, in case of earthquake, urban flooding, cyclone, tsunami, extreme weather etc.:
i. Sufficient power back up should be provided. There should be an alternative source of power.

ii.   As factor of safety, power supply may have to be shut down in certain circumstances to avoid any mishap.

iii.   Proper earthing and safety against short-circuiting / electrocution is needed.

iv.   Power source, equipment, poles, cables, etc., should be accessible only to authorized personnel.

v.   Periodical inspection and maintenance of power source, transmission system, transformers, equipment, poles, cables, etc. is important.

vi.   Suitable warning signs should be put up in local language.

Machines and Equipments

i.   In the operational control room/ centralized control room in any industrial plant, all the appropriate machines and equipments should be available to operate any kind of eventuality, arising out of nature induced event.

ii.   There should be specially designed machine guards and separators to take care of safety of critical machines and equipments.

iii.   Machines should be located at proper places; they should be accessible during events of natural hazards for operating.

iv.   Machines should be protected from extreme weather conditions.

v.   Official in-charge of the operation should be trained to take decision to stop a machine in the event of a hazardous event. For example, the fans in a cooling tower may have to be stopped during a cyclone.

vi.   Proper foundations should be designed taking into account prevailing hazards.

vii.   The connection of a machine with its foundation should be provided with some flexibility to accommodate movement due to earthquake.

viii.   The foundation of a machine should be free from water inundation, and free draining.

ix.   Frequent inspection and regular maintenance is important.

x.   Specialized manpower should be designated to operate critical machines and equipments. The specialized persons should be physically available 27X7 on rotation basis/ on call.

Industrial building

Industrial buildings should be constructed taking into account localized risks, also including the extreme events:

i.   During the design stage of the building, necessary precautions should be taken about the hazards such as flood, cyclone, earthquake, etc.

ii. Safety of existing buildings should be evaluated; and if needed, necessary retrofitting should be done to make the buildings resistant to these hazards.

iii. The construction of industrial building should also be in line with safety specifications prescribed in the National Building Code (NBC) 2005, to avoid any future risk.

iv. Floor level of the industry should be kept well above the expected flood level of the location; roofs of the structures should be strong enough to withstand the cyclone winds; the structural elements should be able to resist the earthquake forces.

v.   Roof of the building should be leak-proof.

vi. Good drainage should be provided from the floor as well as from the open area.

vii. Basement and any underground tanks should be protected from ingress of ground water by proper waterproofing arrangement.

viii. Special paints and coatings may have to be used on the walls and floor.

ix. Floor should be able to take heavy loads and wear and tear.

x.   Periodic inspection and regular maintenance is needed.

xi. There should be couple of safe zones inside the industrial building for safety of employees as well as the contract workers. So that at the time of emergency these place can act as the assembly points or safe zones.

Conveyor, Piping System

i. Conveyor should be properly guarded through the side railing etc. from security point of view, so that any damage to the others can be prevented.

ii. Conveyor at the lower level should be protected from water.

iii. Conveyors should not be accessible to unauthorized persons.

iv. Conveyors should be suitably covered so that the material moving on top of it, can't harm to any passerby.

v. Conveyors should conform to the standards of Conveyor Equipment Manufacturers' Association (CEMA).

vi. Flexible connection should be provided for pipelines at critical locations in order to make them resilient to earthquake shaking.

vii. Piping should conform to the ASME standards.

viii. Physical inspection of pipes, joints, etc. should be done periodically.

ix. Special care of the piping supports to be taken.

x. For assuring health of pipeline, the Pipeline Integrity Management System (PIMS) should be institutionalized.

Waste Disposal

i. Make specific provisions so that industrial hazardous waste can't get mixed with process condensate, water and other utilities.

ii. Reduce the toxicity of waste and make appropriate changes in the processes. For example, having sufficient height of the chimney; use of filters, etc.

iii. All types of wastes – solid, liquid, and gas – should be disposed of properly and safely.

iv. Take suitable adaptive measures in order to reduce the waste materials if possible.

v. The construction and maintenance of hazardous industrial waste sites/ installations should be periodically supervised by experts so that gaps, if any can be identified and addressed well in time.

Transportation

i. Vehicle drivers and accompanying staff should always carry the Material Safety Data Sheet (MSDS) while movement of any hazardous industrial material. These MSDS Sheets should be made available in the local language, so that precautionary measures can be taken by the driver and staff itself.

ii. Workers handling chemical containers (cylinders, drums) should be trained for loading, unloading, moving, etc.

iii. The drivers and support staff should carry TREM (Transport Emergency) Card; they should be trained in the precautions to be taken while transporting the hazardous industrial materials.

iv. Suitable warning signs should be displayed on the containers and vehicles.

v. Location in the industry for loading and unloading the hazardous materials should have proper flooring and access.

vi. Symbols of dangerous industrial goods to be displayed on the vehicle (truck/ railway wagon) while transportation of the same either through rail or by road.

Surroundings

i. Inculcate the concept of Community Based Disaster Management (CBDM) at the community level, to last mile connectivity, with the help of Multi Stakeholder Partnership (MSP) with all concerned stakeholders.

ii. Institutionalize the offsite emergency plan with the help of District Administration, District Crisis Group (DCG) and Local Crisis Group (LCG).

iii. Industries should utilize the Corporate Social Responsibility (CSR) and Responsible Care (RC) initiatives for the safety the surroundings and wellbeing of the nearby residents/ villagers.

iv. The public awareness should be conducted for sensitization of the people residing in the vicinity.

v.   Form the disaster management teams in the villages, including the Community Information Representatives (CIRs) as the nodal persons (they should be from the nearby villages and adequately trained w.r.t. to deal with the nature induced any eventuality/ disaster).

vi.   Liaison with the local administration for receiving early warning of hazards and when offsite drills are organized.

vii.   Provide the transport vehicles for evacuation of people, if needed.

viii.   Provide awareness on the hazardous industrial waste disposal sites.

ix.   Use the platform of local NGOs and volunteers for guiding the people about evacuation.

Conclusion

Though it is not possible to stop the natural calamities and climate change, but a systematic approach can be adopted at our end to minimize the impacts of natural hazards and climate induced extreme events, in context of industries. The key prevention and adaptation measures discussed in previous sections can be very useful at the industrial level, in order to deal with flooding, cyclonic storm, tsunami, earthquake, cloudburst and also the other extreme weather events.

In today's scenario of globalization, especially the industrial automation, it is need of the hour; to take the mission focused, target oriented, voluntary and time bound approach to cope with the threat of climate induced extreme events and natural hazards by taking prompt steps at the level of industries, with support from all other stakeholders.

However, in order to institutionalize the suggested measures on the ground, some investment will be required, but ultimately it will be worth to go for it rather than waiting to look at the consequences of such calamities.

References

1. IPCC (Intergovernmental Panel on Climate Change) Fifth Assessment Report: Climate Change 2014

2. "Industrial sitting in multi hazard environment: application of GIS and MIS" by Dr. Anil K.Gupta and Ms. Sreeja Nair, NIDM, published in International Geoinformatics Research and Development Journal, Vol 1, Issue 2, June 2010.

3. TOT Manual on Climate Change and Industrial Disaster Risk Management, 2009

4. Vulnerability Atlas of India, by BMTPC, 2007.

Chapter- X

Environmental Impacts of Disasters: Can the loss of Natural Capital be Substantially Reduced?

Jayashree Parida & Niharranjan Mishra*

Abstract

The environmental impacts of disasters on natural capital become major threat for economies and political agendas today. Particularly in the developing countries, the magnitude of disaster-related natural capital disruption influences a lot on the primary livelihood patterns of people like agriculture, fishery, forest product collection etc. Natural capital comprises the stock of natural resources like water, air, land and habitat, together with the flow of environmental services to the people by which households engage in agricultural pursuits and/or resource collection for both sustenance and income generation. In spite of its potential significance, relatively few studies have attempted to focus on the effects of disasters on natural capital which directly and indirectly affects the livelihood patterns of affected population. So this paper attempts to highlight the disaster-impacted loss of natural capital and to discuss the issues and challenges related to policies and programmes to sustain natural capital in the context of disaster management.

Keywords: Environment, Livelihoods, Natural Capital, Natural Disaster

---

*National Institute of Technology, Rourkela, Odisha, India

Introduction

The effects of climatic variability manifested in disaster occurrences afflict many regions of the world, particularly the developing countries. The magnitude of these impacts in terms of lives lost and livelihoods disrupted affects mostly the poor because of their limited adaptive capacity. This in turn poses multiple threats to economic growth, wider poverty reduction, and the achievement of the Millennium Development Goals [1], [2]. It is also reflected in the words of Intergovernmental Panel on Climate Change (IPCC):

> *Populations are highly variable in their endowments and the developing countries, particularly the least developed countries...have lesser capacity to adapt and are more vulnerable to climate change damages, just as they are more vulnerable to other stresses. This condition is most extreme among the poorest people [3].*

These climatic events adversely impact the sectors of agriculture, fishery and thereby the livelihoods of several coastal communities which undermine local and national development efforts to support livelihoods, promote economic growth and achieve overall human well-being. Disasters have strong and mostly negative impact on livelihood assets, leading to outcomes of increased vulnerability, reduced food security, and more fragile institutions. The agriculture and natural resources sectors (natural capital) are highly vulnerable because they are continuously exposed to natural disasters. Natural resources are considered as natural capital that people use those goods and services for their own livelihood purposes. The disruption of natural capital becomes a serious threat because the rural poor mostly rely on unsteady and highly vulnerable livelihoods related to natural capital like land, water, soil etc. in areas prone to drought, flooding and other hazards.

The analysis of weather-related natural capital disruption has naturally been retrospective because the ability to predict the scale and timing of extreme weather events is challenging. Although natural resources play crucial role in rural livelihoods, little research has explored the relationship between disaster and rural livelihoods with special focus on natural capital. Linkages between environment and disasters are now acknowledged, yet are poorly reflected in disaster management and disaster plans [4]. In report of Intergovernmental Panel on Climate Change (IPCC), environmental accounts have not yet been included in the national accounts of countries, although some of the value of environmental services is included in the statistics of such sectors such as agriculture and tourism. The widespread loss of natural resources and biodiversity by natural disasters is much more important than conservation issue because these provide socially and economically valuable services. For example, more than two hundred million people in Asia depend directly on local marine and coastal resources for their income, livelihoods and food security.

The present paper raises and tries to answer questions about the environmental impacts of disasters on natural capital and how the livelihood patterns of household are impacted by these effects. It also focuses on issues and challenges related to policies and programme to sustain natural capital to improve the livelihoods of affected communities. "A keynote on natural capital" will briefly review the available literature on five capitals of livelihoods followed by "environmental impacts of disasters" which will show the impacts of different natural hazards on different livelihood patterns particularly related to natural capital. The final section will deal with certain recommendations.

Natural Capital and Livelihood

The concept of livelihood with sustainability was first defined by Chambers and Conway (1991) as 'a livelihood comprises the capabilities, assets (stores, resources, claims and access) and activities required for a means of living: a livelihood is sustainable which can cope with and recover from stress and shocks, maintain or enhance its capabilities and assets, and provide sustainable livelihood opportunities for the next generation; and which contributes net benefits to other livelihoods at the local and global levels and in the short and long term

[5]. Based on this definition, Scoones (1998) and Department for International Development (1999), introduced five capitals of sustainable livelihoods: i) natural capital (soil, water, air and other natural resources); ii) human capital (skills, knowledge, health and labour); iii) social capital (social networks, social relations, affiliations, associations etc.); iv) financial capital (cash, credit, saving and other economic assets); and v) physical capital (housing, infrastructures, production equipments and technologies, livestock and domestic utensils) [6], [7]. A livelihood is sustainable if it can cope with, recover from and adapt to stresses and shocks, maintain and enhance its capabilities and assets, and enhance opportunities for the next generation [5]. Rural households pursue diverse livelihood strategies including farming, herding and the exploitation of natural resources based on the relative availability of capital assets. Natural capital includes access to land, water and wildlife from which households engage in agricultural pursuits or resource collection for both substance and income generation [7]. There are four general services provided by natural capital, each of which need to be considered from the perspective of criticality:

1. Provisioning Services (which provide resources used in production (timber, fish, etc.)
2. Regulating Services (which regulate ecosystem processes, such as decomposition of organic wastes, cleansing of the air (by oxidation, etc.)
3. Cultural Services (providing benefits of a spiritual, aesthetic, recreational or psychological nature; giving meaning to place, etc.)
4. Supporting Services (which regulate processes necessary for all the other ecosystem services)

Environmental Impacts of Natural Disasters

Disasters have adverse environmental consequences and also degraded environment also cause and exacerbate the negative impacts of disasters.

Impact on Natural Resources and Biodiversity

Natural resources are not the only type of natural income which flow from ecosystems. Forests, for example, are not simply wood production units. They also prevent soil erosion, absorb rain water and provide flood control, they provide habitat for a diversity of plant and animal species which may serve as foods or medicines for other species, they absorb the natural wastes of these diverse life forms, they generate oxygen and sequester carbon from the atmosphere, they affect the microclimate of their area, they are a key component of the hydrologic cycle, as well as providing aesthetic enjoyment and spiritual inspiration. These forest ecosystem functions evolved to maintain the overall health of the forest environment and the creatures in it. Ecosystem functions are another form of natural income derived from the same natural capital of the forest ecosystem that generates timber for economic use. The loss and damage of mangroves has a devastating impact on households due to their high dependence on the natural environment as a source of livelihoods and food security. Mangroves are the important source of subsistence and income for local communities, particularly for landless laborers, through the collection of firewood, production of charcoal, and the harvesting of fisheries as well as material for shelter. They also serve as natural barriers to surges and floods and as fish breeding grounds.

Impact on Agriculture

Agriculture is the major source of income in most developing countries. Agricultural production is highly dependent on weather, climate and water availability and is adversely affected by weather and climate related disasters. The rural people are more exposed to disasters because they live in disaster-prone areas and depend on high-risk and low return livelihood system such as rain-fed agriculture [8]. Floods make land unsuitable for agricultural production [9]. These can restrict food production by damaging seeds either on-farm or off-farm [10]. Floods and droughts reduce the impact area's total vegetative cover; typhoons and floods lead to soil erosion, higher coastal tides and storm surges; floods result in siltation and sedimentation, accumulated waste, polluted water and deformed land topography; and droughts reduce rainfall, lower soil fertility [11]. Taken together, all three natural disasters indirectly reduce the viability of both land and water ecosystems as suppliers of ecosystem services and endanger human health and safety. Disasters like flood or drought decrease the soil fertility which makes the land incongruous for agricultural yields [9], [12].

Impact on Fishing

Local livelihoods are severely affected by these environmental damages. Fisheries is considered to be one of the important sectors contributing to the economic growth, livelihood support and poverty alleviation in the country like India. India is the second populous country in which around 11 million people are supported by fishery activities. With changing consumption pattern, fisheries play an important role in food security and livelihood security. Fisheries and fishing-dependent people are often located in places that are at particularly high risk of extreme events. Coastal fisheries and floodplain fisheries can, for example, be subject to flooding, cyclones and tsunamis while inland fisheries can be significantly affected by droughts and floods. Fishing communities situated in low-lying coastal areas are exposed to a number of natural hazards and are consequently more vulnerable. Fishers are highly dependent on fishing for their livelihoods with little possibility of finding alternative employment. Their access to land is generally limited and their assets, in the form of boats and gear, are more exposed to natural hazards. Disasters affect the fishing communities in different ways [13]. These extreme events can destroy or severely damage infrastructure and livelihood assets such as boats, landing sites, post-harvesting facilities and roads. Loss of life can be the most severe impact in fishing communities, affecting not only surviving household members but also potentially upsetting economic and social activities and systems outside the immediate family [14].

Impact on Eco-tourism

Globally tourism contributes 8 per cent of global employment and 9 per cent of the world GDP and over 9 per cent of the world investment [15]. In India, the travel and tourism industry accounts for nearly 4.8 per cent of GDP, taking into account direct and indirect employment. The local economy of most of the developing countries relies heavily on tourism for the livelihood of its people. In most cases, natural disasters have a negative impact on the economy and on the people who depend on tourism for livelihood. As a result, the unemployment rate raises and the disposable income of local people decreases. Tourists do not visit those places as a result of the disaster, they lack jobs and income opportunities as well as businesses also definitely decline. For example, in Uttarakhand flood 2013, Uttarakhand incurred a loss of about Rs 12,000 crore, based on Gross State Domestic Product (GSDP) figures from the state budget for 2013-14. Eleven per cent of the GSDP was washed away in terms of prospective tourism earnings due to floods. A large number of people employed in tourism and related sector lost their source of livelihood. The livelihoods of 83,320 households from the affected five districts of the state depended on the tourism sector. This included small businesses such as hotels and restaurants (6500), petty traders (23,000) such as road side tea stalls and roadside eateries (Dhabas), fruit and vegetable vendors, handicraft vendors, taxi and bus drivers, palanquin bearers(dandi kathi) and mule owners who carry pilgrims and goods up the steep slopes of the two dhams, and the priests [16].

In this context, it is important for the tourism industry to take into account the possibility of natural disasters to ensure business sustainability. This will make it easy for the place as a whole to recover faster from the disaster and at the same time, it will mitigate the damage from the disaster.

Natural Disasters, Gender and Natural Capital

Particularly women from developing countries are suffered most by natural disasters like flood, cyclone etc. They are dependent on natural resources first hand to sustain their lives. They are more vulnerable to natural disasters because of the socioeconomic inequalities between men and women in terms of rights and social norms of society, social rules and restrictions. On the other hand, rural women have extensive local knowledge on environment for sustainable living. So women are more capable to cope with the deterioration in the environment or to take precautions in changing conditions with these crises.

Issues and Challenges

Maintaining natural capital or ecosystem management in a sustainable way is particularly critical for the rural poor, whose livelihoods and ability to cope with natural disasters directly depend on the availability of local natural assets and resources. It is very difficult to quantify and monetize the environmental impacts of natural disasters. So it is a challenging issue for policy makers to devote more attention and perhaps research to these issues. The scientific community now stresses that both the underlying causes of human vulnerability to hazards, and the role of environmental conditions in exacerbating those hazards should be taken into account. The attempt was made by the Partnership for Environment and Disaster Risk Reduction (PEDRR) comprised of UN agencies, international and regional NGOs as well as specialists that collectively aim to influence policy, enhance implementation and better coordinate efforts in environmental management for disaster risk reduction, climate change adaptation and sustainable livelihoods. It promotes ecosystems management as the key strategy to reduce disaster risk, increase local resilience and adapt to a changing climate [4]. Following are certain issues and challenges to sustainability of natural capital in disaster risk reduction.

First, Environmental conservation and disaster management are important to the livelihoods of local people who often live in hazard-prone areas. They have built up, through thousands of years of experience and intimate contact with the environment, a vast body of knowledge on hazards and the environment events. It is a challenge to maintain the continuity of traditional knowledge through transmission from generation to generation. Indigenous knowledge should be considered as a complement to scientific knowledge in the development of community-based disaster risk management plans and programmes.

Second, involving local communities in disaster risk reduction is the main enabling factor for successful management of natural capital in disaster risk reduction. Beck et al. (2013) described their successful experiences of working with local decision-makers and community residents in developing environmentally sustainable and risk-sensitive solutions to coastal zone management [17].

Third, Disaster Risk Reduction (DRR) is a fundamental development issue. There should be bridging the gaps between policy and institutions. Therefore two conditions are required to fulfil such as i) an enabling policy environment is needed with integrated policies and legislations; ii) these policies and legislations need to be acted upon and enforced [18].

Fourth, although implementation of DRR projects and initiatives has increased over the years, the monitoring and evaluation of DRR interventions have always posed a major challenge. Monitoring and evaluation needs to be incorporated as part of implementation and adjusted according to scale depending on the level of intervention, types of stakeholders involved and the ecosystem services for DRR.

As Hyogo Framework for Action 2005-2015 recommends certain priorities such as sustainable use and management of ecosystems, integrated environmental and natural resource management etc, but in a review report of the United Nations Office for Disaster Risk Reduction (UNISDR, 2011), many countries still have inadequate or no policies that address both environmental management and DRR [19].

Conclusions

The literature on natural disasters and natural capital that has been reviewed in this paper describes that disaster-related bio-diversity loss impact a lot on the different livelihood strategies of communities. Natural capital provides the environmental basis for the development of country. So disaster risk reduction should aim to protect the capital assets of communities which in turn promote more livelihood options and underpin the sustainable development process. Various kinds of conservation activities should be adopted to protect mangroves and coastal dunes which play important role in cyclone or other natural extremes. Post-disaster strategies should incorporate livelihood restoration which can minimize the damage to natural capital. And lastly greater attention and investment are needed to support national and local efforts to mainstream ecosystem management in DRR in different sectors of development planning like agriculture, tourism, forestry etc.

References

1. ADB et al., Poverty and climate change: reducing the vulnerability of the poor through adaptation. VARG Multi Development Agency Paper. United Nations Development Project (UNDP) United Nations, New York. 2003. Retrieved from www.undp.org/energy/povcc.htm

2. Stern, N. et al., Stern review on the economics of climate change. (HM Treasury, London: Cambridge University Press, 2006).

3. Intergovernmental Panel on Climate Change. (2001). Climate change 2001: impacts, adaptation and vulnerability, summary for policymakers. A Report of Working Group II of the IPCC. Geneva: Intergovernmental Panel on Climate Change (IPCC).

4. The Partnership for Environment and Disaster Risk Reduction, Demonstrating the role Chambers, R. & Conway, G. R.. Sustainable rural livelihoods: practical concepts for 21st century, IDS Discussion Paper 296, Brighton: Institute of Development Studies.1991.

5. Scoones, I. , Sustainable rural livelihoods: A framework for analysis. IDS working paper, 72. Brighton: Institute of Development Studies. 1998.

6. Department for International Development, Sustainable livelihoods guidance sheets. London: Author. 1999. Retrieved from www.ennonline.net/ pool/files/ife/dfid-sustainable-livelihoods-guidance-sheet-section1.pdf

7. Sivakumar, M. V. K., Impact of natural disasters in agriculture, rangeland, forestry: An overview. In

M. V. K. Sivakumar, R. P. Motha & H. P. Das (Eds.), Natural Disasters and Extreme Events in Agriculture, (Netherland: Springer,2005) 1-22.

8. Das, H. P. (2005). Agrometerological impact assessment of natural disasters and extreme events and agricultural strategies adopted in areas with high weather risks. In M. V. K. Sivakumar, R. P. Motha & H. P. Das (Eds.), Natural disasters and Extreme Events in Agriculture, (Netherland: Springer. 2005) 93-113.

9. Armah, F. A., Yawson, D. O., Yengoh, G. T., Odoi, J. O., & Afifa, E. K. A., Impact of floods on livelihoods and vulnerability of natural resource dependent communities in Northern Ghana. Water, 2, 2010, 120-139. doi: 10.3390/w2020120

10. Israel,D.C. & Briones, R. M., Impacts of natural disasters on agriculture, food security, and natural resources and environment in Philippines. Discussion Paper Series No. 2012-36, Philippines: Philippines Institute of Development Studies.2012.

11. Popp, A., The effects of natural disasters on long run growth. Major Themes in Economics, Spring. 2006. Retrieved from http://business.uni.edu/economics/themes/popp.pdf

12. Gaillard, J. C. Maceda, E. A., Stasiak, E., Berre, I. L., & Espaldon, M. V., Sustainable livelihoods and people's vulnerability in the face of coastal hazards. Journal of Coastal Conservation, 13(2/3), 2009, 119-129.

13. Food and Agricultural Organization of the United States, Disaster response and risk management in the fisheries sector, FAO Fisheries Technical Paper, 479. 2007. Retrieved from ftp://ftp.fao.org/docrep/fao/010/a1217e/a1217e00.pdf

14. Kapur, A., Insensitive India: Attitudes towards disaster prevention and management. Economic and Political Weekly, 40(42), 2005, 4551-4560.

15. The World Bank, Draft Project Appraisal Document on India: Uttarakhand Disaster Recovery Project. 2013. Retrieved from http://dmmc.uk.gov.in/files/pdf/UDRP-Draft_PAD-Oct_8.pdf

16.   Beck, M. W., Gilmer, B., Ferdaña,Z., Raber,G. T.,
           Shepard,C. C., Meliane, I., Stone,J. D.,Whelchel,
           A. W., Hoover, M. & Newkirk, S., Increasing the
           resilience of human and natural communities to
           coastal hazards: Supporting decisions in New
           York and Connecticut, In F. G. Renaud, K.
           Sudmeier-Rieuxand M. Estrella(Eds.), The Role of
           Ecosystems in Disaster Risk Reduction, (New
           York: United Nations University Press, 2013) 140-
           163.
17.   Papathoma-Koehle, M. & Glade, T., The role of vegetation
           cover changes in landslide hazard and risk. In F.
           G. Renaud, K. Sudmeier-Rieuxand M.
           Estrella(Eds.), The Role of Ecosystems in Disaster
           Risk Reduction, (New York: United Nations
           University Press, 2013). 293-320.
18.   United Nations International Strategy for Disaster
           Reduction, Global assessment report on disaster
           risk reduction: Revealing risk and redefining
           development. Switzerland, Geneva: Author. 2011.
           Retrieved from
           http://www.unisdr.org/we/inform/publications/198
           46

Chapter- XI

The Role of Carbon Capture Technologies in Mitigation of Climate Change: A Restoration Perspective

Hemlata Lohar*

Abstract

The Global warming is attributed to increasing greenhouse gas emissions and mounting concentrations of carbon dioxide and other gases in the atmosphere. The earth's climate is dynamic and always changing through a natural cycle which is speeded up because of anthropogenic activities. Abnormal climate change phenomenon resulting from greenhouse gas emissions have been emerging since the 1990's. Cutting down emissions of global greenhouse gases can reduce the extent of climate change. There are a number of relatively low cost CO_2 mitigation technologies. Carbon capture and sequestration (CCS) has been recognized as a key mitigation option that could reduce CO_2 emissions. "Carbon capture and sequestration (CCS)", refers to a set of technologies designed to reduce carbon dioxide (CO_2) emissions from large point sources to mitigate climate change. CCS technology involves capturing CO_2 and then storing the carbon in a reservoir other than the atmosphere, instead of allowing it to be released into the atmosphere where its accumulation contributes to climate change. Three main approaches are available to capture CO_2 from large scale industrial facilities i.e. Post-combustion Capture, Pre-combustion Capture and Oxy-fuel Combustion Capture. In carbon sequestration, CO_2 is sequestered in geological media including depleted oil and gas reservoirs, unminable coal seams, and deep saline porous formations.

Keywords – Anthropogenic activities, Carbon capture, Carbon sequestration, Climate Change, CO_2 emissions

*Department of Environmental Sciences, MLS University, Udaipur, Rajsthan, India

Introduction

Global Warming is the increase of Earth's average surface temperature due to effect of greenhouse gases, such as carbon dioxide emissions from burning fossil fuels or from deforestation, which trap heat that would otherwise escape from Earth. This is a type of greenhouse effect. This hurts many people, animals, and plants. Many cannot take the change, so they die. The greenhouse effect is when the temperature rises because the sun's heat and light is trapped in the earth's atmosphere. Greenhouse gases in the earth's atmosphere, collect heat and light from the sun. (A greenhouse gas (GHG) is a gas in an atmosphere that absorbs and emits radiation within the thermal infrared range. This process is the fundamental cause of the greenhouse effect.) The primary greenhouse gases in the Earth's atmosphere are water vapour, carbon dioxide, methane, nitrous oxide, and ozone. The most significant greenhouse gas is actually water vapor. However, even slight increases in atmospheric levels of carbon dioxide can cause a substantial increase in temperature. This enormous input of CO_2 is causing the atmospheric levels of CO_2 to rise dramatically. CO_2 tends to remain in the atmosphere for a very long time (time scales in the hundreds of years). Human beings have increased the CO_2 concentration in the atmosphere by about thirty percent, which is an extremely significant increase, even on inter-glacial timescales. It is believed that human beings are responsible for this because the increase is almost perfectly correlated with increases in fossil fuel combustion, and also due other evidence, such as changes in the ratios of different carbon isotopes in atmospheric CO_2 that are consistent with "anthropogenic" (human caused) emissions. Climate change refers to any significant change in measures of climate (such as temperature, precipitation or wind) lasting for an extended period (decades or longer). Past changes are not unusual as they were of natural origin. But most of the changes within the last 50 years were very unusual as they were human-induced. The cause of these changes has been under extensive study. One factor is the steady increase in carbon dioxide which has been observed, presumably as a result of the combustion of fossil fuels. In 1958 the observed concentration was 315 ppm, which suggested an increase of about 0.5 ppm per year in the initial half of the 20th century. In 2005 the measured concentration of CO_2 was 374 ppm, suggesting an increase of about 1 ppm per year in the latter part of the 20th century (Malti Goel, 2010). At present; the atmospheric CO_2 concentration has crossed the limits up to 401 ppm (www.CO2NOW.org). To overcome the problems related to increasing CO_2 concentration, CO_2 mitigation options must be checked. There are a number of relatively low cost CO_2 mitigation technologies. They include improving energy supply and end use efficiency, switching from coal or oil to gas where possible, forestation, and inexpensive renewable energy applications (White paper report). A common mitigation measure to reduce carbon emissions is thus to use natural gas in place of other fossil fuels. Carbon capture and storage (CCS) has been recognized as a key mitigation option that could reduce CO_2 emissions. It refers to a set of technologies designed to reduce carbon dioxide (CO_2) emissions from large point sources or it is the process of capturing waste carbon dioxide (CO_2) from large point sources, such as fossil fuel power plants and transporting it to a storage site. There are two parts of CCS process. First, CO_2 is captured using different technologies and second, CO_2 is sequestered in geological media including depleted oil and gas reservoirs, unminable coal seams, and deep saline porous formations (Bachu et. al., 2003). Currently, three main approaches are available to capture CO_2 from large scale industrial facilities or power plants: Post-combustion Capture, Pre-combustion Capture and Oxy-fuel Combustion Capture.

Why CCS is required?

CCS is one of a suite of technologies that will all be required to combat climate change, including renewables, nuclear and energy efficiency. The importance of CCS as one of the tools against global warming is highlighted in a report by the International Energy Agency, which found that CCS could contribute to a 19% reduction in global CO_2 emissions by 2050, and that fighting climate change could cost over 70% more without CCS. Rising CO_2 concentrations in the atmosphere from pre-industrial levels of 280ppm to a present day value of 401ppm has led to increasing ocean acidification and may be contributing to climate change and a rising of global temperatures. A doubling of man-made CO_2 emissions since the 1970's coupled with geological evidence, which shows that changes of this magnitude usually occur over timescales of 5,000 to 10,000 years, suggests that it is likely that man-made CO_2 is contributing significantly to this rise in atmospheric CO_2. If fossil fuel combustion is allowed to continue to grow unabated then it is projected that CO_2 emissions will reach 35.4 Gt a year by 2035. This is in line with the worst case scenario in the IPCC 2007 Climate Change report which couples CO_2 rises to a world average temperature increase from 2.4-6.4°C by 2100. If the world is to maintain its current dependence on fossil fuels then CCS is a necessary technology for tackling rising atmospheric CO_2.

What if we do nothing?

The longer we wait, the worse it gets. You may not believe in climate change, but most scientists believe that the evidence of high CO_2 levels and hot climates in the past is compelling. You may not care if the summers get a few degrees warmer, but the ocean will inevitably become more acid, and the last time that happened it became a layered green soup (about 50 Million years ago). Like all preventive medicine, it's easier to put off the fateful day. But when that day arrives, it causes you more pain, and costs more, compared to early actions. It's important to realize that, even if we act now, the climate will carry on warming for another 3 or 5 degrees Centigrade. By acting now, we have a chance to limit that rise to less than 5 Centigrade, by keeping atmospheric CO_2 less than 550 parts per million.

What is CCS?

CCS is essentially a three stage technology where CO_2 is captured from large man-made CO_2 emission sources, transported via a network of pipelines and stored in deep subsurface geological formations. The capture process can potentially remove 90% of the CO_2 generated from fossil fueled (coal, oil and gas) electricity generation and industrial processes (such as steel and concrete manufacture)- based on the most recent estimates of CO_2 emission from fuel combustion this would represent a mass of CO_2 into the thousands of millions of tons. In order to prevent this large volume of CO_2 reaching the atmosphere it can be injected and safely stored in depleted hydrocarbon reservoirs, non-potable saline aquifers or unmineable coal seams. Methane gas is produced from offshore gas fields, and is brought onshore by pipeline. Using existing oil-refinery technology, the gas is 'reformed' into hydrogen and CO_2. The CO_2 is then separated by a newly-designed membrane, and sent offshore, using a corrosion-resistant pipeline. The CO_2 goes to an oilfield. The CO_2 is stored in the oilfield, several km below sea level, instead of being vented into the atmosphere from the power station.

Types of carbon capture technologies

Pre-combustion CO_2 Capture: The pre-combustion capture technology aims to remove or minimize CO_2 from the fuel before it is combusted. From natural gas CO_2 separation is routinely done by scrubbing before it is combusted. Coal needs to be, gasified before CO_2 separation. Integrated Gasification Combined Cycle (IGCC) technology is an appropriate choice. The CO_2 from coal gas should be removed at the higher temperature of gasification so as to reduce overall energy consumption. The CO_2 sequestration studies to find the materials—rare earths, composites and absorbents—which can perform at these high temperatures has been a research challenge. The development of the right materials that can withstand the required temperature for capturing CO_2 emanating from the coal Syngas is the foremost requirement. Other requirements are re-generality of the material and the cost-effectiveness of the separation method. After removing CO_2 hydrogen remains as pollution free fuel.

Post Combustion CO_2 Capture: The post-combustion CO_2 capture technology is concerned with CO_2 separation from the flue gas of a conventional power plant. The flue gas is dirty since it contains many other pollutants besides CO_2. The CO_2 can be captured by using techniques of chemical absorption, physical adsorption, cryogenic separation and membrane separation. The amine based solvent separation is well known technology, but the challenge lies in regeneration of the solvent and development of cost-effective adsorbents. New techniques like pressure and volume swing absorption cycles and use of polymeric membranes are being investigated. Vast possibilities exist for materials development in CO_2 sequestration research. The estimated cost of post combustion CO_2 capture and storage has also been worked out. In electricity generation, the application of CCS may double the cost of generation, depending on the technology used. CO_2 capture is estimated to cost about 70% of the total (the remaining is for transportation and storage) and the energy penalty is also significantly high.

Oxy-fuel combustion capture: In oxy-fuel combustion, nearly pure oxygen is used for combustion instead of air, resulting in a flue gas that is mainly CO_2 and H_2O. If fuel is burnt in pure oxygen, the flame temperature is excessively high, but CO_2 and/or H_2O-rich flue gas can be recycled to the combustor to moderate this. Oxygen is usually produced by low temperature (cryogenic) air separation and novel techniques to supply oxygen to the fuel, such as membranes and chemical looping cycles are being developed. The power plant systems of reference for oxy-fuel combustion capture systems are the same as those noted above for post-combustion capture systems.

Methods of carbon sequestration technologies

Biological Route: The biological route to capture CO_2 from flue gas requires an algae pond in the vicinity of a thermal power plant. Development of strains with high productivity appears to be the most cost-effective solution. But the greatest challenge is to isolate algae and genetically improve algal strain for both higher oil content and overall productivity. Marine algae could also form a possible solution for thermal power plants situated along the sea coast. Micro-mediated CO_2 sequestration using carbonic anhydrase offers another option. A proper understanding of enzymes and hetero-trophic microbial systems would help in stabilizing atmospheric carbon through photo-autotrophic and

245

non-photosynthetic CO_2 fixation processes.

Ocean Sequestration: Oceans are vastly unexplored option for CO_2 storage. Oceans have higher CO_2 flux than the atmosphere. The options for storing CO_2 can be on the surface, below the surface and on the deep sea floor. However, its effect on the marine ecosystem and living resources is yet to be assessed. The lowest estimate of CO_2 that can be stored in the Sea floor of ocean basins in a super cooled liquid state permanently is approximately 5000 giga tones (Gt).

Terrestrial Sequestration: Some other methods for CO_2 sequestration and storage are also under investigation. Terrestrial sequestration aims at biological amplification of carbon fixation in soil and biota. Increasing forest cover is considered the most appropriate and cost-effective proposition as a means of mitigation of climate change. However, it requires enormous data on carbon stocks, rate of sequestration and soil emission over different land covers. Recent advances in modern biology, including advancement in genomic sciences, provide new methods for enhancement of the photosynthetic reaction rate in plants for CO_2 sequestration. Such genetic approaches are expected to increase crop productivity in the long-run.

Underground Storage: Many new concepts and also being developed for CO_2 sequestration and storage. For example, the use of deep underground formations like saline aquifers and basalt rocks for storage of bulk of CO_2. While saline waters at a depth of 800m or more could safely dissolve CO_2 without contamination of ground water, basalts are expected to provide solid cap rocks and thus a higher level of integrity for CO_2 storage on geological time scales. Basalt rocks react with CO_2 and can convert it into mineral carbonates. Such inter-trappean zones between basalt flows are considered to be most stable. The Columbia River basin in USA has shown encouraging results in CO_2 storage in basalts.

Enhanced Oil Recovery: CO_2 injection as a secondary method of enhanced oil recovery is another promising technology. The CO_2 injected in depleting oil or natural gas reservoirs is expected to increase the viscosity of leftover crude and result in oil recovery. Enhanced oil recovery from oil fields and coal bed methane recovery in coal seams are additional options for CO_2 storage. Business models on these lines are also being developed. However, very little knowledge base exists in these areas and results are still in their infancy. It requires a greater thrust to make CO_2 sequestration commercially viable.

Conclusion

The above mentioned research on carbon capture and sequestration has focused on capture from large point sources. Each of the capture options has its particular benefits. Post-combustion capture and oxyfuel have the potential to be retrofitted to existing coal-fired power stations and new plants constructed over the next 10-20 years. Pre-combustion capture utilising IGCC is potentially more flexible, opening up a wider range of possibilities for coal, including a major role in a future hydrogen economy. All the options for capturing CO_2 from power generation have higher capital and operating costs as well as lower efficiencies then conventional power plants without capture. Capture is typically the most expensive part of the CCS chain. Costs are higher than for plants without CCS because more equipment must be built and operated. Around 10-40% more energy is required with CCS than without. Energy is required mostly to separate the CO_2 from other gases and to compress it, but some is also used to transport the CO_2 to the injection site and inject it underground. As CCS and power generation technology become more efficient and better integrated, the increased energy use is likely to fall significantly below early levels. Much of the work on capture is focused on lowering costs and improving efficiency as well as improving the integration of the capture and power generation components. These improvements will reduce energy requirements.

References

1. Anand B. Rao, Edward S. Rubin, David W. Keith, M. Granger Morgan. Evaluation of potential cost reductions from improved amine-based CO_2 capture systems. *Energy Policy, 34(18),* 2006, 3765-3772.
2. Anand B. Rao and Edward S. Rubin. A Technical, Economic, and Environmental Assessment of Amine-based CO2 Capture Technology for Power Plant greenhouse Gas Control. *Environmental Science and Technology, 36(20),* 2002, 4467-4475.
3. Audus H., Freund P. The costs and benefits of mitigation: A full fuel-cycle examination of technologies for reducing greenhouse gas emissions. *Energy Conversion and Management, 38,* 1997, S595-S600.
4. Bachu, S., & Adams, J. J. Sequestration of CO_2 in geological media in response to climate change: capacity of deep saline aquifers to sequester CO_2 in solution. *Energy Conversion and Management, 44,* 2003, 3151-75.
5. Bettina Susanne Hoffmann, Alexandre Szklo. Integrated gasification combined cycle and carbon capture: A risky option to mitigate CO_2 emissions of coal-fired power plants. *Applied Energy, 88(11),* 2011, 3917-3929.
6. Davison J. Performance and costs of power plants with capture and storage of CO_2. *Energy, 32,* 2007, 1163-1176.
7. Duan H. The public perspective of carbon capture and storage for CO_2 emission reductions in china. *Energy policy., 38(9),* 2010, 5281-9.
8. Douglas Aaron and Costas Tsouris. Separation of CO_2 from flue gas: A Review. *Separation Science and Technology, 40(1-3),* 2005, 321-348.

9. Elizabeth J. Wilson, S. Julio Friedmann and Melisa F. Pollak. Research for development: Incorporating Risk, Regulation and Liability for Carbon Capture and Sequestration. *Environmental Science and Technology, 41(17),* 2007, 5945-5952.

10. Eric Favre. Carbon dioxide recovery from post-combustion processes: Can gas permeation membranes complete with absorption? *Journal of Membrane Science, 294(1-2),* 2007, 50-59.

11. Green D. A., Brian S. Turk, Raghubir P. Gupta, Jeffery W. Portzer, William McMichael, Douglas Harrison. Capture of carbon dioxide from flue gas using solid regenerable sorbents. *International Journal of Environmental Technology and Management, 4(1-2),* 2004, 53-67.

12. Herzog H., Drake E., Adams E. CO2 Capture, Reuse, and Storage Technologies for Mitigation Global Climate Change, A White Paper Final Report, energy laboratory, Massachusetts Institue of Technology, Massachusetts Avenue Room E40-455, Cambridge, MA. 1997.

13. Herzog H.J. and Drake E.M. Carbon dioxide recovery and disposal from large energy systems. *Environment and Resources, 21,* 1996, 145-166.

14. Hitchon B. Aquifer Disposal of Carbon Dioxide: Pilot Experiment for Geological Sequestration of Carbon Dioxide in Saline Aquifer Brine Formations Hydrodynamic and Mineral Trapping–Proof of Concept; Geoscience Publishing, 1998, Sherwood Park, Alberta, Canada.

15. Houping Huang and Shih-Ger Chang. Method to regenerate ammonia for the capture of carbon dioxide. *Energy and Fuels, 16(4),* 2002, 904-910.

16. Ishibashi M., Ota H., Akutsu N., Umeda S., Tajika M., Ijumi J., Yasutake A., Kabata T., Kageyama Y. Technology for removing carbon dioxide from power plant flue gas by the physical adsorption method. *Energy Conversion Management, 37(6-8),* 1996, 929-933.
17. Jennie C. Stephens, Carbon Capture and Storage, 2009, http://www.eoearth.org/article/Carbon_ca pture_and_storage
18. Jin H., Gao L., Han W., Hong H. Prospect option of CO_2 capture technology suitable for china. *Energy. 35,* 2010, 499-506.
19. Jose D. Figueroa, Timothy Foult, Sean Plasynski, Howard Mcllvried, Rameshwar D. Srivastava. Advances in CO_2 capture technology- The U. S. Department of Energy's Carbon Sequestration Program. *International Journal of Green house Gas Control, 2(1),* 2008, 9-20.
20. Juan C. Abanades, Edward S. Rubin, Edward J. Anthony. Sorbent Cost and Performance in CO_2 Capture Systems. *Industrial and Engineering Chemistry Research,* 43(13), 2004, 3462-3466.
21. Kanniche M., Rene Gros-Bonnivard, Philippe Jaud, Jose Valle-Macros, Jean-Marc Amann, Chakib Bouallou. Pre-combustion, post-combustion and oxy-combustion in thermal power plant for CO_2 capture. *Applied Thermal Engineering, 30(1),* 2010, 53-62.
22. Ki Bong Lee, Michael G. Beaver, Hugo S. Caram and Shivaji Sircar. Reversible Chemisorbents for Carbon dioxide and their Potential Applications. *Industrial and Engineering Chemistry Research, 47(21),* 2008, 8048-8062.
23. Nakagawa K. and Ohashi T. A Novel Method of CO2 capture from High Temperature Gases. *Journal of Electrochemical Society, 145(4),* 1997, 1344-1346.

24. Plasynski S. I., Litynski J. T., McIlvried H. G. and Srivastava R. D. Progress and New Developments in Carbon Capture and Storage. *Critical Reviews in Plant Sciences, 28(3),* 2009, 123-138.
25. Raihi K., Edward S. Rubin, Schrattenholzer L. Prospects for carbon capture and sequestration technologies assuming their technological learning. *Energy, 29,* 2004, 9-10.
26. Renato Baciocchi, Giuseppe Storti, Marco Mazzotti. Process design and energy requirement for the capture of carbon dioxide from air. *Chemical Engineering and Processing: Process Intensification, 45(12),* 2006, 1047-1058.
27. Reeve D.A. The Capture and Storage of Carbon Dioxide Emissions; Office of Energy Research and Development Natural Resources, 2000, Ottawa, Ontario, Canada.
28. Richard S. Middleton, Jeffrey M. Blielicki. A scalable infrastructure model for carbon capture and storage: *SimCCS. Energy Policy, 37,* 2009, 1052-1060.
29. Schell J., Casas N., Pini R., Mazzotti M. Pure and binary adsorption of CO_2, H_2, and N_2 on activated carbon. *Adsorption, 18,* 2012, 49-65.
30. Stephens, J. Growing interest in carbon capture and storage (CCS) for climate change mitigation. SUSTAINABILITY: SCIENCE, PRACTICE, & POLICY *2(2),* 2006, 4–13.
31. Steven J. Davis, Ken Caldeira, H. Damon Mathews. Future CO_2 emissions and climate change from existing energy infrastructure. *Science,* 329(5997), 2010, 1330-1333.
32. Terry F. Wall. Combustion processes for carbon capture. *Proceedings of the Combustion Institute, 31(1),* 2007, 31-47.

33. VanderWiel D.P., Zilka-Marco J.L., Wang Y., Tonkovich A.Y., Wegeng R.S. Carbon Dioxide Conversions in Microreactors; Pacific North-west National Laboratory, 1999, Richland, WA.

34. White Curt M., Strazisar Brian R., Granite Evan J. and Hoffman James S. Separation and capture of CO2 from large stationary sources and Sequestration in geological formations – coal beds and deep saline aquifers. *Journal of the Air & Waste management Association, 53,* 2003, 645-715.

35. Wilson M. A., Wrubleski R. M. and Yarborough L. Recovery of CO_2 from power plant flue gases using amines. *Energy Conversion and Management. 33(5-8),* 1992, 325-331.

Chapter- XII

Impact of Displacement, Resettlement and Rehabilitation on Happiness and Life Satisfaction among Residents in Town of Harsood (M.P.)

Ushakiran Agrawal*

Abstract

Narmada valley development in Madhya Pradesh and Gujrat has caused mass scale displacement, resettlement and rehabilitation. The entire town of Harsood has been shifted as the old settlement got submerged in Indira Sagar dam built across Narmada river This town is situated almost 200 Kms south west of Bhopal and remained a center of Narmada Bachao Aandolan. The displacement, resettlement and rehabilitation has direct impact on human psychology which is measurable in terms of happiness and life satisfaction. Although the problem is wide spread and it has given rise many movement across the country, there has always been a need of systematic psychological studies. Usually during displacement the villages and towns are scattered over different places disturbing the entire socio-cultural and economic life style of displaced communities. But such kind of compensation may not satisfactorily counter balance for the social, cultural, psychological and ecological disturbances, they need to be rehabilitated in other senses that is socially, economically, psychologically and ecologically as well. The town of Harsood is systematic resettlement site where the entire community has been shifted and therefore I found it perfect case for study. Sample of 100 persons were tested on happiness and life satisfaction scale and the results will definitely show changes in some dimensions of the scale , as well as happiness level will be low among such persons.

Key words–*Happiness, Life Satisfaction, Resettlement, Rehabilitation*

*Department of Psychology, Govt. D. B. Girls P.G. College Raigarh Chhatish Garh, India

Introduction

Ideologically, this line of research is rooted in 18th century enlightenment thinking. From this perspective, the purpose of existence is life itself, rather than the service of King or God. Self-actualization and happiness become central values. Society itself is seen as a means for providing citizens with the necessities for a good life. In the 19th century, this conviction manifested itself in the utilitarian creed that the best society is one which provides 'the greatest happiness for the greatest number'. In the 20th century it has inspired large scale attempts at social reform and influenced the development of the welfare state. Efforts towards the creation of a better society manifested themselves in attacks on the evils of ignorance, illness and poverty. Consequently, progress was measured by literacy, control of epidemic disease and the elimination of hunger. Social statistics were developed to record the extent to which progress in these areas had been achieved. Advances in the combat of these social ills were followed by efforts to create welfare-states that ensure a good life for everybody, in particular a good material standard of living. The extent of progress in that area was expressed in terms of monetary gains, security of income and the degree of income-equality. This gave rise to an abundance of social research on poverty and social-inequality, which today is still a major research tradition.

When used at the societal level, only the former meaning applies. When it is that the quality of life of the people in a country is poor, it means that essential conditions are lacking, such as sufficient food, housing and health care. In other words: the country is not 'live able' for its inhabitants. At the individual level, the term quality of life can take on both meanings. When we say that somebody doesn't have a good life, we may mean that he/she lacks things deemed indispensable and/or that this person does not thrive. These conditions may coincide, but this is not necessarily the case. A person can be rich, powerful and popular, but still be troubled. On the other hand, someone who is poor, powerless and isolated, may nevertheless be thriving both mentally and physically. I refer to these variants as respectively: 'presumed' quality of life and 'apparent' quality of life.

Life-satisfaction is one of the indicators of 'apparent' quality of life. Together with indicators of mental and physical health, it indicates how well people thrive. Data about life-satisfaction is used for several purposes. The most elementary use of life-satisfaction data is to estimate apparent quality of life within a country or a specific social group. This is typically done to assess the extent of a social problem or issue and to recommend possible policy interventions.

High satisfaction suggests that the quality of life, in the population concerned, is good. Though conditions may not be ideal, it is apparently acceptable for most of the population. Low satisfaction marks serious shortcomings of some kind. For example the assessment of life-satisfaction among single people. In all modern nations, single persons express less pleasure with life than married persons, and the divorced and widowed frequently express the lowest levels of satisfaction with life.

This difference in life-satisfaction between those who are single and those with a partner is in fact greater than that expressed between rich and poor (Veenhoven, 1984:6/4). This is commonly explained in terms of 'deprivation'. Apparently, singles lack something essential in life. A problem is that dissatisfaction with life means that *something* is wrong, but it does not indicate *what*. The discontent of the unmarried could be due to negative labeling, but it can also be attributed to loneliness and lack of social support. A related application of life-satisfaction data is the monitoring through time. If average satisfaction levels increase, this suggests that the quality of life in the country or social group has improved.

Definition of Life Satisfaction

"Life satisfaction "is one among a range of concepts that is assumed to reflect the conditions of 'a good life'. This section aims to clarify the relationship between life satisfaction and the two related concepts of quality of life and subjective well-being. Subjective well-being also provides the theoretical context for the definition of life satisfaction applied in the thesis. The distinction between a top-down and bottom-up theoretical framework for life satisfaction judgments is also addressed. The concept of quality of life is frequently used to describe "the good life" within several disciplines such as economy, sociology, psychology, medicine, and health-care. The contents and specific measures of quality of life, however, vary both between and within disciplines (Farquhar, 1995). The emphasis ranges from standards of living in economy to perceived health status in medicine. In fact, more than 1000 measures of various aspects of quality of life have been identified (Hughes & Hwang, 1996) and more than 100 definitions of quality of life have been proposed (Cummins, 1997). In spite of the lack of a widely accepted definition most definitions of quality of life include a multidimensional functional status aspect and a subjectivity aspect (Muldoon, Barger, Flory, & Manuck, 1998). Multidimensional functional status incorporates physical well-being, functional ability, emotional well-being, and social well-being and subjectivity refers to the individual's own perception of his or her quality of life (Muldoon et al., 1998). Accordingly, whereas the subjectivity aspect of quality of life resembles life satisfaction, there is a multidimensional functional status dimension of the quality of life concept that life satisfaction clearly excludes.

Life satisfaction is the way a person perceives how his or her life has been and how they feel about where it is going in the future. It is a measure of well-being as well as a cognitive, global judgment. It is having a favorable attitude of one's life as a whole. Life satisfaction has been measured in relation to economic standing, amount of education, experiences, and the people's residence as well as many other topics.

Life satisfaction can reflect experiences that have affected a person in a positive way. These experiences have the ability to motivate people to pursue and reach their goals There are two emotions that may affect how people perceive their lives. Hope and optimism both consist of cognitive processes that are usually oriented towards the reaching of goals and the perception of those goals. Previous modelling showed that positive views and life satisfaction were completely mediated by the concept of self-esteem, and the different way ideas and events are perceived by people. Several studies found that self-esteem plays a definite role in influencing life satisfaction. There is also a homeostatic model that also supports these findings. One's mood and outlook on life can also influence one's own perception of their life satisfaction. It is proposed that overall life satisfaction comes from within an individual based on the individual's personal values and what he or she holds important. For some it is family, for others it is love, and for others it is money or other material items; either way, it varies from one person to another. Economic materialism can be considered a value. Previous research found that materialistic individuals were predominantly male, and that materialistic people also reported a lower life satisfaction level than their non-materialistic counterparts. The same is true of people who value money over helping other people; this is because the money they have can buy them the assets they deem valuable. Materialistic people are less satisfied with life because they constantly want more and more belongings, and once those belongings are obtained they lose value, which in turn causes these people to want more belongings and the cycle continues. If these materialistic individuals do not have enough money to satisfy their craving for more items, they become more dissatisfied. This has been referred to as a hedonic treadmill. On the contrary, if an individual does not hold the acquisition of wealth as a high priority, his or her personal financial state will not make a difference on how happy he or she is with life overall. Individuals reporting a high value on traditions and religion reported a higher level of life satisfaction. This is also true for reported routine churchgoers and people who pray frequently. Conveniently, the idea of religion and church are selfless, non-materialistic acts, which logically concludes why the opposite effect is true of people who hold opposite values as priority. Other individuals that reported higher levels of life satisfaction were people who valued creativity and people who valued respect for and from others—two more seemingly qualities not related to material goods. Because hard times come around and oftentimes people count on their peers and family to help them through, it is no surprise that a higher life satisfaction level was reported of people who had social support, whether it be friends, family, or church. The people who personally valued material items were found to be less satisfied overall in life as opposed to people who attached a higher amount of value with interpersonal relationships.

Life satisfaction is an overall assessment of feelings and attitudes about one's life at a particular point in time ranging from negative to positive. It is one of three major indicators of well-being: life satisfaction, positive effect, and negative affect (Diener, 1984). Although satisfaction with current life circumstances is often assessed in research studies, Diener, Suh, Lucas, & Smith (1999)also include the following under life satisfaction: desire to change one's life; satisfaction with past; satisfaction with future; and significant other's views of one's life." (Beutell), Indeed, Suh et al. (1998) found that the correlation between life satisfaction and the prevalence of positive affect is higher in individualistic cultures, whereas in collectivistic cultures affect and adhering to norms are equally important for life satisfaction.

Life satisfaction is a more complex concept than the attainment of goals or the feeling good about oneself. It has the following five variables. Neugarten, Havighurst, and Tobin's (1961) theoretical framework provided an operational definition of the latent variable of life satisfaction which consists of the five following variables.

The five factors while determine the life satisfaction are (Neugarten et al., 1961) –

1. Zest vs. apathy relates to an enthusiasm of response to life in general and was not related to any specific type of activity, such as social or intellectual engagements. A subject who was enthusiastic about sitting home reading was scored as high as an energetic person was on this scale. Physical energy as well as intellectual energy and other highly involved pursuits contributed to a high score.
2. Resolution and fortitude measures the respondents' active acceptance of personal responsibility for their lives rather than passively accepting or condoning what has happened to them. Erikson's integrity is similar in conceptualization and relates to the meaningfulness of life and the lack of fear of death.
3. Congruence between desired and achieved goals measures the relative difference between desired and achieved goals

caused one to be satisfied or dissatisfied with life in this rating

4. Self-concept is based on one's present emotional, physical, and intellectual dimensions. Persons who do not feel old but are concerned with their appearance and judge themselves to be wise and competent tend to rate themselves higher on this factor. Past successful living may contribute to this component but only indirectly.

5. Mood tone. The final factor, mood tone, relates to optimism and happiness and other positive affective responses. Depression, sadness loneliness, irritability, and pessimism are feelings that would result in very low scores. Assessing life satisfaction is more complex than just measuring happiness but happiness with the present life state is an important contributor.

6. Life Satisfaction is "an operational definition of 'successful aging'" (Neugarten at al., 1961).

Happiness

Happiness is a mental or emotional state of well-being characterized by positive or pleasant emotions ranging from contentment to intense joy. A variety of biological, psychological, religious, and philosophical approaches have striven to define happiness and identify its sources. Various research groups, including positive psychology.

The Three Dimensions of Happiness

[Positive Psychology] takes you through the countryside of pleasure and gratification, up into the high country of strength and virtue, and finally to the peaks of lasting fulfillment: meaning and purpose (Seligman 2002, p. 61).

According to Seligman, we can experience three kinds of happiness: 1) pleasure and gratification, 2) embodiment of strengths and virtues and 3) meaning and purpose. Each kind of happiness is linked to positive emotion but from his quote, you can see that in his mind there is a progression from the first type of happiness of pleasure/gratification to strengths/virtues and finally meaning/purpose.

The Pleasant Life: Past, Present & Future

Seligman provides a mental "toolkit" to achieve what he calls the pleasant life by enabling people to think constructively about the past, gain optimism and hope for the future and, as a result, gain greater happiness in the present.

Dealing with the Past

Among Seligman's arsenal for combating unhappiness with the past is that which we commonly and curiously find among the wisdom of the ages: gratitude and forgiveness. Seligman refers to American society as a "ventilationist society" that "deem[s] it honest, just and even healthy to express our anger." He notes that this is often seen in the types of therapy used for issues, problems and challenges. In contrast, Seligman extols the East Asian tendency to quietly deal with difficult situations. He cites studies that find that those who refrain from expressing negative emotions and in turn use different strategies to cope with the stresses of life also tend to be happier (Seligman 2002,).

Optimism about the Future

When looking to the future, Seligman recommends an outlook of hope and optimism.

Happiness in the Present

After making headway with these strategies for dealing with negative emotions of the past and building hope and optimism for the future, Seligman recommends breaking habituation, savoring experiences and using mindfulness as ways to increase happiness in the present.

The Role of Positive Emotion

Many studies have shown that positive emotions are frequently accompanied by fortunate circumstances (e.g., longer life, health, large social networks, etc.). For example, one study observed nuns who were, for the most part, leading virtually identical lifestyles. It seemed that the nuns who expressed positive emotions more intensely and more frequently in their daily journals also happened to outlive many of the nuns who clearly did not. Another study used high school yearbook photos of women to see if the ultimate expression of happiness (a smile) might also be used as an indicator as to how satisfied they might be 20 years later. When surveyed, those who were photographed with genuine, "Duchenne" smiles were more likely to find themselves, in their mid-life, married with families and involved in richer social lives.

In short, positive emotions are frequently paired with happy circumstances. And while we might be tempted to assume that happiness causes positive emotions, Seligman wonders, instead, whether positive emotions cause happiness. If so, what does this mean for our life and our happiness?

The Good Life: Embodying 6 Virtues & Cultivating The 24 Strengths

The strengths and virtues [...] function against misfortune and against the psychological disorders, and they may be the key to building resilience (Seligman 2002).

Virtues

One notable contribution that Seligman has made for Positive Psychology is his cross-cultural study to create an "authoritative classification and measurement system for the human strengths". He and Dr. Christopher Peterson, a top expert in the field of hope and optimism, worked to create a classification system that would help psychologist measure positive psychology's effectiveness. They used good character to measure its efficacy because good character was so consistently and strongly linked to lasting happiness. In order to remain true to their efforts to create a universal classification system, they made a concerted effort to examine and research a wide variety of religious and philosophical texts from all over the world (Seligman 2002, p. 132).

They were surprised to find 6 particular virtues that were valued in almost every culture, valued in their own right (not just as a means to another end) and are attainable.

These 6 core virtues are:

1. wisdom & knowledge
2. courage
3. love & humanity
4. justice
5. temperance
6. spirituality & transcendence

Strengths

For Seligman, the strengths are the "route" through we achieve virtues in our life.

Seligman clarifies the difference between talents and strengths by defining strengths as moral traits that can be developed, learned, and that take effort. Talents, on the other hand, tend to be inherent and can only be cultivated from what exists rather than what develops through effort (Seligman 2002). Seligman sees the healthy exercise and development of strengths and virtues as a key to the good life – a life in which one uses one's "signature strengths every day in the main realms of your life to bring abundant gratification and authentic happiness." The good life is a place of happiness, good relationships and work, and from this point, Seligman encourages people to go further to seek a meaningful life in the continual quest for happiness (Seligman 2002, p. 161).

The Meaningful Life

Meaning & Flow

Positive emotion alienated from the exercise of character leads to emptiness, in authenticity, depression and, as we age, to the gnawing realization that we are fidgeting until we die (Seligman 2002).

Here Seligman states, rather dismally, that there are no shortcuts to happiness. While the pleasant life might bring more positive emotion to one's life, to foster a deeper more enduring happiness, we need to explore the realm of meaning. Without the application of one's unique strengths and the development of one's virtues towards an end bigger than one's self, one's potential tends to be whittled away by a mundane, inauthentic, empty pursuit of pleasure.

Seligman expands on the work of his contemporary and colleague, Mihaly Csikszentmihalyi, in the area of "flow" to explain, in part, what he means by the meaningful life. Investing oneself into creative work creates a greater sense of meaning in life and accordingly, a greater sense of happiness.

Altruism

Kindness [...] consists in total engagement and in the loss of consciousness (Seligman 2002).

The exercise of kindness is a gratification in contrast to pleasure. As a gratification, it calls on your strengths to rise to an occasion and meet a challenge, particularly in the service of others.

Previous Study: Review of Literature

Martin and Jiménez (2012) studied on - An Evaluation of Life Satisfaction within the Migratory Experience According to Psychosocial Variables This study attempts to discover which psychosocial variables effect whether a displaced person evaluates their migratory experience and their life in the new context as positive. The psychosocial variables studied are: social support, individual self-esteem, social identity, analysis of endo \group and exo group, assimilation of host culture, and perception of the assessment of the host culture and level of retention of the original culture. The general objective is to discover to what degree these variables predict the level of life satisfaction in the new city of residence. Following an analysis of the data, we find that social support predicts satisfaction in 23.3%. Furthermore, in order to generalise these findings across the overall immigrant population, resident in Spain, a comparison of three Spanish cities is carried out: Barcelona, Madrid and Málaga. The results show that although an identical pattern cannot be applied to all three cities, but in conclusion we can say that the variables with greater success in predicting life satisfaction are: social support, assimilation and assessment of host culture and self-esteem.

Methodology

Nature of the Problem

i. To study the impact of displacement, resettlement and rehabilitation on different dimensions of life satisfaction on the five dimensions namely -Mental, Family, Job, Social, and Marital as a function of gender.

ii. To study the happiness level in the displaced, resettled and rehabilitated in the town of Harsood (M.P.) as a function of gender.

Hypotheses

i. Displacement resettlement and rehabilation has an impact on the different dimensions of life satisfaction i.e. mental, family, job, social and marital, especially on mental and family dimensions as a function of gender.

ii. Happiness will become less after displacement, resettlement and rehabilitation and its amount will vary with gender.

Sample

Consists of 99 residents 68 male and 31 female, of new Harsood their age ranging from 30 to 65 yrs of Harsood shifted in to new place near Chhannera , sampling was done on incidental –cum- random basis.

Tools

Pramod Kumar and Jayshree Dhyan's. Life satisfaction Scale having 54 items , having 5 dimensions-Mental, Family, Job, Social, and Marital will be used for measuring life satisfaction, happiness will be measured by using a scale by Dr J.C. Ajwani And Amba Sethi.

Statistical Treatment

Mean differences will be computed with the help of using t- test, and differences will be observed among five dimensions of life satisfaction among male and female residents of Harsood similarly differences in happiness levels will be studied with reference to gender.

Procedure

Data will be collected in small groups after giving instructions and making rapport with them.

Result and Discussion

 i. On the mental dimension of life satisfaction (TABLE 1) t value 11.17 was found to be significant at .01 level showing that male and female residents of Harsood differ in this dimension, however the mean of women's is found to be higher i.e. 12.54 than men i.e. 9.89 showing that women have more mental - life satisfaction than men.

 ii. On job dimension, the amount of life satisfaction is (TABLE 2) the t value 14.48 was also significant at .01 level showing difference in amount of life satisfaction (on job dimension) among males and females. On this dimension the means are found to be higher for men (7.25) as compares to women (2.62) showing that men have more life satisfaction on job dimension.

 iii. On social dimension of life satisfaction the t value is 60.89 (TABLE 3) again significant at higher level i.e. .01 on the basis of gender. In this dimension mean for women is found to be higher (10.93) as compared to men (8.94) showing women have more life satisfaction on social dimension.

 iv. The t value on marital dimension of life satisfaction among males and females is 63.58 significant at higher level (TABLE 4), On this dimension again women are found higher i.e.10.67 as compared to the mean of men i.e.8.36, showing higher satisfaction on this dimension than males, related to their compassionate nature and adjustment which they receive from their childhood during sex role training.

v. While seeing the difference in family dimension of life satisfaction the t value is 166.48 significant on higher level, (TABLE 5) for men 4.92 and for women 5.92 women slightly higher on this dimension. See Fig 1 a pie diagram t values on all five dimensions namely (mental, job, social, marital and family)

vi. When happiness was analyzed the mean is higher in the cases of females, (76.67) and lower on the side males , showing that women in our society are nurtured to feel happy even in difficult situations they are taught in childhood to be accommodative , in nature and they are trained to adjust in all circumstances while receiving sex role training , but in case of males mean is 71.57 , (TABLE -6) males are taught to be competitive,   less accommodative hence in difficult situations they are prone to be less happy as compared to women, t value was significant at .01 level showing a remarkable difference in men and women in happiness confirming the hypothesis   that Happiness will become less after displacement, resettlement and rehabilitation, it became less as the results are on the lower side of happiness however the pre data was not collected i.e. before the displacement, resettlement and rehabilitation however it showed difference in gender and its amount varied as a function of gender , see Fig 2, bar diagram showing mean differences in happiness among males and females

Figures and Tables

TABLE -1

T-test

Differences between Male and Female Life Satisfaction in Mental Dimension

Mental	N	Mean	Sd	Mean Difference	T-Value	Sig.
Male M 9.89	68					
Female M 12.54	31	12.17	2.06	11.17	53.94	.01**

TABLE-2

T-test

Differences between Male and Female Life Satisfaction in Job Dimension

Job	N	Mean	Sd	Mean Difference	T-Value	Sig.
Male M 7.25	68					
Female M 2.61	31	6.84	4.09	5.83	14.48	.01**

TABLE -3

T test

Differences between Male and Female Life Satisfaction in Social dimension

Social		N	Mean	Sd	Mean Difference	T-Value	Sig.
Male M 8.94		68					
Female M 10.93		31	10.71	1.58	9.70	60.89	.01**

TABLE-4

T Test

Differences between Male and Female Life Satisfaction in Marital Dimension

Marital		N	Mean	Sd	Mean Difference	T-Value	Sig.
Male M 8.36		68					
Female M 10.67		31	10.16	1.43	9.16	63.58	.01**

TABLE -5

T- test

Differences between Male and Female Life Satisfaction in Family Dimension

Family		N	Mean	Sd	Mean Difference	T-Value	Sig.
Male M 4.92		68					
Female M 5.92		31	5.93	.295	4.92	166.48	.01**

Figure 1; a pie diagram t values on all five dimensions namely (mental, job, social, marital and family)

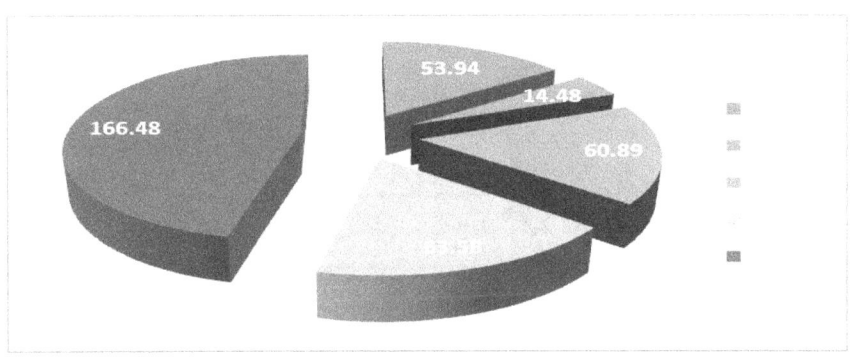

TABLE -6

T-test

Differences between Male and Female of Harsood   in Happiness.

Happiness	N	Mean	SD	Mean Difference	t-Value	Sig.
Male	68	71.57				
Female	31	76.67	9.99	71.91	71.20	.01**

Figure 2: bar diagram showing mean differences in happiness among

269

males and females

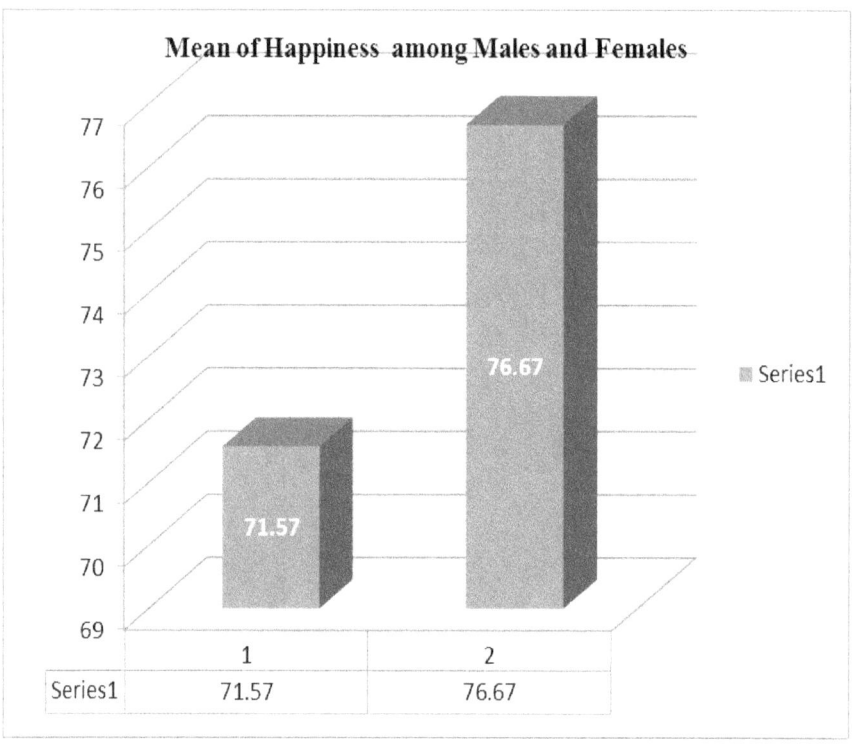

Conclusion

i. In mental, social marital and family dimensions women were found to be higher except in job dimension men showed more life satisfaction thus confirming the hypothesis, Displacement resettlement and rehabilitation has an impact on the different dimensions of life satisfaction i.e. mental, job social marital and family especially on mental social marital and family dimensions as a function of gender.

ii. Results of were on the lower side in happiness however the pre data was not collected i.e. before the displacement, resettlement and rehabilitation but results on happiness was on the lower side after displacement, resettlement and rehabilitation ,and it showed difference as a function of gender .

References

1. Operbacks mpany.website: Veenhoven.R. (1984) Conditions of Happiness, Dordrecht: Reidel, (reprinted 1991 by Kluwer Academic.)
2. Veenhoven.R. (1996). Developments in Satisfaction Research. Social Indicators Research, 37, 1-46
3. Farquhar, M. (1995). Definitions of Quality of Life: taxonomy, Journal of Advanced Nursing, 22(3), 502- 508.
4. Hughes, C., & Hwang, B. (1996). Attempts to Conceptualize and Measure Quality of Life. (Vol.1). Washington: American Association on Mental Retardation
5. Cummins, R. A. (1997). Assessing Quality of Life for People with Disabilities. In R. Brown (Ed.), Quality of Life for people with disabilities: models research and practice. (2nd ed., pp. 116-150).
6. Muldoon, M. F., Barger,S. D., Flory, J. D., & Manuck, S. B. (1998). What are Quality of Life Measurements Measuring? British Medical Journal, 316(7130), 542-545.
7. Diener E. (1984). Subjective well-being. Psychological Bulletin, 95(3), 542-575.
8. Diener, E., Emmons, R. A., Larsen, R. J., & Griffin, S., (1985). The Satisfaction with Life Scale. Journal of Personality Assessment, 49, 71-157.
9. Buetell, N. (2006). Life Satisfaction, a Sloan Work and Family Encyclopedia entry. Retrieved May 10, 2007, from the Sloan Work and Family Research Network website.
10. Suh, E., Diener, E., & Fujita, F. (1996). Events and Subjective Well-being: only recent events matter. Journal of Personality and Social Psychology, 70(5), 1091-1102.

11. Neugarten, B. L., Havighurst, R. J., & Tobin, S. S. (1961). The Measurement of Life Satisfaction. Journal of Gerontology, 16, 134-143.

12. Seligman, Martin E.P. (1991). Learned optimism: how to change your mind and your life New York, NY: Pocket Books.
13. Seligman, Martin E.P. (1996). The optimistic child: proven program to safeguard children from depression & build lifelong resilience. New York, NY: Houghton Mifflin.
14. Seligman, Martin E.P. (2002). Authentic happiness: using the new positive psychology to realize your potential for lasting fulfillment New York, NY: Free Press.
15. Seligman, Martin E.P. (2004). "Can happiness be taught?" Daedalus, Spring 2004.
16. Seligman, Martin E.P. Doing the Right Thing: Measuring Well Being for Public Policy. International Journal of Wellbeing Vol. 1, No. (2011)
17. Seligman, M.E.P. (2004). Can Happiness be Taught? Daedalus journal, Spring 2004. Escape from Freedom (U.S.), The Fear of Freedom (UK) (1941) ISBN 978-0-8050-3149-2
18. Martín, M. & Moreno-Jiménez, M. (2012). An Evaluation of Life Satisfaction within the Migratory Experience According to Psychosocial Variables. Psychology, 3 , 1248-1253. doi: 10. 4236/ psych. 2012.312A185.
19. Macarena Vallejo Martín, Maria del Pilar Moreno- Jiménez (2012).An Evaluation of Life Satisfaction within the Migratory Experience According to Psychosocial Variables, Psychology 2012. Vol.3, No.12A, 1248-1253 Published Online December 2012 in SciRes (http://www.SciRP.org/journal/psych)
20. Erich Fromm (1947) Man for himself, an inquiry into the psychology of ethics Henry Holt and Company.
21. Erich Fromm (1990) The sane society Holt Paperbacks. ISBN 9780805014020.

Chapter- XIII

Socio-ecological Implications of Hydro-power Generation: A Study of Power Projects in Himachal Pradesh

Anjali Chauhan*

Abstract

Himachal Pradesh is situated in the lap of Himalayas. Nature has compensated hill states with vast hydropower potential due to perennial rivers. Himachal Pradesh has massive hydroelectric power potential and may become the first hydropower state of India by 2020. In the present developing state of country's economy, there is a great requirement of electrical power for both industrial and agricultural use. So we need to find alternative sources so that our environment is clean and safe and protected. In Himachal Pradesh 95% of the hydropower generation is through run of river projects, though some are storage dam projects also. 120 power projects with a capacity 17,000 MW across five river basins of the state which are Satluj, Beas, Ravi, Chenab, and Yamuna have been identified by The Himachal Pradesh Power Department. Out of these 70% have been allotted and are under different stages of execution. These projects shall provide boost to States economy and earn good revenue, however these have their concerns also. The hill state of Himachal Pradesh is ecologically and geographically a fragile region. The aim of this paper is to find a judicious approach for sustainable development of hydropower and to mitigate its long-term impact on the life and environment of the people of the state of Himachal Pradesh.

Key words: Hydropower, Dams, Climate change, Environment and Sustainable development

*Assistant Professor, Department of Sociology, Govt. College Sunni, Himachal Pradesh University, Shimla, India

Introduction

Hydroelectric power is renewable and environmentally safe source of energy. It provides 1/5 of world's total electricity. In India there is an ever increasing demand of electricity for industrial, agricultural purposes and as well as for rural electrification and presently most of the energy is produced from fossil fuels mainly coal. The potential of hydroelectric energy in India is reportedly massive, and particularly in the Himalayan states, of which Himachal Pradesh constitutes an important part. The need of the hour lies in exploring into some alternative methods of energy generation which can cater to the needs of Indian population as well as help keep our environment clean safe and protected and lead to sustainable development.

The hill states of India have been compensated by nature with vast hydropower potential in lieu of sound agricultural system available in the plains. The state of Himachal Pradesh with hilly terrain abounds in this natural wealth and is making earnest efforts to exploit its water resources for developmental purposes by constructing hydropower dams. Though these dams are serving as agents of development but they have serious impacts on the lives, livelihoods, culture of local people as well as on the physical environmental conditions and the biodiversity of the concerned area. Himachal Pradesh has a power potential of about 27,000 MW. About 6,480 MW has been harnessed till now by public sector units and private and joint venture companies. The basin wise potential are; Satluj (13332 MW), Beas (5,995MW), Chenab (4032MW), Ravi (3237MW) and Yamuna (840MW) (Sharma & Rana, 2014). Looking at the fragile ecology of Himachal Pradesh it becomes pertinent to ask whether the state in the long run shall be able to sustain the increasing spate of construction of hydropower plants. Though it is true that the state needs to tap on this rich resource with which it is blessed, so as to generate revenues and help the state in reducing its financial burden. But we also need to assess the gravity of the situation and ponder in all its seriousness whether development brought about by these projects is sustainable without hampering the ecology and ecosystem of the affected areas. The question which also catches my attention is why the production of energy which is considered safe clean and renewable, is subject to increased public concerns? This paper is an attempt to find all these answers and is based on primary and secondary data. The source of primary data primarily is one on one interaction with some project affected people and interaction with members of co-operative society involved in hydropower projects in the state.

Himachal Pradesh

Himachal Pradesh known as 'abode of snow" is bound between 30°22' to 33°12' N latitude and 75°47' to 79°04' E longitude. To the east and the northeast the state forms India's border with Tibet, towards its north and northwest lies the state of Jammu & Kashmir, in the south-east is Uttaranchal, Haryana in the south and Punjab in the west and southwest. Himachal Pradesh is a mountainous state, right from the Shiwaliks and spreading up to the trans-Himalayan heights of Zanskar range with altitudes varying from 350 m to 7000 m above the mean sea level. The total geographical area of Himachal Pradesh is 55,673 sq km. Total population of the State is 68.65 lakhs (Census, 2011).The state is divided into four major physiographic zones namely Shiwalik Hills, Lesser Himalaya, Greater Himalaya and Trans Himalaya.

Himachal Pradesh is gifted with rich water resources, such as glaciers, rivers and lakes. The high altitude areas in the Lesser Himalaya and the Greater Himalaya region constitute the origins of a number of perennial rivers. The monsoon rains, in the Shiwalik hills and the Lesser Himalayan regions significantly contribute to the water yield in the rivers in Himachal Pradesh.There are more than 2500 glaciers in the state located mostly above 4000 m elevation in Pir Panjal, Greater Himalaya, Dhauladhar and Zanskar ranges. In addition, there are many smaller glaciers in Ravi basin, Dhauladhar and Pir Panjal mountain ranges. In Satluj basin there are more than 200 glaciers.

The climate of Himachal Pradesh is influenced by variation in elevation and the slope. The high mountain ranges and the southwest monsoon modify the climate of Himachal Pradesh. The weather is a cold temperate one in the middle region, humid in the southern region and cold desert in the Kinnaur and Lahaul-Spiti region. The rainfall in the state is uneven. In the Shiwalik hills the average annual rainfall is more than 2000 mm, whereas in the Trans- Himalayan region the average annual rainfall is less than 500 mm. In the Satluj valley average annual rainfall ranges from 813 to 1280 mm. At the higher altitudes the precipitation occurs as snow.

The State is home to a large variety of plant and animal species, endemic as well as which have migrated from the far off regions like Mediterranean, Tibetan region of Trans Himalaya, The Indo-Malayan, Caucasia, Northeast Asia and the Eastern Himalayan region. The vast variations in the altitude and precipitation in the State offer diverse microclimatic conditions. This results in multiplicity of habitats and ecological niches for different plant and animal species. The higher altitudes are known for a large variety of plant species, which have medicinal properties.

Major Hydropower Projects in Himachal Pradesh

Himachal Pradesh has five major river basins which are fed by five perennial rivers. Majority of Hydro power plants are on these five rivers and their tributaries. These rivers are Satluj, Ravi, Beas, Chenab and Yamuna. The Himachal Pradesh Power Department, with the help of the Himachal Pradesh State Electricity Board Corporation, has done a commendable job of identifying 120 power projects with a capacity 17,000 MW (50 per cent projects would be of 5 to 50 MW) across five river basins of the state. Ninety-five per cent projects are run-off-the-river (R-o-R) type and are located across the rivers Sutlej, Beas, Ravi, Chenab, Pabbar (a tributary of Yamuna) and their tributaries. Out of 120 projects, at least 70 per cent have been allotted and these are under different stages of execution. These projects have been initiated both by private and public sector players (SVJN, NTPC, NHPC, HPPCL, and HPSEB) almost in equal proportion.

India's first Bhakra-Nangal dam on river Satluj in Himachal Pradesh is a multipurpose dam. Similarly, many hydro-projects have been started, like; Jai Parkash Associates has already started its 1000 MW Karcham-Wangtu project across the Satluj River. As such, by 2020, Himachal Pradesh will have an additional power generation of 17,000 MW and earn good revenues. Successfully operating is the country's largest 1500

MW Nathpa Jhakri Hydropower Station and is setting new benchmarks in generation and maintenance year after year, after having tackled the silt erosion problems in under-water turbine parts.

There is no world consensus on definitions of hydro-power plants mainly because of different development policies in different countries. Based on installed capacity of hydro-power projects, classification of hydropower plants varies in countries. A general classification may be taken as: Micro: 100KW and below; Mini: 2000KW and below; Small: 25000KW and below; Medium: 100000KW and below; Large: above 100000KW (Saxena & Kumar, 2010).

Table 1: Some of the Hydro-power projects (functional) in Himachal Pradesh

Sr. No.	Name of Power Project	Installation Capacity in MW	Classification	Name of River	District
1.	Nathpa Jakhri	1500	Large	Satluj	Kinnaur
2.	Karcham Wangtu	1000	Large	Satluj	Kinnaur
3.	Chamera St-1	540	Large	Ravi	Chamba
4.	Baspa-2	300	Large	Baspa	Kinnaur
5.	Bhaba-2	120	Large	Bhaba`	Kinnaur
6.	Sanjay Vidyut Pariyojna	120	Large	Bhaba	Kinnaur
7.	Bassi	66	Medium	Beas	Mandi
8.	Girinagar	60	Medium	Giri	Sirmaur
9.	Andhra project	16.5	Small	Pabbar	Shimla
10.	Baner & Neugal	12	Small	Baner Khad	Kangra

Table 2: Hydro-power projects under execution in Himachal Pradesh

Sr. No	Name of Power project	Installation Capacity (in MW)	Classification	Name of River	District
1.	Parbati Stage-2	800	Large	Pabbar	Kullu
2.	Parbati Stage-3	520	Large	Pabbar	Kullu
3.	Kol dam	800	Large	Satluj	Bilaspur-Mandi
4.	Rampur	412	Large	Satluj	Shimla-Kullu
5.	Shongtong Karcham	450	Large	Satluj	Shimla
6.	Sainj	100	Medium	Sainj	Kullu
7.	Sorang	100	Medium	Sorang Khad	Kinnaur
8.	Uhl-3	100	Medium	Beas	Mandi
9.	Kashang 1	65	Medium	Kashang Stream	Kinnaur
10.	Kashang 2&3	130	Large	Kerang Stream	Kinnaur
11.	Sawra Kuddu	111	Large	Pabbar	Shimla
12.	Tidong 1	100	Medium	Tidong Khad	Kinnaur
13.	Tangnu Romai-1	44	Medium	Pabbar	Shimla
14	Chanju -1	36	Medium	Chanju Nallah	Chamba

Types of Hydropower Generation

Hydropower generation is carried out in three ways:

Storage dams-where a dam collects water in a reservoir and then releases it to drive turbines producing electricity. Pumped storage-where water is pumped to a higher reservoir usually during times of low priced electricity, then released to lower reservoir, again driving a turbine, usually when the electricity price is higher. Run-of-river –where the natural flow of river is used to drive a turbine.

In Himachal Pradesh most of the hydropower projects are of run of river type. Such projects get kinetic energy of rivers without building dams. A weir/barrage is constructed across the river and the flow is diverted through a long straight RCC-lined tunnel at a slope gentler than that of the river, so that the end of the tunnel reaches a far higher elevation than the bed of the river. This level difference is utilized to lead the flow to the turbines of the powerhouse to generate electricity. The water in such projects is continuously used for power generation and released simultaneously. However, the underground balancing reservoir accumulates a very negligible amount of silt in its bottom for which silt flushing is done at intervals. This system faces two inherent deficiencies. Firstly, the rivers carry very high discharge during the monsoon season and very low flows during the remaining nine months of the year. The powerhouse does not get full supply of water round the year and the installed capacity remains under-utilized. Secondly, in the absence of a storage dam, the silt in the flowing water during rainy season is not entrapped and quite often the concentration goes very high. This results in huge revenue loss.

In order to offset these two deficiencies, it is essential that one or two storage dams, are constructed in the upstream reaches of the river to entrap silt (eg:khab project on Satluj).This also helps store flood water during high flow season to be released later during the lean flow period to increase the power generation of all downstream projects by at least 30 per cent. The storage dam also prevents floods particularly in the Satluj River, where these have been attributed due to release of water from the Parchu Lake in China.

Benefits of Hydroelectric Power

Energy is important for industrialization, employment generation and overall development. Hydropower is the energy that comes from the force of moving water. The amount of electricity produced depends on the head and flow. The head being the height of water or the distance from the highest point of water to where it goes through turbine. Flow is how much water moves through the system. A typical hydroelectric plant has three parts: an electric plant where electricity is produced, a dam that can be opened or closed to control water flow and a reservoir where water can be stored. Following are the benefits of hydroelectric power. It is considered to be the cheapest way to produce electricity today, because once the dam has been built and equipment installed, the energy source that is free flowing water, is free. These plants do not emit pollutants into air as they burn no fuel. Therefore it is clean fuel source that is renewable yearly by snow and rainfall. Hydro plants produce power cheaply due to their sturdy structures and simple equipment. They are dependable and long lived and their maintenance costs are low in comparison to coal and nuclear plants. Water can be kept in reservoirs and released when needed to generate electricity, thereby making it an intermittent and flexible source of energy. Beside this the reservoirs holds water for irrigation and provide recreational opportunities such as boating.

Social Implications of Hydro-power Projects

The construction of hydro projects tend to bring about adverse social and environmental impacts, which makes people question the sustainability and legitimacy of large dams as vehicles of development. The constructions of storage dams have their own shortcomings.

Dams leads to the submergence of vast land mass causing displacement and impoverishment of large number of families. Relocation and rehabilitation of communities at locations nearby or elsewhere is a herculean task. It results in landlessness of displaced people. The land is often lost forever and only in few cases partially replaced. Relocation further results in joblessness leading to unemployment and underemployment of displaced population. Homelessness is another major side effect due to displacement. For few it may be temporary but for many it may stretch long, thereby resulting in loss of their identity and cultural impoverishment. As relocated families lose their economic power it creates social and psychological problems accompanied by feeling of injustice and vulnerability. This causes severe health problems. Their uprooting diminishes their self- sufficiency and tends to make them victims of food insecurity, as their system of local arrangements of food supply is dismantled. Further the dislocation of families brings about loss of their access to common property especially the poor and marginal families e.g. loss of forests and grazing grounds. The dispersal of their formal and informal network, local associations, community structures and social organizations all lead to loss of social capital; this tends to be the cause of their disempowerment and impoverishment.

Boomtown formation around these projects site is another adverse social impact. Due to under training and unavailability of local labor it is substituted by over importation of labor from other areas (eg labor from Bihar in Himachal).This has its own socio cultural impacts and tends to create problems of social, economic, cultural nature and health problems to local people.

Besides this construction of dams bring about unanticipated downstream changes in agricultural system as the limited floods get restricted downstream and the disruption in the flow of rich nutrients deeply affects the agricultural production, which thereby affects the livelihood and lifestyle of people.

Another social impact is the loss of cultural heritage assets as the place which before dam construction, had cultural, spiritual and religious meaning and sanctity for e.g. places of worship, symbolic markers are at times lost in dam construction and this hurts the sentiment of local people.

Ecological Implications of Hydro-power Projects

Constructions of hydro projects have negative impact on the surrounding environment. Construction of dams results in loss of wild lands and wildlife habitat. Dams lead to flooding of massive area thereby causing decomposition of vegetation and production of greenhouse gases. The water quality changes due to lack of dissolved oxygen near the bottom of reservoirs. This is toxic to fish and can lead to death of aquatic life. It is also corrosive to turbines. Dams block fish migration as they have to swim upstream to reproduce and this disrupts their spawning and migratory patterns bringing about their depletion (e.g Trout and Mahaseer).

In the present times of social, environmental and political activism it is not easy to get clearance for big projects. Obtaining environment and forest clearances from the Ministry of Environment and Forests (MoEF) and other agencies has become a big challenge. These projects are being objected to by local residents and environmentalist. They are concerned about the fallout of impounding of rivers and ruthless tunneling of hills, deforestation, and drying up of water sources. There is concern among local people that these rivers would virtually disappear from the scene. People are dependent on small streams for their needs of drinking water and irrigation, which would be affected by construction of small projects on these. The projects are being implemented in haphazard manner.

Tunnel digging and blasting leads to cracks in the houses in project vicinity. This further leads to drying of springs, grazing and agricultural fields. For e.g. 43 out of 167 water sources have dried up in villages affected by the Karchham Wangtoo project, and discharge in another 67 has gone down (tribune India). During the making of tunnel to give water a slope, the excavation material is directly dumped into river or near road side, which not only causes deterioration of water quality but also air pollution. Transmission tower lines are used to transmit electricity to other states and districts. During making of these towers many forest lands have so far been cleared. EIA reports of felling of unbelievable number of trees by individual projects including highly endangered species like Chilgoza trees. In Shimla, Kullu, Sirmaur and Bilaspur around 1,19,292 trees have been cut to construct these power lines. Apple which is the main cash crop of district Shimla and Kinnaur has witnessed decrease in crop production due to air pollution, decrease in precipitation and lack of moisture in the soil. The main reason behind the decrease in crop production and small size of apples are the dust which arises from dumping of excavation material, which results in air pollution. The dust affects the flower of plant during its time of pollination, as it settles down on the stigma of the flower.

Shimla and Kinnaur and Chamba especially are known for their natural beauty and cool and pleasant temperature. But due to construction of these hydro projects the temperature in these areas has been increasing. The main reason behind it is greenhouse gasses that are released into the atmosphere from air pollution. Global warming is changing climate globally and is causing significant changes to various regions of the project affected area. Weather cycle is changing, as a result it sometimes leads to excessive rains and at times create drought like conditions. An irony of the state of affairs is that, these projects are constructed on faults which means that the risk of earthquakes always loom large in these hydro project sites. Frequent landslides are another problem in such areas and it disrupts the normal life of the inhabitants as it disconnects people with other areas.

To run the projects large number of laborers' are hired who live in labor camps along the banks of stream or river and pose significant environmental threat, as most of these labor camps do not have adequate provision for wastewater and sewage. Consequently the adjacent stream, which is invariably used downstream for washing, irrigation and other purposes, and stream bank, are severely contaminated. The negative environmental, health impacts of these labor camps are felt and complained about by the local residents. The habitat around the project site is affected and there is decline in diversity due to increase in the collection of fuel wood.

Most of the sites where these projects are located have social and cultural importance to the local population due to sense of identity to their native place. Moreover, these project sites are rich in natural resources. Therefore, it becomes imperative to minimize the loss of such habitats and prevent the destruction of ecosystems upon which the region's social, ecological and economic wellbeing depends. The adjoining areas of major hydropower projects in Himachal Pradesh provide food, fodder and fuel wood to the local people because of the presence of large number of species. Therefore in order to sustain the livelihood of the rural population of these areas massive plantation of plants having medicinal, fuel wood, fodder values should be carried out in suitable areas as an alternative arrangement. It is argued that in order to keep a balanced environment, a green belt rich in ground vegetation should be created around these project areas.

Hydro-power Policy of Himachal Pradesh-2006

The 2006 Hydropower Policy seeks to bring about development in local area where the hydro projects are located. For this it requires the project developers to deposit one percent of the project cost into an account with the district commissioner. These funds, known as Local Area Development Funds, are to be allocated by the Local Area Development Authority (LADA) in order to bring about developmental activities in infrastructure and services in the project affected areas. The most important feature of the new guideline is one per cent free power to be made available by the power producer in addition to the 12 per cent free power to the state government shall be allocated for the project affected families. This one percent free power will be distributed annually as a cash transfer to every family in the project affected area to the extent of 85 per cent. And the remaining 15 per cent will be distributed among the BPL (below poverty line) families.

Under the amended power policy, the government will get free power and upfront premium from all the allotted projects. The quota of free power fixed for projects up to 5 MW is 6 percent for the first 12 years, 15 percent for up to 30 years and 24 percent for up to 40 years. After 40 years, the projects will be handed over to the government. To encourage small entrepreneurs, the government is not charging any upfront premium for projects up to 2 MW. These projects would only be allotted to residents of the state. Not more than two projects would be given to independent power producers. The new revised LADF guidelines seek the formation of separate committees under the district administration for each project with the project developer as Member Secretary. Concerned MLA shall be represented on all these Local Area Development Committees. The guidelines enhance the autonomy of Gram Panchayats to decide on schemes to be taken up and the selection of implementation agencies. They will clarify the concept of project affected area and project affected zone and make a provision of normative allocation of funds for schemes in the project area during the construction of a project. For smaller projects below 5 MW, care has been taken to ensure that wards of Gram Panchayats can alone be defined as project affected areas so that funds are not spent in other places (sndrp.in).

In addition the 2006 Hydropower Policy seeks to generate local benefits by stipulating that 70% of the project's workers be from Himachal Pradesh. Along with this it wants that permanent jobs be provided to local people by these project developers so that they do not have to leave their native place in search of steady income. These workers shall have to be registered with labor department so as to provide them with compensation in case of any untoward happening.

Himachal Pradesh has developed incentive packages to encourage private investors to develop small-scale hydroelectric- projects. Its aim is to maximize benefits from these projects and to bring about reduction in fossil fuel use, greenhouse gas emissions and thus protect forests and biodiversity in this fragile region. The policy also seeks enhancement of local economic opportunities, freeing women from the burden of collecting fuel wood and doing other household tasks, and capacity-building benefits. Keeping in mind these benefits small hydel projects are being initiated. The state Government has taken several initiatives to encourage private sector participation in small hydro power development. Himachal Pradesh is among the few States, which has streamlined and is continuously refining the various procedures/processes to minimize the bottlenecks (Himurja).

The process of exploitation of hydro potential in small hydro sector through private sector participation began during 1995-96. Since then, the allotment of project sites has been a continuous process. Till 30th November 2011, 468 small hydroelectric projects (upto 5MW capacity) with an aggregate capacity of 1176 MW have been allotted. Out of these 45 projects with an aggregate capacity of 177.55 MW have been commissioned. A goal of 500 MW through small hydro projects by the end of 2014 has been fixed (Himurja).In Himachal Pradesh small hydro power potential is more than 2000 MW. Such projects offer an attractive package of incentives. The state has well developed road network which makes easy accessibility to the sites. Moreover the peaceful industrial climate -excellent rapport between workforce and industry, cooperative labor pool/workforce, congenial climate, and well-knit communication network with FAX/ STD/ISD facilities available in all corners of the State, in all, provide conducive environment for small hydropower projects in the state.

Himachal Pradesh has already taken lead in environment protection measures and is all set to become the country's first carbon neutral state by 2020.The state government has got the World Bank sanction 1000crore loan that will enable the state sustainable management of natural resources and heritage with a focus on forests, wildlife, wetlands, livestock, mining, fisheries, waste disposal and architecture and small hydro projects.

Benefits of Small Hydro-power Projects

Small hydro projects are reliable, eco-friendly, mature and it is proven technology. They are more suited for the sensitive mountain ecology of Himachal Pradesh and can be exploited wherever sufficient water flows - along small streams, medium to small rivers. Such projects do not involve setting up of large dams or problems of deforestation, submergence or rehabilitation. Moreover they are non-polluting, and entail no waste or production of toxic gases, thereby these are environment friendly. Other benefits of small hydro projects are that they require small capital investment, have short gestation period and minimal transmission loss.

Institutional Models

Two institutional models for small hydropower development exist that have the potential to realize more sustainable, effective and equitable hydropower outcomes. These models are represented by the Sai Engineering Foundation and the Churah Cooperative Floriculture Society. Sai Engineering Foundation is a registered charitable foundation and has been involved with hydropower development since the 1990s. They own and manage their own projects and provide consulting services for other private power developers. They invest the revenue from hydropower production in social service and welfare programs in Himachal Pradesh. These activities include medical and blood donation camps, financial assistance to low income students, community-based welfare programs, working with government programs to deliver services to low income communities, and promoting cooperative societies in the field of power generation, construction, and floriculture (Sai Engineering Foundation 2011). Sai Foundation develops small hydropower projects, in a manner that prevents or mitigates the negative impacts on local livelihood strategies and is responsive to local concerns and issues.

The other is the Churah Floriculture Cooperative Society. Churah cooperative society is working to promote the economic development of low income families in the Churah Valley, a remote area in Chamba District. The cooperative's initial and on-going work involves developing floriculture using greenhouses, and marketing cut flowers to cities, as well as off-season vegetable production in neighboring Pangi Valley. They are also working to develop a small hydropower project under the framework of the 2006 Hydropower Policy. Four hundred Below Poverty Line (BPL) households, all members of the cooperative society, are involved in this effort. The cooperative society is making efforts in securing NOC from the government. The revenue from the small hydropower project, once it is commissioned, will be shared among the participation parties.

Another example is of Greenko, one of the largest operators of small hydro projects in India and continues to add medium sized hydro projects. They selectively choose projects that can be developed within a cluster, thereby increasing developmental and operational synergies. Their projects have minimal social & environmental issues as well as low gestation period due to fewer clearances and predictable construction. Many small hydel projects are run by its subsidiaries in Chamba and Shimla and Kangra districts of Himachal Pradesh, which are primarily run of river projects.

Conclusion

Both the Sai Engineering Foundation and the Churah Floriculture Cooperative Society lay emphasis on corporate ownership of small hydropower facilities and are seen as viable alternatives to current hydropower policy. Both of these organizations are accountable to local concerns and interests. Along with this, these organizations prioritize on issues that are local, social and environmental friendly.

In cases where projects do negatively affect local livelihoods, e.g. when a project renders gharats defunct, disrupts a community-managed irrigation system, or disturbs grazing or cultivated areas, then adequate compensation should be provided through a government-facilitated process. Similarly, negative environmental effects should be mitigated, for example by requiring manual cleaning of desilting tanks, installation of fish-friendly diversion weirs, adequate supply of water to support ecosystem needs, and taking care of muck depositing sites.

Measures that strengthen small hydropower projects' accountability should be developed. Measures such as requiring Environmental Impact Assessments, along with the requisite public hearings, as well as obtaining environmental clearance from the state, would go a long way to improving the sustainability of small hydropower projects in Himachal Pradesh. Such alternatives should be adopted which makes hydro project owners accountable to local communities and towards environmental concerns. The State Govt. should offer more support to cooperative societies and NGO's like Sai Engineering Foundation. Along with this the governance measures should be strengthened and the civil society should be aware and active towards environmental concerns. Before sanctioning any project, recommendations of world commission on dams must be taken into consideration which emphasized on equity, efficiency, participatory decision making, sustainability and accountability. The negative social impacts need to be pre-empted by government through proper planning and legislation; otherwise the development brought about by these hydro projects shall bring about increased social, political and environmental opposition. However, it also remains to be seen to what extent the government of Himachal Pradesh shall embrace this approach and give more teeth to its currently progressive, but not enforced, power policy which shall brighten the future of the state.

References

1. Baker, J. Mark (2014):"Socio-Ecological Impacts of Small Hydropower Projects in Himachal Pradesh." Viewed on 11June 2014. Website:http://sandrp. wordpress. com/ 2014/06/11/the-socio-ecological-impacts-of-small-hydropower-projects-in-himachal-pradesh.

2. EIA Report KWHP(2005).Comprehensive Revised EIA for 1000 MW Karcham-Wantoo Hydroelectric project, District Kinnaur, Himachal Pradesh, Jaypee Karcham Hydro Corporation Ltd, New Delhi.

3. Gaur, V.K (ed.) (1993): Earthquake Hazards and large Dams in the Himalaya, INTACH, New Delhi.

4. Harnot, S.R & Verma, R.P (2004): Himachal at a Glance, Shimla. Minerva Book House.

5. Himachal Pradesh Energy Development Agency (2000). Brochure for Entrepreneurs: Small Hydro Development in Himachal Pradesh. Shimla, India: Himachal Pradesh State electricity Board.

6. Khera, D. & Singh, M. (2001):'New Trends in the Development of Hydropower Projects in India' in Honningsvag, B et.al. (eds.), Hydropower in the new Millennium, Lisse, Balakema.

7. Kumar, A & Prasad, K. (2002): Dialogue on Dams and Development-Criteria and Guidelines for Dams, Institute of Resource Management and Economic Development.

8. Sai Engineering Foundation (2011):"Karmayoga,"Quaterly Newsletter of Sai Engineering Foundation, 1(11) New Shimla, Himachal Pradesh.

9. Saxena, Praveen and Kumar Arun2010"Hydropower Development in India" IGHEM-2010, Oct21-23, 2010, AHEC, IIT Roorke, India.

10. Sengupta, N. et.al. (2000): "Large Dams: India's Experience", a case study prepared as an input to World Commission on Dams, Cape Town.

11. Sharma, H.K & Rana, P.K (2014): Assessing the Impact of Hydroelectric Project Construction on Rivers of District Chamba of Himachal Pradesh in the Northwest Himalaya, India, International Research Journal of Social sciences, Vol. 3 (2), 21-25.

12. Sinclair, John (2003):"Assessing the Impacts of Micro Hydro Development in Kullu District, Himachal Pradesh,

India", Mountain Research and Development, Vol.23, No.1, pp.11-13.

13. WCD (2000): Dams and Development: A new framework for decision making, World Commission on Dams, Earthscan, London.

14. http://www.censusindia.gov.in/

15. http://www.ireeed.gov.in

16. http://www.tribuneindia.com

Chapter-XIV

Scenario of Dams and Fish Biodiversity in the Rivers of Himachal Pradesh

Krishan   Lal*

Abstract

Himachal Pradesh is located in the northern region of India, in Himalayas and has rivers like Sutlej, Beas, Ravi, Yamuna, Chandrabhaga and Pabbar etc. flowing through it. There are many dams like Bhakra dam, Pong dam, Pandoh dam, Chamera dam, Kol dam and Nathpa Jhakri dam etc. constructed across the rivers in Himachal Pradesh. Dams are providing clean energy needed for development but these are also causing the degradation of ecology. Fish migrates for feeding and breeding purposes. Fishes like Mahseer (Tor putitora) and Silver carp (Hypophthalmichthys molitrix) etc. shows migration. Muck and material gets released in the river during the construction of dam. Soil erosion due to construction of roads & dams, flash floods and deforestation etc. causes the deposition of silt in the reservoirs and it is degrading the ecosystem. Sufficient water should be released from the dams so that level of water may be maintained for the survival of aquatic fauna and flora downstream. Conservation measures should be taken for protection of environment. People should be educated about the importance of degrading ecology and measures for its protection. Habitat loss and habitat degradation is major reason for the decline of species. Conservation of habitat is necessary for biodiversity conservation.

Key words – Dams, Ecology, Rivers, Fish Diversity

---

*Assistant Professor, Department of Zoology, Netaji Subhash Chandra Bose Memorial Govt. College, Hamirpur, Himachal Pradesh University

Introduction

Himachal Pradesh consists of 12 districts and has an area of 55, 673 square kilometres. Many dams have been built across the rivers in Himachal Pradesh especially for the purpose of hydroelectric power generation and many more are under construction or being planned by the state government. Himachal Pradesh is rich in fish resources as it has different climatic conditions. Cold, fast flowing waters of the streams and rivers in districts Kullu, Shimla, Kinnaur and Chamba harbours the trout fishes. Carp fish farms at Deoli (Bilaspur), Alsu (Mandi), Kangra (Kangra) and Sultanpur (Chamba), Trout fish farms at Patlikuhul (Kullu), Barot (Mandi), Holi (Chamba), Sangla (Kinnaur) and Dhamwari (Shimla) are some of the fish farms in Himachal Pradesh. Fish are reared in farms for the purpose of stocking of rivers and reservoirs, for selling for culture and consumption purpose etc. Dams have different types of effects on the ecology. Dams adversely affect the fish migration due to physical obstruction. Mahseer (Tor putitora) and Silver carp (Hypophthalmichthys molitrix) are the fishes which migrates from one region of the river to the other region of river. Silver carp catches got increased to 846 t (78 %) in the year 2000-01, 974 t (83 %) in 2001-02, 1083 t (85 %) in 2002-03 due to obstruction in their migration due to the construction of Kol Dam across the river Sutlej which affected the migration and more fish got caught but this catch dwindled to 726 t (76.98 %) in 2003-04 due to failed migration and breeding [1]. Construction of dams and barrages have affected the upstream migration of Tor putitora needed for spawning, it caused depletion in population of this fish in Himachal Pradesh [2]. Fishes are getting declined from the reservoirs, rivers and streams due to the changed habitat. Density of the dams is increasing day by day. Downstream the dam, dewatering is becoming a common feature which is affecting the floral and faunal life. Life of fish depends on the phytoplanktons and zooplanktons so their less productivity affects the life of fishes adversely. Fishing is the occupation of poor people. Government is earning revenue from fisheries and also from hydroelectric power generation. There is a need to strike a balance between the two. Muck and material should not be released in the rivers. Reforestation will help in the checking of soil erosion. More silt gets deposited in the rivers and reservoirs due to deforestation, agricultural operations, construction of roads and buildings etc. Deposition of silt in the reservoirs creates hindrance to the development of fishes. Vegetation is getting submerged in the reservoir. Habitat of the terrestrial animals is getting destroyed due to damming because of water covering the terrestrial areas. Great emphasis should be given to the protection of endangered Mahseer. It is famous for the sport fishing. Close season should be continued to be followed every year in which no fishing is allowed as it helps in more production of fishes. People should be educated about the environmental problems and aesthic value of flora and fauna. Hill streams fishes have modifications like adhesive suckers in their body so that these can attach their selves with the rocks and stones. Fishes like Barilius sp., Nemacheilus sp. And Danio rerio etc. have potential of being cultured for ornamental purposes. Himachal Pradesh attracts many tourists every year to the religious places. Dams also attract the tourists. Many of the tourists want to have more and easy information about the available fish fauna of the region. Tourists may be attracted by establishing aquaria showing different types of fishes of the local region so that tourists can get the knowledge of local fishes. Habitat protection is most essential requisite for the protection of any species. Himachal Pradesh government is aware of this fact and had made it mandatory to release sufficient water (minimum fixed quantity), downstream the dams and weirs for protection of biodiversity downstream.

Materials and Methods

Information included in this paper was collected from fishermen, interaction with public of the area, visits to some sites up stream and down streams the dams and fish landing centres in Himachal Pradesh. Measures for conservation of ecosystems and fish biodiversity are recommended.

Dams in Himachal Pradesh

Gobind Sagar Reservoir across the river Sutlej, Pong Reservoir across the river Beas, Pandoh Reservoir created by damming the river Beas, Chamera reservoir across the river Ravi are some of the reservoirs in Himachal Pradesh. The dams have been created in Himachal Pradesh especially for the purpose of hydroelectric power generation. Rivers are flowing through the deep gorges in Himachal Pradesh hence these rivers have a great potential of hydroelectric power generation through damming. Though the hydro electric energy is considered the clean energy but creation of dams is causing the changes in environment. Flow of water gets obstructed hence the flora and fauna which needs water permanently gets completely eradicated or their composition gets affected due to alteration in habitat.

Impact of Dams on Fish Habitat

During the construction of a dam and also thereafter, roadways are an essential requisite for carrying the construction material and heavy machinery to the dam site. Muck have been added into the rivers because most of the roads have been constructed alongside the rivers, in the Himalayan region. Construction of roads increases the soil erosion. Soil after getting washed into the rivers and reservoirs adversely affect the spawning, breeding and consequently decline in the fish fauna. Deforestation decreases the vegetation cover and increases the soil erosion. Some fishes are common in the flowing water of rivers but these fishes gets eradicated due to formation of reservoir. Habitats of the animals and plants gets submerged due to reservoir creation.

Rivers are drying downstream, filled with more water upstream hence drowning the area. Dam construction attracts the people from different places hence mounts more pressure on the limited available resources. Due to the increased settlement of labour colonies near the rivers and streams it has been found that the small fishes of the streams were caught indiscriminately resulting in the decrease in biodiversity.

Potential of the dams to disasters

Reservoirs have a great potential for disasters especially if dam gets broken or during the sudden release of water. Reservoirs and dams have a great potential to cause man made as well as natural disasters. Earthquakes, heavy floods can enhance the disasters.

Alteration in the Habitat

Dams changes the composition of flora and fauna of a place because of the changed physico-chemical characteristics of the river. During the early days of Gobindsagar reservoir formation, Tor putitora was an important fishery in Sutlej river but due to changed physico-chemical conditions and introduction of exotic species catch of this fish dwindled to 2-3 % in the year 1984 -85 which was 20 % in the year 1974-75 [3].

Due to the formation in dams, habitats of the rivers have got changed. Temperature, intensity of light penetration in water due to conversion of river into a reservoir gets changed and it changes the productivity of the reservoir. Silt deposition causes the alteration in the habitat.

Adverse effects of dams on fish migration

Fish migrates for feeding and breeding purpose. Hindrance in the migration adversely affects the spawning hence fish population decreases. Migration of the fish gets obstructed hence productivity of the fish got adversely affected. More fish become vulnerable to fishing in the area from which it is unable to migrate. Fish passes should be created so that fish can migrate from one side of the dam towards the other side when it desire.

Knowledge of fish community in rivers, their biology and migratory behaviour should help to better understand and define the need of the fish pass and other structures needed for fish migration in rivers [4]

Some commercial fishes in Himachal Pradesh

Catla catla (catla), Labeo rohita (rohu), Cirrhina mrigala (mrigal), Tor putitora (mahseer), Cyprinus carpio (Common carp), Ctenopharyngodon idella (grass carp), Hypophthalmichthys molitrix (silver carp) , Labeo dyocheilus, Labeo calbasu (kalbans), Labeo dero (gid) , Schizothorax richardsonii (snow trout), Garra gotyla gotyla, Crossochilus diplochilus, Aorichthys seenghala, Wallago attu and Salmo trutta etc. are some of the important fishes in the rivers of Himachal Pradesh.

Hill streams are rich in fishes like Barilius sp., Garra gotyla gotyla, Crossocheilus sp. Etc.

TABLE 1. - Ecological Problems imposed by Dams on the fishes in the rivers in Himachal Pradesh

Ecological Problems imposed by Dams on Fishes	Effects on Fishes	Recommendation
Change of lotic water conditions into lentic water conditions	Change in fish composition, adverse effect on stream fishes	Density of dams should be low, dams should be constructed when and where absolutely necessary
Physical barriers for fish migration	Hindrance in fish migration adversely affects the breeding and feeding migration of fishes	Construction of fish passes
Deposition of silt after slowing down of water flow	Silt deposition adversely affects the fishes	Checking the soil erosion, reforestation especially near the river banks, silt removal
Destruction of spawning ground	Destruction of Spawning grounds, difficulty in attachment of eggs with vegetation etc.	Identification and Conservation of spawning grounds
Change in physico-chemical conditions of water body	Water temperature, light penetration, dissolved nutrients etc changes the fish composition	Protection of fishes having potential threats due to reservoir formation
Drying the stretch of the rivers downstream	No survival of flora and fauna, eradication or adverse effect on fishes	Continuous release of water to check the drying of the river stretches
Change in fishing method so change in fish population	Different fishing methods in the reservoirs may affect some of the fishes but some of the fishes escape the nets	Mesh size regulation as per available fish species, Stocking the declining fishes
Change in fish population due to changed conditions of ecosystem	Due to changed conditions of ecosystems population of fish gets changed as the new	Regulating the fishing methods and policies as per local needs, Continuous research

	ecosystem may be suitable for some fishes but unsuitable for others	work on fish and environment

TABLE 2. – Some Power Projects in Himachal Pradesh

Name of Dam / Hydro Project	River basin
Nathpa Jhakri	Sutlej
Baspa	Sutlej
Bhakra	Sutlej
Kol Dam	Sutlej
Rongtong	Sutlej
Bhaba	Sutlej
Pong	Beas
Larji Dam	Beas
Pandoh Dam	Beas
Dehar	Beas
Giri	Yamuna
Gumma	Yamuna
Andhra	Yamuna
Chamera –I	Ravi
Chamera- II	Ravi
Holi	Ravi

Conclusion

Downstream flow of water should not be stopped completely. Water should be released continuously downstream to avoid complete drying of river so that vegetation and animals can survive. Reforestation should be done to protect the forest. Fish passes should be formed to allow fish migration. Stretch of rivers having more biodiversity should be protected. Dam density across the rivers should be appropriate so that damming can have minimum effect on the local fauna and flora. Habitat loss should be avoided as far as possible as it is most important factor for the survival of any plant or animal species. Breeding and spawning grounds for fishes are located in the streams; hence streams which are tributaries to the rivers should also be conserved for fish conservation.

Animals and plants having potential threats of getting destroyed due to dam formation should be conserved at some alternative site. Fishermen operating in the rivers and streams should be organized in the form of co-operative societies. Mesh size regulation, close season should be continued to be observed during the breeding season of the fishes. Removal of sand, coarse sand and stones etc. should be regulated and when it is necessary to remove, it should be removed only from such places where it cannot alter the fish habitat. Killing of fishes through dynamiting should be checked strictly. Fish having size less than minimum size allowed legally to catch, should not be caught.

References

1. B. D. Sharma. Fisheries Development of Gobind Sagar Reservoir. Fishing Chimes 27 (1), 2007, 112- 114.
2. J. R. Dhanze and R. Dhanze, Depleting fish genetic resources of H. P, in P. V. Dehadrai, P. Das, S. R. Verma (Ed), Threatened Fishes of India, Natcon Publication 4 (Muzaffarnagar: NATCON, 1994) 197-204.
3. A. Dua, Fisheries in Gobindsagar, Fishing Chimes 13 (9), 1993, 53-54.
4. M. Larinier, Environmental issues, dams and fish migration, in G. Marmulla (Ed.) Dams, fish and fisheries - Opportunities, challenges and conflict resolution, FAO Technical Paper 419 (Rome: FAO , 2001) 45 -90.

Chapter- XV

Development of viable and vital town centre- Case Study of Delhi City

Krupesh Chauhan & Yamee Thakkar*

Abstract

The town centre is the term used to refer to the commercial or geographical centre or core area of a town. Town centres are traditionally associated with shopping or retail. The potential benefits from town centre management are highlighted as 'There is increasing evidence that effective town management and promotion of town centres brings positive benefits. Town centre management programmes'. It should form part of a wider commitment and partnership between local authorities, retailers and other private sector and community interests. They should be based on a long term town centre strategy agreed by both public and private sectors, supported by ongoing monitoring of its health to ensure long-lasting success. The Study also identifies that there is a need to encourage the provision of a wide range of everyday needs, the conservation and maintenance of the built fabric and the public realm, the generation of local pride and confidence and the emergence of new uses of space. This paper includes the study of necessary qualities required for creating a vital and viable town centre. It shall further discuss the case of town centre of Delhi city.

Keywords – town centre, built fabric, conservation, vital and viable town centre

*Professor and Research Scholar, Department of Civil Engineering Department, Urban Planning, SVNIT, Surat, India

Introduction

They are also the centre of communications with major public transport hubs such as train or bus stations In the Indian context Town centre served as the nuclei for business activity of the cities. Town centres have a role that extends far beyond places in which people shop and transact business. They are, literally and metaphorically, at the heart of the communities they serve. The importance of town centres is therefore not simply their commercial viability but also their contribution as a location for jobs, services, community development, marketing and promotion. With the introduction of fast modes of transport coupled with phenomenal growth in economic activities, these areas degenerated into problem areas. With the result, restructuring of the cities became crucial and various planning authorities developed new growth centres to act as counter-magnets to the traditional city bazaars. In the context of large metropolis the urban sprawl being very large necessitating the creation of more than one growth centre. The structure of the cities has been changing through the ages and so have the theories of urban structure and growth. Hence, policy entered land development, despite the good intentions behind it, works against the interest of poor in an average Indian city.

Town and city centres are complex places that serve as places that serve a wide range of people and purposes. The importance of healthy vibrant town centres has been highlighted in recent years in certain locations due to the visible effect of vacant shops and a perception among some that their towns are not providing them with all the services they want or need, with a negative impact on their quality of life. Town centres, and those who operate in and manage them, are having to adapt to changing circumstances as global issues impact on local conditions. Similarly, local authorities are also having to adapt to rapid changes in the fiscal climate and increasingly challenging budgetary constraints. As with any change process it is important to be able to measure where we are, monitor progress, learn from others and realistically compare and measure performance. This report and accompanying tool kit aims to facilitate and support all those with an active interest in improving the experience and vitality of town centres so that they, in turn, provide a healthy sustainable operating environment for the businesses and communities who depend on them.

Whatever the real or perceived drivers behind town centre change, it is clear that they are nothing if not complex. Instead we must recognise the probable influence of a multitude of factors such as the economy, changing lifestyles, an ageing population, technological advancement, and the rise of highly effective convenience led retailing. The Government are committed to sustainable development and a view that embraces economic growth and social progress as well as a concern for the environment. The aim is to promote economic activity by establishing favourable economic conditions for the market to exploit. As part of its policies related to welfare to work and overcoming social exclusion, the Government wants as many as possible to take advantage of the changes in retailing and leisure, and to ensure that most people, including the disabled, have access to them. Promotion of and greater reliance on public transport forms an important part of this approach. This paper shall include the discussion of various essential features and objectives that a town centre must incorporated.

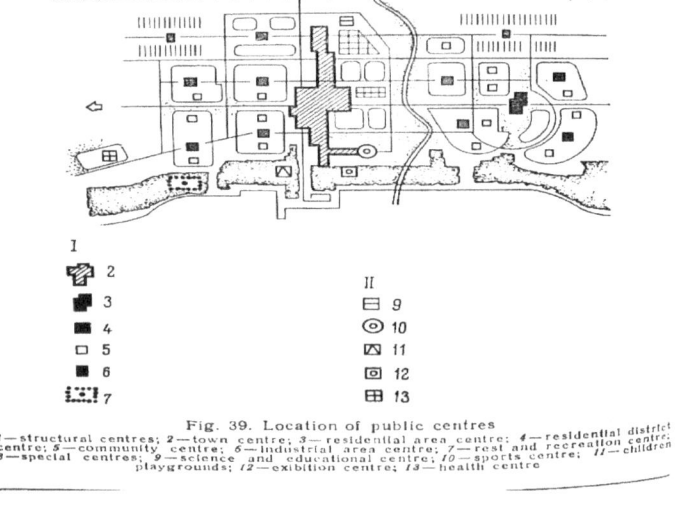

Fig. 39. Location of public centres
1—structural centres; 2—town centre; 3—residential area centre; 4—residential district centre; 5—community centre; 6—industrial area centre; 7—rest and recreation centre; 8—special centres; 9—science and educational centre; 10—sports centre; 11—children playgrounds; 12—exhibition centre; 13—health centre

Fig 1: Components of a typical town centre

Objectives of a vital and viable town centre

The major objective is to sustain and enhance the vitality and viability of town centres. The vitality of town centres should, it is suggested, be monitored by undertaking 'health checks' focussing on a number of key indicators. These are: accessibility, customer views, diversity of uses, environmental quality, pedestrian flow, retailer profile, retailers views and shop rents.

Principles of achieving a perfect town centre

Ensuring the availability of a wide range of shops, employment, services and facilities to which people have easy access by a choice of transport; Minimising transport impacts; and Promoting quality –through urban design, environmental improvements, and promoting individuality.

Need of the study

a) District centres have thrown up substantial debate on the concept behind them. As is obvious, the urban planning concepts-adopted by the first Master Plan are alien to the city's climate and cultural context, as it was based on modern urban planning theories. Many cities have condemned them on the basis of their alianneess to its surrounding residential fabric, their inaccessibility and their being a cause for environmental stress to its surroundings due to excessive traffic around them. Also a District Centre is supposed to:

    i.   Decentralise places of employment.

    ii.   Serve certain number of population

    iii.   Create work-home relationship in the intended influence area.

    iv.   Furnish essential and high unit value merchandise and shopping facilities.

    v.   To accommodate work-cum-industrial centres.

b) To be centre of cultural activities and entertainment for the District,

c) In order to achieve all these features certain assumptions were made for Delhi in the First Master Plan on the basis of changing trends observed at that period of time. These assumptions were for the structure and structural changes in Delhi's working force, state income of Delhi and the fast growing population. In consideration of these features, Delhi was divided into 8 planning divisions.

One of the major objectives for establishing these planning divisions was to make them, self-contained in employment and community facilities. These divisions to have population ranging from 3.7 to 4.0 lakhs. Hence, each division to have 2-3 district centres which are composite retail shopping centre with commercial and service uses. In most cases they will also have a smaller area for Govt. offices and an industrial cum work centre to provide employment.

Presently, the situation is different and moreover drastic changes are going to come with the economic reforms. New commercial districts are now being developed in the periphery of Delhi, principally in the suburbs of Gurgaon in the south west and Noida to the south east, which increasingly attract multinational occupiers. It is important to note that Gurgaon and Noida are located in the neighbouring States of Haryana and Uttar Pradesh respectively. Hence it has become essential that "The District centre in Delhi has to be revived if the capital does not wish to keep losing out on investments and job generation to Gurgaon and Noida."

Fig 2- study area Delhi

Factors operating in Metropolitan areas which create trends of
Decentralisation

It is natural, that the American cities of twenties and thirties, which
provided the data upon which these models were built, would be
undergoing important structural changes i.e. the form and structure of the
Modern American city is the result of numerous economic, social and
cultural factors operating on them through many decades.

Some of the most significant of these factors are:

- Rapid and massive growth,

- A heterogeneous population,

- The changing forms of urban transportation.

The American urban population has not only been growing but it also has
been unusually heterogeneous with a great volume of internal migration.
This succession of people results not only in shift in living quarters but
also in changes of shops, schools and religious buildings. But even
where, assimilation has taken place, cities remain heterogeneous, with
the segregation of income replacing that by ethnic group.

During the twentieth century there had also been a phenomenon rise in
number of automobiles in the urban areas. Here, the urban transport not
only laces the urban structure together, but it also affects the arrangement
and function of elements in the structure of the city. Now, two opposing
forces are identified to have an impact on the growth of the city. They
are:

Push forces: Which push to migrate from the central area to the
peripherals of the city,

Pull forces: That tends to hold certain functions in the central
zone and attract others to it.

The Indian Situation

From 1941 to .1951; the population of India increased by 13.3% but the urban population increased by almost three times. Cities with population up to 1 lakh have suffered the increase in population by 23.2% and in cities with population size of over 1 lakh, the increase was 12.3%.Inspite of the phenomenal increase in population size in Metropolitan areas and that is population was heterogeneous, it did not create conditions for centrifugal forces, a desire to leave one part of the city and the urge to settle in the suburban areas to act.

The major reason was that urban transport system in the cities was not developed adequately so people tended to remain near the central core of the urban areas, where they work, in order to save time and money. More emphasis was on living around places of work rather than own a single family house on a large open plot.

Thus aiding the centripetal forces in Indian cities is an inadequate urban transport system and poorly developed suburban areas which obviously lack the proper infrastructure to support a population. Therefore, in spite of forces like high land values, high taxes, which create a desire in the people to move out, there is no alternative site to the central core for residing. Moreover, a traditional Indian city form is quite unacceptable to western oriented physical planning principles. In the west, zoning or marking out land uses is based on 'transportation system with the commuting time being the determinant or where each type of activity will be located, whereas, in India, resource constraints prevent the development of effective mass transportation system. Moreover, half the workforce in a city finds employment in the informal sector.

In Delhi itself about 53% of work force is employed in informal sector. It naturally follows that at least half of the work sites will be scattered throughout the city rather than concentrate in specific work zones. Thus in an average Indian town, the emphasis should be on orienting the plans for the poor by correlating the employment structure and land use, instead on the preoccupation with the poly-centred land development.

Conclusion

Occupying an important place in the plan structure of any town is the system of town centres differing in their function and location. The town centre as a place of greatest concentration of public life is of particular importance. As a rule town centres are built up with administrative and commercial buildings, public and cultural establishments, large shops, and places of entertainment in a unified architectural ensemble dominating the urban pattern and in harmony with its general plan structure. Hence it proves to be a significant factor to be considered while undergoing the process of planning for the entire town.

References

Thesis on – Marketing of Bandra Kuala complex as an alternative CBD for Mumbai metropolis by: Vaidya B. Negi, School of Planning cept Ahmedabad

Thesis on - Impact of corporate sector on commercial development- Ankush agarwal, SPA New Delhi. A study of methodology an its application in forecasting a viable commercial development investor's perspective: Rishika urp-1499, School of Planning cept Ahmedabad Metropolitan City centre of Delhi, study on Traffic and Transportation: SPA New Delhi

Kashyap, Rajesh (1999); "Study of District Centre in New Delhi", School of Planning and Architecture, New Delhi.

Thesis on- "Readdressing District Centres, Case study New Delhi"; Kashyap Shabha (1979); School of Planning and Architecture, New Delhi. Reading borough council local development framework town centre uses background paper, July 2011.